Inside Monte Carlo

The Grimaldi coat of arms commemorates the seizure of the Monaco fortress in 1297 by a Genoese force disguised as Franciscan monks.

Inside Monte Carlo

STANLEY JACKSON

W. H. Allen · London
A division of Howard & Wyndham Ltd
1975

© STANLEY JACKSON, 1975

THIS BOOK OR PARTS THEREOF MAY NOT BE
REPRODUCED WITHOUT PERMISSION IN WRITING.

PRINTED AND BOUND IN GREAT BRITAIN BY
W & J MACKAY LTD, CHATHAM, FOR THE PUBLISHERS,
W. H. ALLEN & CO LTD, 44 HILL STREET,
LONDON W1X 8LB

ISBN 0 491 01635 2

Contents

Acknowledgment

For permission to reproduce in this book photographs which are their respective copyrights, I am indebted to Gianni Bozacchi, Centre de Presse, Photo Détaille, George Lukomski, Mander and Mitchenson, Paris Match, the Radio Times Hulton Picture Library, Sarelli and SBM.

'A sunny place for shady people'
          – Somerset Maugham.

'Here the arts can still flourish in the
shade of the olive groves, by the edge of
the Latin sea; here, where the rightful
power of one ensures the freedom of all . . .'
                              – Marcel Pagnol.

Foreword

Monaco, smaller than London's Hyde Park or a Texan oilman's front lawn and paddock, even with the acreage recently won from the sea, offers a remarkable case of historical survival. Prince Rainier III is the 31st heir of the Grimaldi dynasty which, apart from a short break during the French Revolution, has ruled continuously for close on seven centuries. Such a phenomenon, unique in Europe's saga of power struggles and toppled monarchies, cannot be entirely equated with the relatively modern emergence of its famed Casino, the subject of so many biographies, novels and films.

Without minimising the influence of gambling, which attracted Grand Dukes and Hollywood tycoons alike, or the aura of gilded sophistication symbolised by Diaghilev's Ballet Russe, international yachtsmen and racing drivers, my primary objective has been to focus and analyse the crazy logic which transformed a barren promontory, worth only a few centimes a square metre little over a century ago, into one of the world's most prosperous countries with a buoyant economy and real estate ranking in value with Manhattan, Mayfair and the Champs Elysées.

Once the carnation in Europe's tourist lapel, Monte Carlo is now more akin to an apparently ageless charmer, who still enjoys an occasional flutter at the tables but has shrewdly sunk her earnings, moral and otherwise, into prime land sites or other lucrative outlets. Her vicissitudes of fortune and resistance to such formidable suitors as Zaharoff, de Gaulle and Onassis form the main subject matter of this volume.

During the past 40 years I have met many of the personalities, ranging from the Windsors, Randolph Churchill, the Aga Khan and leading members of the 'Jet Set' circuit to most of the prominent hoteliers and officials who have played their parts in Monte Carlo's continuing fascination. Above all, my talks with Prince Rainier almost exactly span his entire reign, from his accession to the recent celebration of his Silver Jubilee. I owe a special debt to him for answering my questions with patience and frankness and also for affording me generous access to the family's photographic records and albums.

Many others gave very helpful assistance or advice. They include Prince Louis de Polignac and his fellow-directors, who allowed me to consult and quote from the files of the Société Anonyme des Bains de Mer; Josianne Mérino, the company's Publicity Director, and Laurent Savelli, Chef du Service Historique; Nadia Lacoste and the staff at Monaco's Centre de Presse; Gabriel Ollivier, principal of the Musée National; Georges Lukomski, Prince Rainier's aide; Jean Broc, former director of the Hotel de Paris, and Jacques Simon, manager of the Métropole; Douglas Keay; and my daughter, Tisha Browne.

Prologue

A cliff-bound enclave, with its toes dipping into the Mediterranean and shoulders screened by the Alps from cold north winds, Monaco's only asset until modern times was a natural harbour easily defended by a fortress on the Rock. Inevitably, it became a strategic prize for warring neighbours but without justifying direct annexation once the Grimaldis had established their sovereignty. The family coat of arms portrays two bearded monks defending the Grimaldi shield with drawn swords above the pious motto, *Deo Juvante*. It recalls a stratagem which founded the ruling house without much serious claim to divine intervention. On the evening of January 8, 1297 François Grimaldi, aptly nicknamed 'Malizia' (the Spiteful), entered the courtyard in Franciscan robes to open the gates for his followers. They brutally massacred the garrison manned by a rival faction of fellow-Genoese.

Long before the Christian era many others had coveted this sharp rock jutting 500 metres into the Mediterranean. The Phoenicians first settled there, followed by the Romans, many of whom built handsome villas overlooking 'the Port of Hercules' from which Julius Caesar embarked on his campaign against Pompeii.[1] Monaco was occupied after the collapse of Rome by

[1] Legend maintains that Monaco was founded at least 16 centuries B.C. by the Phoenician sun god, Melkarth. Others associate its name with the Grecian deity,

various warrior races including the Saracens, who were expelled in 975, and the Moors. Towards the end of the 12th century the Republic of Genoa persuaded the Holy Roman Emperor to concede them the Rock (at that time a dependency of the Counts of Provence) subject to its being fortified. The fortress, built in 1215 on the remains of a former Saracen citadel, is the site of the present-day palace.

Although the Counts of Provence had relinquished their rights, Genoa was split between Holy Roman Empire supporters and those who gave allegiance to the papacy, among them the Grimaldi clan of wealthy shipowners who had long served the Republic as consuls or ambassadors. The ruler of Anjou and Provence, backing each of the Genoese partisans in turn, had finally forced François Grimaldi to seize Monaco at sword's point. He was driven out by the other faction and overlordship shuttled for some years between the rival parties, until another Grimaldi, henceforth known as Rainier I, strengthened his claim by placing galleys at the disposal of the King of France.

He was awarded the title of 'Admiral General of France' for his services in helping to defeat the Flemish fleet and also given the lordships of Villeneuve in Normandy and Cagnes in Provence. He failed to regain uninterrupted control of the fortress during his lifetime but his exploits as fighting sailor and lover are embedded in Monegasque folk lore. He is said to have kidnapped and betrayed a Flemish maiden during one of his assaults on the Schelde with a landing party. She was supposed to have turned into a witch and cursed him and his descendants with a prophecy often fulfilled in the centuries ahead; 'never will a Grimaldi find true happiness in marriage'.

Rainier's son, Charles, established his family as full masters of Monaco for the first time after resisting an attack by marauding Catalans. He thought it wise to refortify the Rock while simultaneously building up a sizeable army and fleet subsidised by the *droit de mer* which gave Monaco 2% of the cargo value of all ships

---

Herakles Menouakh, or the Roman Hercules, and link the principality with the site of a Roman temple to the god of strength; Portus Hercules Monoeci.

passing through the port. This source of revenue was lucrative but the economy still relied mainly on a few goatherds and peasants who scratched a bare livelihood from the scrub.

The Grimaldis already had a keen eye for percentages long before the casino days. They seldom failed to back the winning side, traditionally France, by giving the highest bidder access to a safe harbour together with the services of their fighting men. In October 1338, after various raids on Venetian shipping, Monegasque mercenaries joined the French and Genoese in an audacious attack on Southampton which they looted, returning safely to Dieppe with their plunder. They helped briefly to sweep the badly-equipped British Navy from the Channel and arrived back in Calais with ears and fingers as trophies from a surprise raid on Thanet ports. The English took vengeance at Crécy where Charles was badly wounded and most of his crossbowmen massacred. Soon afterwards, however, he used his plunder from Southampton to acquire the lordships of Menton, Roquebrune and Eze, then part of Provence.

Within a century finances were once more dangerously stretched after a rash military adventure against the Duke of Milan. The seigneur, Jean I, even offered to sell Monaco for 15,000 gold *écus* to the Dauphin, who had thought of using it as a base for invading Italy but abandoned that plan. Jean then attempted, also without success, to interest the Venetians in buying the Rock, but he secured the protection of the Duke of Savoy by handing over part of Menton and all Roquebrune.

The Grimaldis, whose capital resources and manpower were totally inadequate either for the large ships or the heavier artillery in a new age of warfare, had long outlived their usefulness as mercenaries. The Port was their one asset but it could only be fully exploited by a diplomatic finesse which few seigneurs exhibited. During the 16th century they almost wrecked the dynasty with inter-family plots on a Borgian scale. Three rulers in turn came to a violent end. Jean II, who seemed chiefly concerned with embellishing his palace, was stabbed to death by his brother, Lucien, while dining with him at their castle in Menton. Lucien was immediately faced with attack by the Genoese who failed to take the Rock after a siege of 102 days, but this resistance had sparked off renewed interest in Monaco's strategic value. Spain began to make overtures and the Republic of Florence sent Niccolo Machiavelli to negotiate a Treaty of Alliance and Navigation. King Louis XII of France soon granted letters patent acknowledging the seigneur's independence and a suzerainty which derived 'solely from God and by the Sword'.

Lucien was also murdered by a jealous kinsman. His younger brother, who had unwisely abandoned the French alliance, died mysteriously of poison after accepting a Spanish garrison. They remained in control for more than an uneasy century during which Honoré II was first given the title of 'Prince and Lord of Monaco' by the protecting Power. He made the secret Treaty of Péronne in September 1641 with Cardinal Richelieu, who not only needed to contain Spanish aggression but required a sea base for bottling up Savoy and the always troublesome Italian republics. He therefore guaranteed Monaco's full sovereign independence and agreed to provide a defence force of 500 men whose officers would be nominated by France but remain under the prince's orders. Three days later the Spanish garrison was overcome in a surprise attack by a mixed force of French artillery, concealed outside the ramparts, and a number of local patriots. The prince returned his Spanish Order of the Golden Fleece but he was more than compensated by the French titles of Duc de Valentinois and Marquis des Baux among other valuable lands and lordships. He now attended the Versailles Court, and King Louis XIV later became godfather to his grandson.

From a troubled and backward territory of no more than 500 souls, living in poverty and menaced either by foreign invaders or harsh garrison troops, Monaco had at last emerged as a small but respected principality.[2] Secure in defence and with unexpected wealth, the ruler made costly additions to his palace which he

---

[2] Although the French franc would remain Monaco's monetary unit, the ruler now had the right to issue his own coinage so long as it was struck by the Paris Mint and had the same size, weight and metal content as the French unit.

seemed to visualise as a Mediterranean Trianon. New gardens with ornamental fountains were laid out and statue-lined arcades led to a graceful *Pavillon des Bains*. Several hundred superb paintings now hung on the walls of the royal apartments and guests occupied sumptuous chambers in a new extension which overlooked the Cour d'Honneur dominated by an imposing marble staircase. A contemporary French historian, who stayed at the palace, entered his room and was 'astonished to see a large table and two benches of solid silver, and a huge ewer, the height of a man, with a round basin which four men could not lift – all this admirably worked with the princely arms in relief.'

This taste for grandeur encouraged the Grimaldis to seek marriage alliances to strengthen their social position and finances. Honoré's grandson, Louis (whose father had been accidentally shot dead), succeeded to the throne in 1662 and had the misfortune to marry Charlotte de Gramont, daughter of the celebrated Field-Marshal. She was a flighty young woman with a keen appreciation of her own charms ('my eyes are dazzling . . . my lips are crimson, and there is something captivating in my smile'). Her full-blooded sexual appetites demanded more satisfaction than Prince Louis – and most other mates – could provide. She tired quickly of her dull marriage of convenience and returned to Versailles as the favourite of Louis XIV, who compensated his cuckolded godson by appointing him Envoy to the Holy See during the negotiations over the Spanish Succession.

The Prince of Monaco took his new appointment as a cue for riotous ostentation. He attempted to outshine all the other ambassadors and had his carriage adorned with curtains of cloth of gold. For his triumphal ride into the Vatican his escort had their horses shod with silver but so loosely nailed that the crowd could scramble gratefully for fragments. King Louis rewarded his services with the cannon which stand to this day on Monaco's ramparts.

Charlotte did not confine her favours to the French king. She seduced the famed soldier, de Lauzun, and used to admit him, sometimes disguised as a footman, to her boudoir until the jealous monarch sent him to cool off in the Bastille for six months. 'Madame de Monaco' consoled herself so vigorously in his absence that bawdy writers began building highly-coloured plots about her exploits. Prince Louis, enraged with his rôle of Europe's leading cuckold, started hanging effigies of de Lauzun and several others, all wearing court dress, on gibbets at the French frontier. This childish vengeance caused Madame de Sévigné to report that 'more than half the courtiers of Versailles are now dangling along the borders of Monaco'.

His son, Antoine I, was another victim of 'the witch's curse'. He too married an heiress, Marie de Lorraine, daughter of the wealthy Comte d'Armagnac, who deceived him so blatantly that he spent many years with the French Army. After fighting at the sieges of Mons and Namur, he returned to a principality threatened from the sea by the British Navy and on land by the soldiers of Savoy, who had taken up arms against France during the War of the Spanish Succession. He was forced to confirm the Duke of Savoy's overlordship of Menton and Roquebrune but remained obsessed by fears of attack. He melted down his palace silver and sold the family jewels to erect Fort Antoine, complete with gunproof underground shelters overlooking the port.

His passion for engineering had one useful long-term bonus; he built a much-needed road to Menton. He had hoped to improve his palace but could only afford to convert a large room into a concert hall where he sometimes conducted the orchestra. Soured in his last years by an unhappy marriage, he became a puritanical recluse.

He had no male issue and was succeeded by his eldest daughter, Louise-Hippolyte, whom he had prudently married off to Jacques de Goyon-Matignon, Comte de Thorigny, a member of France's oldest and richest nobility. Their marriage contract was signed by the young Louis XV and the Regent of France. She died of smallpox after reigning for less than a year, the throne then passing to her husband, who duly renounced his name to assume the Grimaldi title and arms. But as he had little taste for Monaco, he stayed mostly on his fine estate in Normandy and was therefore more than willing to leave all administration to the former prince's natural son, the Chevalier de Grimaldi, who for the next half-century virtually ruled the principality. He acted as regent when Jacques decided to abdicate in favour of his 14 year-old son, Honoré III.

The young prince was educated by Jesuits and then soldiered in the French King's Guard with whom he fought at Fontenoy. He later had his horse shot from under him in battle and returned home, severely wounded, but with the rank of Marshal. Honoré followed family tradition by taking an aristocratic and wealthy bride, but with no more luck than his ancestors. Catherine de Brignole, descendant of Genoese doges, was a proud and vivacious woman 20 years younger than her dreary husband. She dutifully presented him with a son and heir but her tantrums often sent him hurrying off to the comparative peace of his Normandy estate while she continued to entertain her lovers. Poor Honoré had one brief moment of glory when the Duke of York, brother of King George III, was carried ashore at Monaco after becoming ill at sea. Honoré at once arranged for him to be quartered in one of the most handsome palace apartments where he received every care but died within a few days.[3] King George showed his appreciation by sending him some racehorses, hunters and six of his brother's carriage horses.

Princess Catherine parted from her husband three years later. Already a saddened recluse, he suffered a far more crushing blow when the aged Chevalier de Grimaldi died in 1784, leaving him quite incapable of riding the coming storm. With the fall of the Bastille the Grimaldi estates were confiscated, but the National Assembly later agreed to respect Monaco's neutrality and pay him an annual pension. He showed his gratitude by subscribing to revolutionary funds and also made the French Army a gift of all

[3] According to Monegasque folklore, the Duke of York's beautiful mistress lodged in a house off the headland from which she could see the palace. When the Royal Standard of England was flown at half mast she is said to have flung herself into the sea. For years afterwards, the local peasantry thought the Pointe de la Veille was haunted by 'The Woman in White' and would cross themselves as they hurried past.

his horses. But the Monegasque National Convention still dethroned him and voted unanimously for incorporation in the Republic. Monaco was then renamed 'Fort Hercules'. Once the Danton régime had taken over in Paris, Honoré was arrested and spent his last months in a military barracks. His home in Monaco was pillaged but loyal servants salvaged a few works of art and stored them in the chapel. The palace became a military hospital for wounded soldiers from the Italian battlefields, and later an almshouse. Much was allowed to fall into ruin including the beautiful *Pavillon des Bains* which would never be restored.

Honoré's eldest son, the Duc de Valentinois, also suffered imprisonment. He was separated from his wife, but she managed to go into hiding with her infant son, Florestan, and remained under cover. The prince's youngest son, Joseph, had escaped to London with his wife, Françoise-Thérèse, leaving their two daughters in the care of an old family retainer, but she became anxious for their safety and rashly returned to France where she was arrested and sentenced to death as an *emigrée*. She cut off all her golden hair with a piece of broken glass and sent it to the revolutionary tribunal, explaining that it was a legacy for her children from 'a foreign princess dying through the injustice of French judges'. She then applied a little rouge to her cheeks before riding defiantly to the guillotine.

Her husband returned from exile with his second wife, an English girl, when Napoleon showed more tolerance towards the Grimaldis. They received back a few parcels of land to keep them from destitution. Prince Joseph at once pledged his allegiance and was granted a commission in the Imperial Guard, later serving the Empress Joséphine as her devoted chamberlain. His nephew, Honoré-Gabriel, son of the Duc de Valentinois who was now a sick man after his life in prison, enlisted in a cavalry regiment and became A.D.C. to General Grouchy.

Following Elba and the coronation of Louis XVIII, the Grimaldis had the liveliest hopes of returning to their principality after over 20 years in exile. Many would have welcomed them, but others saw no future in becoming a vassal of Sardinia which had been promised the county of Nice and might logically claim Monaco as part of their spoils.

It was Talleyrand who restored the Grimaldis to power and re-established the principality's independence by a clause in the Treaty of Paris, confirmed by the Vienna Congress. He had grasped the increasing strategic importance of the Rock as a buffer against Italian aggression. But the Monegasques would still have to submit reluctantly to the 'protection' of the King of Sardinia.

They had other problems. Enthroned as Honoré IV, the Duc de Valentinois was too sick in body and mind to govern. He proposed handing over to his brother, Joseph, who had remained in Paris to bring some order to the depleted Grimaldi finances. But this was opposed by his son, Honoré-Gabriel, whose military service had made him a little power-drunk. His easygoing uncle finally agreed to step down rather than involve himself in an ugly feud. During the last four years of his father's lifetime Honoré-Gabriel assumed all sovereign rights, except the title of ruler.

Like the Bourbons, he could neither forgive nor forget. He had no patience with ideas for reform, seeded during the Revolution and soon fertilised by emergent Italian liberalism. His mother's large fortune had been dissipated by lawsuits, and any hopes of inheriting from his wealthy grandmother, Catherine, were dashed by her second marriage to the Prince de Condé. He had already initiated a policy of crushing taxation when his father was accidentally killed while out driving.

Now in his early forties and still unmarried, Honoré had tried to establish good trade relations with his neighbours but his position was desperate. The pre-revolutionary *droit de mer* had not been revived and the export trade in olive oil and lemons had almost vanished. No longer the protecting power, France saw little reason for tariff concessions, while Sardinia seized every chance to under-mine the little principality's security and economy. With annexa-tion obviously in view, trouble was also being fomented through pro-Italian agents in Menton and Roquebrune.

Soon after his accession and still hoping for diplomatic interven-tion to restrain the Sardinians, Honoré had written privately to the

Duc de Richelieu reminding him of the personal ties which had long united his dynasty with France. The reply was courteous, urbane and quite unfruitful. The prince consoled himself childishly by dressing up his 300 guardsmen, who performed useless ceremonial duties when they were not rounding up civilian 'agitators'. He only saw his advisers to demand still more money for his civil list which had been increased to £12,000 a year, exactly treble the sum voted his grandfather. To raise this amount he increased taxes and also granted a flour monopoly to a grasping businessman from Marseilles. This resulted in poorer quality and dearer bread for his unfortunate subjects. On the credit side he made some effort to start local 'cottage industries' like lace making, but most of the peasants scraped along by picking olives and lemons or grazing their herds on an inhospitable pebbly plateau, the Spélugues, above the almost derelict harbour which had once bristled with Grimaldi galleys and foreign cargo-laden vessels. Only the richer agricultural territories of Menton and Roquebrune, providing almost 80% of the total revenue, kept the principality above a bare subsistence level.

The atmosphere became so uncongenial that he scarcely visited Monaco during the last years of his reign, preferring to strut in Paris society and send irate demands for money to his so-called 'Governor-General'. But he remained too jealous and self-absorbed to accept an unselfish offer to deputise from his younger brother, Florestan, whom he wrongly suspected of plotting to usurp his title.

In fact, Florestan had even less taste for the sullen little principality. Born only four years before the French Revolution, he had renounced his title and reluctantly adopted a military career to please his ailing father. He did garrison duties with an infantry regiment before joining the Grand Army in Russia where he was taken prisoner but released after the fall of Napoleon. He shunned court life and preferred taking minor rôles in the Paris theatre under the name of 'Florestan', without revealing his identity. His prison camp experiences had impaired his health but a modest allowance enabled him to write leisurely verse.

All this changed when he met and married Caroline de Lametz. She was an energetic brunette with a slight squint which had earned her the cruel nickname of 'the one-eyed one' during her convent schooldays. But her rare business vision and intelligence more than compensated for her looks and a slender *dot*. She had soon persuaded Florestan to buy a rundown Paris mansion which she restored at very low cost.[4] After the death of her mother-in-law, the Duchesse de Mazarin, she steadily cleared the estate and even brought some order to the various other Grimaldi estates neglected during the years of exile. She welcomed actors, authors and painters to her salon but usually with a banker or two whose advice might be useful.

This woman, whose financial sagacity would have been remarkable at any time but was almost unique in the mid-19th century, enjoyed a happy marriage for forty years, itself something of a phenomenon for the dynasty. She brought up a son, Charles, born in 1818, and a daughter, Florestine, who arrived several years later, with a firm devotion rarely enjoyed by the Grimaldi children. She also stamped her imprint on the principality's entire economy. Although Monte Carlo would be named in honour of Charles, his mother had first shaped the bold concept of a gambling casino.

Florestan had automatically succeeded after his brother's death in 1841, but he was soon exposed as an amiable small-part actor miscast in a princely rôle. He inherited a near-bankrupt treasury and an over-taxed populace whom he optimistically tried to placate by abolishing the unpopular bread monopoly and reducing customs duties. Recalling his own prison days, he had celebrated his accession by emptying the Monaco gaols of all offenders. He started building orphanages and schools but quickly discovered that his resources would not permit such luxuries in a country

---

[4] The Count and Countess de Grimaldi, as they called themselves, occupied only part of the mansion. Lamartine was among those who rented apartments away from the main wing.

without any profitable industry. In the Condamine port area at the foot of the rock men worked in sheds, cleaning and boxing lemons which the boatmen from Nice picked up for a few francs, while their womenfolk gathered flowers on the Spélugues for Rimmel's perfumeries in Paris and London. Almost one-third of the total population, then under a thousand, served in the Palace Guard while most of the others grazed their sheep and goats. Many died young, the few survivors moving into almshouses which the ruler had built in his first patriarchal flush. He soon gave up handing out free meals to the needy and adopted his late brother's oppressive taxation. Discontent smouldered, notably in Menton and Roquebrune whose citizens, encouraged by the new King of Sardinia's liberal laws, clamoured to secede from Monaco.

The year of revolutions, 1848, proved critical for the principality. Floristan had hastily granted a Charter, but it was too little and too late. A new chamber had power to legislate and authorise the budget, though the sovereign retained his power of veto. He stumbled between benevolent autocracy and a blind panic, merely fanning local discontent by lowering some taxes while arbitrarily raising others. Caroline, adroit with household finances but un-versed in statecraft, remained equally insensitive to the convulsions shaking the whole fabric of Europe. Nearer home, Menton and Roquebrune hoisted the flag of Sardinia and voted unanimously in favour of secession. From Turin came an offer to purchase the principality of Monaco, including the two towns, for six million francs which Floristan refused, though tempted. He was now a very sick man and so exhausted that he appealed to his son to return from Paris and take over all administrative duties.

Prince Charles, a tall handsome young man with a tufted beard and high forehead, had just become a father. He was enjoying Parisian society and the Chateau de Marchais in the Aisne which he had bought with the dowry from his wife, Antoinette-Ghislaine de Mérode, daughter of a Belgian Count. When his wife began to ail following a painful childbirth, she retreated more and more to the peace of Marchais, while Charles continued to cut a figure at Versailles and consoled himself with pretty actresses.

Both were therefore less than enchanted with the move to a squalid little principality and its shabby palace where Princess Caroline swiftly took control of her grandson when Antoinette was confined to her bed.

The imminent annexation of Menton and Roquebrune was only deferred by Sardinia's reckless war with Austria which ended in humiliating defeat. France seized the opportunity to support the Monegasques, who had to be content with the temporary establishment of Menton and Roquebrune as free and independent towns. But they still remained under the protection of Sardinia; an unsatisfactory compromise all round.

Prince Charles grossly misjudged local feeling in 1854 by imagining that the people of Menton would again rally to the Grimaldis if he showed himself among them. He was acclaimed by a few well-wishers but soon surrounded by an angry mob. He had to be rescued by the carabinieri who locked him in gaol for his own safety. His friends in Paris intervened to secure his release. By now his treasury was so empty that he sent emissaries to Turin to offer all rights over the disputed two towns in exchange for four million francs and the withdrawal of the Sardinian garrison from the principality. But the Italians, having meantime formed an alliance with France, were too confident of soon annexing the towns, and perhaps Monaco itself, to give the proposal a second thought.

The principality lapsed into penury and frustration during this period of diplomatic stalemate. The economy was at breaking point and could no longer support the Grimaldis' civil list. Florestan, prematurely senile and almost a dying man, shut himself off from affairs. His wife had become the virtual ruler as Prince Charles was now threatened by blindness although still active in mind and body. The whole family lived in a small wing of the palace and often dined meagrely on fruit, anchovies and occasional game from Marchais. The upholstery had faded and some of the walls disclosed gaps left by magnificent paintings long since sold, together with the family jewels, to meet household expenses.

Princess Caroline began exploring new sources of income. She

looked enviously at Cannes which had no natural port to compare
with Monaco's and could claim no superiority in either climate or
scenery. Yet it attracted the cream of European society, notably
British aristocrats, who regularly occupied its fine hotels during
the mild winter months. An unknown French fishing village in the
Thirties, it owed an almost miraculous transformation to Broug-
ham, Lord Chancellor of England, who had been travelling across
France en route for the Italian Riviera when he was turned back at
Antibes by reports of a cholera epidemic. He stayed overnight at
Cannes and succumbed to the flowers, toy harbour, a ruined
castle and its picturesque views of the Alpes-Maritimes. He returned
each winter and reported his discovery to other would-be refugees
from London's chills and fogs. Hotels and villas were soon built
with a new breakwater to shelter yachts and a small colony of
doctors for wealthy patients suffering from a variety of ailments,
from tuberculosis to chronic hypochondria. An inevitable complement of cocottes appeared for those needing more frivolous
diversion after their medicated sea-water baths.

But Cannes, like all French, English and Italian resorts, still
denied them the delights of gaming. Only the German spas offered
therapeutic waters by day with roulette under the winking lustres
after dark. Tales had already reached Princess Caroline of the gold
being mined by the kursaals at Baden-Baden and Wiesbaden. In
March 1855, she consulted her old friend, Maître Eynaud. He saw
no objection to establishing a gaming house but advised against
using the word 'casino' in publicity to avert ecclesiastical disapproval. He thought up the name, 'Bains de Mer de Monaco', to
stress the spa aspect, but gambling would be the obvious and sole
attraction as the principality boasted neither sea baths nor mineral
waters.

The project was sound in theory but it ignored priorities such as
transport and accommodation which the first concessionaries hopefully expected to provide from their profits. They miscalculated
almost as fatally as the Grimaldis, who were more accustomed to
dealing with diplomats and courtiers than profit-hungry pro-
moters. Prince Florestan, with his wife jogging his elbow, had

signed an ordinance in April 1856 authorising two journalists to exercise a gaming concession for 30 years. He died within a few weeks but his son quickly sanctioned the arrangements to form the new 'Société des Bains de Monaco'. It would have a capital of three million francs (then about £120,000) and guaranteed Prince Charles a minimum of 25,000 frs. a year.[5] The partners cheerfully undertook to build a sea-bathing establishment and an hotel, with transport by steamboat or carriage between Nice and Monaco. They also promised to construct a casino on the Spélugues, the plateau originally cleared for fruit cultivation by Italian convict labourers when the Monaco–Menton road was completed. It was owned by a local landowner, Comte Rey, who disposed of several acres at only 20 centimes (1p) a square metre.

Roulette wheels and tables for faro, whist and écarté had been temporarily installed in a house facing the palace, but gamblers were few and far between. Worse, despite the very modest maximum stakes, some lucky players took 70,000 francs in a single session. The partners hastily reduced the maximum from 170 francs which discouraged even the handful who ventured into Monaco. The owners cut their losses and sold out to a French marquis, but he also panicked after six shaky weeks and transferred his concession to M. Daval, who lacked resources but had some publicity flair. He gave lavish banquets and provided carriages, with horses beribboned in the national colours of France and Monaco, for the convenience of guests from surrounding districts. They were wined and dined but rarely returned.

Transport was an impossible handicap. Those who came by sea from Nice took two hours to cover 15 miles in the ramshackle tub, *Palmaria*, which could only sail in calm weather. And few thought it worthwhile paying 50 francs return fare from Nice to bump along the craggy Corniche road for three hours, followed by a horseback ride or an hour's walk down from La Turbie to the so-called 'Palais de la Condamine'. This grim old building had been rented by Daval, who soon afterwards moved into the Villa

[5] Until the outbreak of the Great War, £1 was worth 25 francs; $1 was worth 5 francs; and a gold louis, 20 francs.

Bellevue but with no more success. He sold out to yet another syndicate, headed by a M. Lefèvre, who pledged himself to start building the promised casino on the Spélugues.

The foundation stone was formally laid by the ten-year-old hereditary prince, Albert, in the presence of his blind father, flanked by Princess Caroline and her daughter, Florestine. It rained pitilessly throughout the ceremony, an unpromising augury for the new casino which duly ran into trouble. Lefèvre engaged an architect who had to work with cheap materials and labourers disgruntled by arrears of wages. When the rocky foundation gave way, he departed suddenly for Abyssinia to take up a more satisfactory assignment.

The gambling concession had become so unfruitful that Lefèvre decided to change the locale to the Villa Gabarini. As an additional attraction he arranged charming concerts but still without any noticeable increase in clientèle. For hours on end the bored croupiers would sit outside, smoking and yawning, while a look-out stationed himself on the ramparts with a telescope to announce the approach of patrons from Nice. Only 155,000 francs in profit accrued for the three months ending in March 1860, by which time Prince Charles, who had so far received hardly a centime, insisted on expediting the new casino. Now almost bankrupt, Lefèvre desperately brought in two more shareholders, the Duc de Valmy and a French notary. They made a start on building the Hotel de Paris near the casino site, but an offer of free land to anyone who put up adjacent villas failed to tempt a single taker.

Princess Caroline again summoned Eynaud, who accepted the post of 'Commissaire du Gouvernement' with special authority to safeguard the Grimaldi interests, now even more precarious since France's recent victorious war with Austria. By the Treaty of Turin signed in March 1860, King Victor Emmanuel ceded Savoy and Nice to France. A month later the people of Menton and Roquebrune voted for incorporation into France. As soon as the Sardinian garrison evacuated Monaco, Prince Charles signed a treaty with Napoleon III, formally surrendering his claim to the two towns in return for an indemnity of four million francs (then

worth about £160,000), together with the restitution of the
Grimaldis' private estates and acknowledgement of Monaco's
sovereign independence. France also promised to build a new
coast road within two years and the prince gladly offered access to
the future railway line linking Nice with Genoa.

With a little more cash in the treasury, Princess Caroline engaged landscape artists to trace out romantic gardens on the site of
the ancient fortifications. Such flourishes gratified family pride but
did nothing to relieve the principality which had lost its most
fertile areas and was now reduced to one-fifth of its former size.

Prince Charles was prodded by his mother and Eynaud into
issuing an ultimatum demanding that the casino should be completed by New Year's Day, 1863, failing which he threatened to
cancel the gaming concession. Driven into a corner, Lefèvre
decided to sound out casino operators in the German spas with a
view to raising investment capital. It so happened that a M.
François Blanc, who had made a vast fortune from the Bad
Homburg Kursaal, had already shown more than a perfunctory
interest in the principality. Masquerading as croupiers, some of his
spies had for some time been reporting secretly on Lefèvre's ups
and downs. He therefore possessed all the background facts when
the Duc de Valmy approached him in Paris towards the end of
1862. By then the new Casino des Spélugues was about to open,
but it had only been possible to furnish the main gaming hall, the
Salle Mauresque, with space for five roulette and trente-et-
quarante tables, a smoking-cum-reading room, and the ballroom.
Funds had almost vanished before the restaurant could be completed, and the modest two-floored Hotel de Paris, designed by
Dutrou, still awaited its finishing touches.

The hard-pressed syndicate had completely misjudged Blanc's
character and background. They were no longer dealing with a
princeling, impatient for a modest supplement to his revenues, but
a rapacious ex-jailbird who had no intention of waving a magic
wand in return for some piddling financial interest in Lefèvre's
shaky enterprise.

Part One

THE BLANCS

Chapter One

FRANÇOIS BLANC and his twin brother, Louis, were born near Avignon in 1806. They inherited a flair for figures from their tax-collecting father but lacked his probity. Working together as dish-washers and waiters in small restaurants, they were light-fingered and never stayed long in any job. Between various shady ventures they became expert baccarat players and amassed enough capital to open a small brokerage office in Bordeaux.

Stock market prices in the thirties were still circulated over the country by a primitive signalling system which relied on carrier pigeons or observers with telescopes stationed on windmills, hills and other strategic points. The Blancs soon bribed a postal official in Paris to add code letters to telegrams indicating share rises and falls. This enriched them by some £20,000 before their accomplice confessed all in a deathbed fit of conscience.

The Blancs were arrested and stood trial in March 1837. François made an eloquent defence, impudently indicting the Bourse itself as no more than 'an infamous gambling-hell'. They were nevertheless found guilty of corrupting a government official, sentenced to seven months' imprisonment, and ordered to pay heavy costs. Although compelled to buy off witnesses who would have testified against them, they still had over £4,000 on leaving gaol. For a while they punted on the Bourse or gambled at a club in the Palais-Royal until Louis Philippe, following England's example, primly banned all gaming. Some of the French club proprietors moved on swiftly to the more tolerant German spas of Baden-Baden, Ems and Wiesbaden, but since the Blancs still lacked the means to compete with such palatial kursaals, they settled for a small-scale establishment in Luxembourg. Here François ran a modest casino and a mistress by whom he sired two sons, Camille and Charles.

With a little more capital and a useful knowledge of gambling operations, he soon headed for Hesse-Homburg which boasted two mineral springs and a pump room but had so far only attracted a few summer visitors. When the brothers arrived on the scene, the Landgrave Philip was straining to make ends meet and relied heavily on an annuity from England dating from the marriage of one of his ancestors to George III's daughter, Elizabeth. Having tried without much success to interest the German Rothschilds in financing a casino, he responded eagerly when François Blanc painted a rosy picture of how he proposed to multiply the number of visitors, then an insignificant 800 or so a year. He offered to build a new pump room and gaming tables which would be run with the utmost gentility, even excluding the prince's subjects to avoid antagonising the Church. The Landgrave would receive a generous rental and a percentage of the profits for a 25-year concession.

The Blancs launched their casino in 1841 with a glittering fête, dinner and ball for several hundred guests, among them notabilities from the neighbouring duchies and principalities. Patrons were tempted by odds more generous than those offered elsewhere. One zero operated instead of the customary two for roulette, and more attractive odds were laid at trente-et-quarante. A mere 1,732 visitors arrived in the first year but reached well over 5,000 within five years.

The Blancs invested most of their early returns in laying out attractive gardens and decking out the casino with tasteful silks and morocco leather. Summer was of course high season, but François soon scored off other spa rivals by keeping Homburg open all the year round. Although this involved a certain loss off-season, it was more than offset by the arrival of the Russian aristocracy, who normally made for Cannes to escape St Petersburg's winters but could not resist a visit to the gaming tables. They included rabid players like the Countess Kisselov, in her wheelchair, on whom Dostoevsky, himself an early visitor to Homburg, based the grandmother in *The Gambler*.

François Blanc's fine-turned publicity sense capitalised on aristocratic names. He mollified the countess for her heavy losses by enrolling her as a shareholder, and she reciprocated by inviting him to her Paris mansion which helped to rehabilitate him socially. He was also careful not to pressure noble losers who would often be given cash advances to continue gambling. When the Kurfürst von Hessen came over from his castle and began plunging wildly at the tables, François good-naturedly accepted 40 trees from his orangery at Hanau as security for a debt which the nobleman had no means of paying.

Prince Charles Bonaparte, Napoleon I's nephew and a cousin of the Emperor Louis Napoleon, was a luckier patron. A florid bull of a man, he arrived after a series of coups at Wiesbaden and with far more cash than the Homburg management had in hand at the time. He had an incredible winning run which netted him over £19,000 and almost emptied the bank's reserves. As Louis had retired from the Board and his brother happened to be away in Paris on business, the manager panicked. François had to wire £12,000 to keep the roulette tables in operation. He also directed his manager to reduce the maximum stake by half and re-introduce the double zero.

Blanc never forgot that very narrow squeak. From that time he enunciated and adopted a cardinal principle now holy writ to every casino proprietor: 'The house must either have more capital than any individual player or must establish a limit so that superior capital can never be brought into play against it'. He needed all his reserves to counter another phenomenal winning run in the summer of 1860, following an already disastrous season which had cut the company's half-yearly profits to a paltry seven guldern once the Landgrave had received his percentage. This time the attack came from Tomas Garcia, a Catalan who had turned professional gambler. He had tried his skill at private clubs in Paris and then made the rounds of the German spas, seldom losing, before scoring his most spectacular triumph at Bad Homburg.

He was a squatly-built man with a brigand's black beard and adorned himself with rings, diamond crosses and lucky charms. He was usually accompanied by his 'mascot', a beautiful fraulein, who followed his signals to play the maximums at trente-et-quarante. Starting with a small stake of less than £100, he won night after night and scooped over £30,000 in a single week. He then lost a substantial amount and went back to modest stakes. He soon hit another winning streak and once more staked maximums with such punishing effect that he hoisted his first week's winnings to almost £120,000. He returned home to instal himself in a magnificent chateau, vowing never again to touch a card or a gambling counter.

Although shareholders received a mere $1\frac{1}{2}\%$ dividend in that bleak year instead of their usual 40%, Blanc planted exaggerated stories of Garcia's coups in the world's newspapers with the hope of enticing less fortunate clients and spared no pains to spread Homburg's fame as a centre of elegance and gaiety whose attractions were not confined to gambling. The parks and gardens had been landscaped by an expert from Berlin and music lovers could revel in the performances of celebrated opera singers or pianists like Anton Rubinstein, who often lost all his fees at the tables. A company from the Comédie Française paid regular visits and few could fault Homburg's concerts or a décor far more artistic than the oriental extravaganzas at Baden-Baden. In this field Blanc owed much to the taste and enterprise of his young wife, undoubtedly one of his shrewdest investments.

After the death of Louis, soon followed by that of Blanc's mistress, he had engaged a pretty dark-haired village girl, Marie Hansel, to act as housekeeper and look after his two natural sons. She was a cobbler's daughter but a most capable bookkeeper and completely bilingual, an asset to Blanc whose German remained sketchy. He was almost thirty years older and unprepossessing with his straggly white moustache, a woodcock's long sharp nose and rheumy eyes behind the thick-lensed spectacles, but Marie accepted gratefully when he decided, with marriage in mind, to send her to a Paris academy for young ladies. By the time she returned to Homburg in June 1854, she had impeccable manners, talked French with a socially acceptable accent, and was quite remarkably poised for a 21 year-old.

In other circumstances she might have ended up a provincial *hausfrau* but French polish and Blanc's millions marked her out for a far more dazzling destiny. They had quietly married at an inconspicuous Town Hall in Paris on 20 June, 1854. Five months later she gave birth to a daughter, soon followed by another baby girl. Her duties as wife and mother did not interfere with her increasing pre-occupation with the Kursaal where she staged excellent concerts and quickly exhibited an artistic flair for décor and landscape gardening. She despised, but knew how to flatter, the crusty Landgrave and tactfully overlooked the excesses of rich titled clients while snobbishly excluding those who might lower the *bon ton*. In the years to come she skilfully directed the casino while her husband took treatment in Switzerland for asthma or visited Paris to invest his gaming profits on the Bourse where he was now a respected figure.

But his personal position was distinctly less comfortable in Hesse-Homburg. The Catholic Church constantly attacked his 'gambling hell' and approved the example of Prussia in closing down the casino at Aix-la-Chapelle. The Landgrave continued to pocket his percentage but pointedly snubbed his French paymaster, who also became a target for abusive or blackmailing letters attacking him as an alien for 'ruining' the country in his greed for easy millions. 'We are guaranteed by the Landgrave' he once reminded his wife when she predicted that Homburg would soon disappear if a militant Prussia took over. 'Yes, *chéri*', she answered sharply, 'but who guarantees the Landgrave?'

Her very practical foresight tilted him finally towards Monaco. He had declined to take the little principality seriously until it came under the protection of France who had promised to build the Nice–Menton road. Having seen a spectacular increase in the number of visitors to Homburg as soon as the tracks were laid to Frankfurt and other cities, he became even more interested in the plan to extend the Riviera railway line from Marseilles. Monaco had suddenly ceased to be a joke. He noted its advantages of climate and scenery and now sensed year-round profits from the slogan, 'Homburg in the summer; Monaco in winter'.

Since the Grimaldis now had their sovereignty guaranteed by treaty with authority to sanction unrestricted gambling, Blanc could rely on security of tenure. He would also be free to exploit the barren but potentially valuable acres on the Spélugues. Monaco admittedly lacked Homburg's spa waters, but his ample reserves of capital, together with likely support from his aristocratic clientèle, would underpin the new venture without much risk.

He was in a splendid bargaining position with advance information of all the stresses suffered by the very nervous syndicate in Monaco. Equally important, he guessed the ruler's own anxiety for a change of direction. The casino's profits in the previous year had increased to only £3,000, which Blanc could clear in an average week at Homburg. He was however far too astute to show his hand prematurely, preferring to strike when Lefèvre's morale and resources would be practically at rock bottom.

In December, 1862, Blanc was playing a few hands of cards at a private club in Paris when the director, one of Lefèvre's friends, confided rather too casually that a syndicate of Frankfurt bankers and directors from the Wiesbaden Kursaal had made a substantial bid for the Monaco concession. Blanc smiled inwardly at this transparent kite-flying, but he agreed to meet the Duc de Valmy, representing the shareholders, and Maître Eynaud, who held a watching brief for the Grimaldis.

The meeting testified to both Blanc's business acumen and his touch of sadism, nourished by the humiliations he had long suffered from the Landgrave. He must have found it particularly congenial to make the Prince of Monaco squirm through his envoys. He elected to stand throughout the meeting, explaining that he had a boil on his behind. It gave him a psychological advantage to talk down (both literally and metaphorically) to his unfortunate visitors. They came away with nothing more than an offhand expression of interest but with just enough bait left on the hook to induce Prince Charles, prompted by his mother, to invite Blanc to visit the principality.

He strengthened his position by stalling. His eagerly-awaited letter of acceptance was peppered with graceful compliments which showed Marie's hand, but he had bluntly stated his intentions. He proposed forming a new company with a capital of £600,000 to equip the casino on the same lavish scale as his Homburg establishment. In addition to building hotels to compete with the finest at Nice and Cannes, he would give the prince a generous percentage of profits and further undertook to provide water, gas and other public utilities. Apart from improving harbour facilities, he would help to finance the proposed road from Nice. Finally, he agreed to buy out the Lefèvre syndicate 'for a reasonable sum' but made it brutally plain that he would not be held up to ransom.

Prince Charles and his mother consulted the Duc de Valmy, who approved, but Lefèvre argued that he and his associates had spent heavily enough on the new casino to justify a good price. Otherwise they threatened to go it alone. The prince, now impatient to complete the transfer, directed de Valmy to pay another visit to Paris. Blanc's boil had apparently subsided but he was still in arrogant mood and flatly rejected a suggested price of £90,000 for the syndicate's shares and debentures. He then wrote tartly to the prince, declaring his firm intention to withdraw altogether. As expected, the Grimaldis became very nervous. Eynaud saw through Blanc's strategy but prudently urged Prince Charles to invite him once more to re-assess Monaco's potential.

The new casino had meanwhile opened with a flourish of galas which attracted many notable gamblers, including none other than Garcia, who had tired of his gloomy chateau and resumed his tour of the German spas. He avoided Homburg and made his way instead to Baden-Baden where he quickly dropped substantial sums. Curiosity, coupled with the hope that a change of scene might improve his luck, led him to Monaco. He promptly won over £2,000 at trente-et-quarante. As others began placing their stakes on the same combinations, Lefèvre saw nothing but bankruptcy ahead. News of this development reached Blanc, who now felt confident enough to pick off Monaco like a ripe fig.

He arrived in the principality at the end of March and was cordially received by the ruler, Princess Caroline, and the watchful Eynaud. Once assured of their support, he made a brief tour of the new casino, the unfinished Hotel de Paris and the still barren Spélugues before presenting himself at the office of Lefèvre, who could not hide his agitation. Blanc almost off-handedly proposed paying £68,000 for the shares and any other assets held by the company. He ignored all arguments and announced briskly, 'Think the matter over. I will return at three o'clock for your final decision. My boat leaves for Nice at four, by which time I must have your answer either way.'

The syndicate caved in without a struggle. Blanc slapped three Banque de France drafts on the table, collected a receipt and sailed off to Nice with a 50-year concession in his pocket. Next day, 1 April, 1863, the articles were drawn up for the new company, the Société Anonyme des Bains de Mer et du Cercle des Etrangers à Monaco, quickly abbreviated to 'SBM'. At the prince's specific request, his subjects were barred from the casino except as employees.

The £600,000 capital was to be divided into 30,000 equal shares of £20 each. Prince Charles received 400 shares, a guaranteed £2,000 a year and 10% of the SBM's profits. All his household expenses were covered, including pay, food and uniforms for the 120-strong Palace Guard. Blanc allotted himself 18,800 shares as managing director. 4,000 of the remainder were speedily applied for and taken up by two nominees on his wife's behalf. His name and the Homburg triumphs over two decades started a stampede for company stock, with Cardinal Pecci (later, Pope Leo XIII) among the earliest investors.

Blanc swiftly summoned his architect, Ludwig Jacobi, from Homburg to report on the new casino and, particularly, the adjacent still-unfurnished Hotel de Paris, since too many gamblers were being driven to Menton or even distant Nice for lack of suitable local accommodation. Jacobi scorned the shabby gaming rooms but, to avoid interfering with play, simply replaced the cheap furniture in the Salle Mauresque with elegant sofas and rich silk curtains. He dismantled or enlarged the other rooms and installed better lighting so that patrons could read their newspapers or drink at the bar in greater comfort. Punters were also tempted by Blanc's decision to abolish the double-zero at roulette and raise the maximum stakes. These concessions were favourably noted in many foreign newspapers which also carried lists of the celebrities who now visited Monaco.

Jacobi joined forces with Dutrou to complete the Hotel de Paris which they modelled on the Grand Hotel in the Boulevard des Capucines instead of the original cheeseparing conception. It opened on New Year's Day, 1864, a tribute to the drive and admirable taste of Marie Blanc, who spent over £8,000 on table silver alone. Many distinguished visitors took rooms, including the Duke of Hamilton and Lord Strafford from England. It soon became an unwritten law to give heavy losers credit until their luck turned, and hotel bills would often be discreetly waived. Madame Blanc also initiated the *viatique* for the benefit of less aristocratic punters. They received second-class fares home, plus an allowance for sandwiches or other light refreshments en route, but strictly on condition that such loans would be repaid before any further visits to the casino.[1]

---

[1] One of the earliest recipients was an English medical student, who had lost £1,000 at the tables. He soon emigrated to Australia and made a large fortune in wool. Returning to Monte Carlo 40 years later, he was politely reminded of his *viatique* by the casino's receptionist, who produced a faded but still legible receipt.

Blanc did not charge for admission but introduced cards of entry to exclude the cheats and adventurers of both sexes who prowled the rooms for likely victims. He also increased the minimum stakes to discourage the indigent. Only ladies of the highest distinction or known personally to the management were at first admitted; even so, their presence at the tables was tactfully ignored by the croupiers who announced 'Messieurs, faites vos jeux', a gallant fiction still preserved by all European casinos. Old friends like the Countess Kisselov had of course been welcomed, and Blanc at once re-imbursed her when a pickpocket lifted her wallet with £1,000 in banknotes.

His most pressing problem was to improve transport pending the completion of the railway and the road promised by France. He scrapped the old boat and chartered a more efficient steamer, with accommodation for 300, on the Nice–Monaco run. Land on the scraggy plateau round the casino had soared almost overnight from 20 centimes to 25 francs a square metre, and speculators were putting up villas or opening stores with a gold rush frenzy.

But there was no Wild West saloon atmosphere in Monaco. Marie Blanc stared wistfully at the natural terraces on the south side of the casino overlooking the sea. In her mind's eye she could already see vast expanses of flower beds which would bloom almost year-round in this sunny mild climate. She soon built five hothouses for imported tropical plants and visited Florence specially to secure rare species from Prince Demidoff's palace at San Donato. Always elegant and serene, she often visited the Grimaldi palace where Princess Caroline, herself a gardening enthusiast, warmly endorsed her plans for beautifying the Spélugues.

Prince Charles also approved, although he was rarely accessible after the death of his long-ailing wife in 1864. He now suffered from attacks of dizziness and insomnia which made him ill-tempered. He neglected his son, Albert, whose boyhood had been dominated by an autocratic grandmother. He later wrote feelingly of what it had meant to him to escape to the Normandy estate with gentle Princess Antoinette. 'My mother', he recalled, 'who was truly a good woman and never spoke a cruel word, opened my eyes in early childhood to the spectacle of human misery. Scarcely a day passed without her showing me those human ills in the poor cottages of the Marchais.'

Adolescent introspection met with little sympathy in the booming first years of the Blanc régime. Even blind Prince Charles had been briefly caught up in the excitement, although he tended to make lengthier visits to his estate which, like the palace in Monaco, he could now afford to maintain in something like its former splendour. In November, 1865, he signed a treaty with France yielding the principality another £8,000 per annum in lieu of salt rights and customs dues. The casino also showed profits of £40,000 by the end of that year.

Now that the Spélugues section, with its casino, shops, two thriving hotels and villas, together with a projected new artery, the Boulevard des Moulins, covered one third of Monaco, Blanc thought it time for a distinctive new name. Prince Charles had agreed to issue an ordinance dividing the principality into three communes; Monaco-Ville, the old settlement on the Rock comprising the palace and a few administrative buildings scattered between narrow cobbly lanes; the Condamine or port district; and the area stretching from the valley of Ste Dévote and the Spélugues promontory to the eastern end of the principality. This would be called Monte Carlo, an adaptation of 'Mont-Charles', in honour of the prince, whose own first preference had been for 'Charleville'.

The SBM grossed two million francs for 1867 and nearly 400,000 more in the following year. Profits soared even higher with an influx of visitors after the completion of the railway from Nice to Vintimille in October, 1868, although the Nice–Monaco road crawled like a tortoise. But Blanc still had the best of reasons to bless his wife's intuitive preference for Monaco. The Seven Weeks War of 1866 had ended with the crushing defeat of the Austrians at Sadowa and the establishment of a North German Confederation. Hesse-Homburg and the other petty principalities were absorbed by Prussia, who had long since abolished gambling in her own territories and now gave Blanc notice to quit by the end of 1872.

Homburg continued to be patronized by gamblers and mineral water addicts, but Blanc had naturally begun to concentrate more capital on Monte Carlo where one of his most trusted lieutenants, Bertora, ran the casino. Madame Blanc supervised the gardens, hotels and other attractions, while preserving a friendly relationship with the Grimaldis. They had quickly restored the cracked marble staircase of the Cour d'Honneur and renovated the dingy State Apartments, several of them now occupied by the early-widowed Florestine, Duchesse d'Urach, and her children. The palace façades had been repainted and the crenellated fishtail towers were extended to conform in style with the original mediaeval fortress.

Blanc had honoured his civic obligations by providing drinking water and street lighting. He financed sewage works and spent liberally to complete the harbour, but he still had to pay a bitter personal price for the gold louis and banknotes which poured into his casino coffers. The English writer, John Addington Symonds, was noting in his diary as early as March 1866: 'There is a large house of sin blazing with gas lamps by night, flaming and shining by the shore, like pandemonium or the habitation of some romantic witch . . . Little can be heard but the monotonous voice of the croupiers, the rattle of gold under their wooden shovels and the click of the ball spinning round for roulette. The croupiers are either fat sensual cormorants or sallow, lean-cheeked vultures or suspicious foxes'.

Blanc defused much adverse publicity, usually inspired by ruined gamblers or jealous Riviera hoteliers, by taking lavish space in London and Paris newspapers. They printed lists of the English milords or Romanovs in residence at the Hotel de Paris. He also bribed hacks, like de Villemessant, to make flattering references to the Prince of Monaco. De Villemessant had failed in the ribbon trade before acquiring *Le Figaro*, then a tabloid scandal sheet. He readily produced stories of elegant parties and dazzling roulette coups.

He was rewarded with a piece of land on the Condamine at a nominal price far below its soaring market value. He was a gorilla-like man whose coarseness offended the finicky Madame

Blanc, but he had to be tolerated for his undoubted usefulness. Apart from his own puffs in *Le Figaro*, he persuaded Blanc to pay the editor of another Paris newspaper a retainer of 25,000 francs a year for a daily mention of Monte Carlo even with nothing more to report than the invariably fine, sunny and warm weather. Tropical thunderstorms would be dismissed as light showers and there was never a hint of the unkind mistral.

The years of pressure on Blanc had left their mark. By his mid-sixties he had become frail and shrunken, blinking suspiciously in the bright sunlight like a man who spends his nights in some dark cell counting great piles of banknotes. He had grown suspicious of would-be friends and almost pathologically vindictive.

He exacted cruel revenge from Garcia for his never-forgotten triumph in Homburg. The Spaniard's return to gambling had lost him his chateau and he plunged even more desperately to make a killing. He was barred by other fashionable spas who found his manners distasteful and drifted to Monte Carlo where Blanc twisted the knife by personally raking in his old enemy's francs. Garcia was reduced to standing outside the casino, babbling of past coups and begging old acquaintances or even strangers for a louis or two to finance his 'infallible' system. One night the doorman, acting on Blanc's instructions, refused him admission. He slunk back to Spain to die in a Trappist monastery.

Madame Blanc, younger than her husband and far more poised, cut a dignified figure at all times but with a sometimes jarring hauteur. At palace receptions her jewels noticeably outshone those worn by the Duchesse d'Urach. She committed an even worse *gaffe* by demanding that the royal guard, who formally saluted François Blanc, should extend her the same courtesy.

Prosperity had increased the population by several thousand, the majority employed by the SBM, but Blanc had unwisely appointed his brother-in-law as *Chef des Jeux* at the casino and given other top jobs to trusted employees from Homburg. He also began to recruit a low-paid labour force from Piedmont to build new villas and roads. Swaggering about like brigands in checked shirts with bright red geraniums in their straw sombreros, they infuriated the

Monegasques who worked less hard but still demanded higher wages. They had other and more justified grievances. The influx of visitors (reaching 150,000 a year by 1870) had made the water supply scarce and often erratic. Some local malcontents threatened to set fire to the casino and others flatly refused to work with the Piedmontese.

Blanc promised to improve the water supply, but he recognised that this was only symptomatic of a deeper unrest which might jeopardise his entire operation. He therefore hinted tactfully to Prince Charles that a few concessions might be to everyone's ultimate advantage. It was duly decreed on February 8, 1869, that the people of Monaco would henceforth enjoy complete exemption from all direct taxes and military service. The fiscal relief immediately attracted foreign capital for new villas, shops and restaurants, but this in turn led to an increase in the resented imported labour. When a noisy protest started outside the palace itself, the National Guard looked the other way to show its sympathy with the demonstrators. Their chief target was a former French officer, Captain Doineau, Blanc's building superintendent, who bullied local workmen and continued to hire still more Italians. The rioters had staged their protest on the Fête of Ste Dévote, confident that their fellow-citizens would be disposed to strike a blow against tyranny while the cannons fired from the palace ramparts in memory of Monaco's patron saint.[2]

The prince, who was anxious both to placate his subjects and assert his authority, expelled Doineau. Blanc hurried back from Paris and protested vigorously, but Prince Charles was only restrained by Maître Eynaud from ending the concession. Blanc yielded rather than risk further antagonising the prince, already

---

[2] According to legend, Dévote, a humble Corsican girl, was converted to Christianity in the third century and refused to give up her faith even under torture. While praying on the rack, her soul ascended to Heaven and her body is said to have been left in a boat, piloted by a dove, safely reaching the Bay of Monaco for Christian burial on 27 January 303. Each year on that day a boat is symbolically burned on the pavement outside the Church of Ste Dévote. Holy relics are carried through the twisting streets of Monaco-Ville and down to the harbour where priests solemnly bless the waters.

incensed by press attacks lampooning him as an indolent ruler who luxuriated in the profits from a vicious gambling hell. These attacks, invariably mounted in Nice, had only been mitigated by the intervention of Napoleon III, who had pleased the Church by refusing to legalise gaming in France but argued that Monte Carlo indirectly benefited resorts like Nice and Cannes by attracting so many rich visitors to the Riviera.

He was also well disposed to the Grimaldis, particularly the young heir, a special favourite with the Andalusian-born Empress. Prince Albert had been granted a commission in the Spanish Navy after graduating from Lorient, but he had resigned after Queen Isabella's dethronement. Tall and thickset, with a shy manner which women found attractive, he enjoyed several amours with Court ladies and actresses. As the future ruler of a now booming principality, he had become a most eligible bachelor with a wide choice of suitable mates.

The bride chosen for him by Napoleon III, prompted by the Empress Eugénie, won full approval from Prince Charles. Lady Mary Victoria Douglas-Hamilton was the daughter of the late Duke of Hamilton, one of Scotland's wealthiest landowners. He had been a notorious drunkard, lecher and gambler, who died after falling downstairs in a Paris brothel. Her mother, a former mistress of the French Emperor, was a descendant of Stéphanie de Beauharnais, Napoleon I's adopted daughter. Lady Mary herself, a pretty and virtuous 18 year-old, had the asset of a handsome dowry but would not inherit the bulk of her huge personal fortune until the age of 24. The couple met and seemed mutually attracted. In August 1869, with his father's consent, Prince Albert visited the Hamilton summer residence at Baden-Baden where he was warmly received. It could not be called a love match, but neither was in any position to withstand parental pressure, reinforced by the Emperor's approval.

The marriage contract was formally signed on 18 September at the summer palace in St Cloud. Napoleon III smiled benevolently although he wore a little rouge on his pallid cheeks and was suffering from stones in the kidney. Twenty years his junior, Eugénie almost skipped with joy as she kissed the young couple and wished them happiness. They married three days later at Marchais in a chapel originally built for the Dukes of Lorraine.

The young princess was already pregnant and dispirited by the time they arrived in Monaco that December. She disliked the gloomy palace and could establish little rapport with blind Prince Charles. Though kindly at heart, he was often irritated by the bickerings of his sister, the Duchesse d'Urach, who wished to run the household, and Princess Caroline. The gentle Scottish girl felt miserably unhappy and isolated between these strong-willed rival châtelaines. Albert, already itching to be back at sea, had no patience with an ailing wife, who was disappointingly cold between the sheets. He would often console himself in Paris. Within a few weeks she had taken refuge with friends in Nice, before going on to Baden-Baden where her son, Louis, was born in July, 1870. Prince Albert made formal if half-hearted attempts at reconciliation, but his relief was obvious when the Franco-Prussian War gave him an opportunity to join the French Navy.

The War proved far less satisfactory for François Blanc. As director of the doomed but still operating Homburg Kursaal, he had been compelled to contribute to the Prussian War Loan which made him even more unpopular when he returned to Monte Carlo. Monaco had not suffered financially. 140,000 visitors arrived in 1871, mainly from Italy, France, England and Germany, with a growing number of titled Russians.

The new government in Paris added to Blanc's troubles by infiltrating the principality with spies, alleging that it had become a haven for enemies of the Republic. They demanded stronger action against the royalist exiles and showed less tolerance of Monaco's gaming monopoly, even hinting at annexation if their little neighbour remained 'unfriendly'. Prince Charles promptly insisted on a much closer scrutiny of casino visitors. Blanc co-operated and had the satisfaction of expelling the notorious adventuress, Cora Pearl, who had snubbed him at Bad Homburg where she had once queened it as the paramour of Prince Jérome Bonaparte, Napoleon III's cousin. She was given twelve hours to leave

Monaco and, for years afterwards, repeated scandalous tales of Blanc's criminal past.

Others added to the quota of malice which soured his last years. He was dogged by blackmailers and slanderers, but they did him and Monte Carlo less damage than the reports of suicides who, according to the thriller writer, William le Queux, averaged one a day throughout the Seventies. Most of these stories were apocryphal, like the well-worn fable that one rogue had smothered himself with tomato sauce and walked off with his wallet, replenished by Blanc's security men, before the police arrived to claim the 'corpse'. And Paris journalists, hired to attack Monte Carlo's monopoly, reported fancifully that a secret little cemetery in French territory, some miles from Monaco, was reserved for suicides who had been carted off at dead of night.

Blanc persuaded the government to ban the issue of poisonous drugs by local pharmacies. All sales of guns were strictly prohibited and hotel chambermaids had instructions to search the luggage of guests and remove bullets from any concealed revolvers. Blanc himself had a sharp nose for potential trouble. One night he recognised a heavy punter as a cashier from the Banque de Paris. He rightly scented embezzlement but waited until the wretch was down to his last few francs before requesting the police to expel him from Monaco. He then wired the Sûreté, who made their arrest as the wanted man stepped from the train in Paris.

Blanc suffered the cruel irony of many another expatriate. He was a patriotic Frenchman but would never be allowed to forget his shady past, whereas his German-born wife, whose elegance and *savoir faire*, backed by well-advertised good works, won her far more popular esteem in Monaco. He had to take the brunt of vicious slanders without winning any credit for the principality's prosperity. Following the final closure of the Homburg Kursaal in 1872, he had added a wing to the Hotel de Paris and extended the casino. Dutrou's new Salle Mauresque would provide ample room for another five roulette and trente-et-quarante tables. Terraces offered a fine view over the Port and Madame Blanc had engaged celebrated experts like Forckel and van den Daele to develop exotic trees, shrubs and giant magnolias for a year-round show. The *plongeurs* of the Hotel de Paris were now sternly discouraged from emptying their slops on the outside terrace to kill plants which had often cost thousands of francs to import.

In 1872 Blanc had started a pigeon-shooting competition with a top prize of 10,000 francs (£400). The birds, with tail-feathers cut to ensure a smaller and more 'sporting' target, were released from five traps on the casino terrace and attracted crowds of sightseers. The first winner, an American named Lorillard, spent 400 francs on cables advising New York friends of his triumph. The Tir aux Pigeons became an annual event and was ritually celebrated with a lavish banquet. Few journalists refused invitations once Blanc began inserting a crisp *mille* in their table napkins. Competitors also received handsome payments for 'endorsing' guns, cartridges and various powders.

Apart from issuing inflated stories of casino coups, Blanc initiated the practice of draping a table in black crêpe and supplying players with free champagne if they had the good fortune to 'break the bank' by exhausting that particular table's reserves of currency and counters. He remained undismayed by these rare triumphs and pooh-poohed the number of so-called 'winning systems' like the Martingale (doubling up on bets in the usually suicidal hope of recouping losses) and the d'Alembert, based on increasing by one unit after a loss and decreasing it after a win.

The inexorable edge in the bank's favour, backed by the cupidity of punters ('money won in a casino is only lent', Blanc used to say after a bad night's play), netted him enough steady profit to advertise a prize of a million francs for anyone who could produce a foolproof winning system at roulette. It was never won but still gave Monte Carlo useful publicity.

As at Homburg, Blanc condoned the presence of pawnbrokers and moneylenders, who encouraged unlucky players to plunge more deeply, but he did all possible to exclude undesirables. He also shared his wife's snobbish penchant for well-dressed patrons. Doormen had strict instructions to turn away shabby-looking visitors. For some years evening dress became *de rigueur* at night and brown boots or knickerbockers were discouraged even for the afternoon sessions. One day an Englishman in rough tweeds was inspected from head to foot and superciliously asked for his passport. 'I haven't got one,' he demurred. 'Indeed, why not?' 'Well, I'm the man who issues them, as a matter of fact.' The receptionist smiled derisively and stood firm. Bertora, manager of the casino, and a quartette of colleagues, all formally dressed in frock coats and silk hats, arrived some days later at the Marquess of Salisbury's villa near Beaulieu to apologise for an unfortunate error. The British Foreign Secretary graciously forgave them.

The Franco–Prussian War had only temporarily checked the annual winter exodus to the Riviera. The Prince of Wales, whose stay in Scarborough had almost ended with his death from typhoid, was among the first of the foreign regulars to return. He had often visited the German spas in the past but gladly sought diversion in Monte Carlo when the wheels stopped turning in Bad Homburg and Baden-Baden. He played for modest stakes at roulette, preferring baccarat, and appreciated the small upstairs room which Blanc had opened for the convenience of aristocratic clients, who could gamble in privacy and comfort without walking through the crowded main salon, contemptuously known as 'The Kitchen' because of its popularity with the servant class.

Blanc introduced another innovation to raise the social status. For some years he had arranged free concerts by a large orchestra in a hall beyond the gaming rooms. As the performances were always well attended, he also occasionally engaged theatrical companies from Paris. These attractions became so popular that the hall could not possibly accommodate all the visitors during high season. Madame Blanc therefore persuaded her husband to build a theatre adjoining the casino. She argued shrewdly that audiences would not only be tempted to play between acts and after the performance, but Prince Charles would surely welcome a refreshing blast of artistic uplift to help clear Monte Carlo's foetid reputation.

The suggestion chimed perfectly with one of Blanc's recent ventures. In the summer of 1874 he had won himself rare esteem in France by lending the Ministry of Works £196,000 to finish building the new Paris Opera House. He had charged an almost nominal 6% interest but cannily demanded, as a *quid pro quo*, that more trains should run between Paris and the principality. The architect, Charles Garnier, also promised to design the Casino Theatre as soon as he had completed his work in Paris.

Blanc did not live to see its opening but survived long enough for the brilliant marriage of his elder daughter, Louise. She and her sister, Marie, were both expensively educated and introduced into the highest Parisian social circles. Louise had made the acquaintance of Prince Constantine Radziwill, scion of a noble if impoverished Polish clan whose title derived from the Holy Roman Empire, but Blanc's long experience of dissipated nobility had made him cautious. He bribed the prince's servants and hired detectives to check thoroughly on the young man's debts, health, friends and habits. He overlooked his mistresses and even a weakness in the lungs but was finally convinced by proof that Constantine had no taste for gambling.

The wedding at the Church of St Roth was the social event of Paris in 1876. The bride wore magnificent diamonds bought indirectly by several of Blanc's patrons in the congregation, including one of the heaviest losers, Count Branicki, the Countess Kisselov's son-in-law. The couple would live comfortably on a huge dowry and also enjoy the Chateau d'Ermenonville, once the home of Jean-Jacques Rousseau. It had been a wedding gift from the bride's parents.

François Blanc was having treatment for asthma at Louèche-les-Bains when he died in July 1877, leaving £3,600,000 of which £40,000 was bequeathed to his parish church, no doubt as a kind of *pour le Personnel* gesture. His widow received the bulk of the estate, but handsome provision had been made in cash and shares for Blanc's two natural sons. The offspring of his marriage each received 4,200 SBM shares.

He was mourned by few outside his family circle, but for good or ill he had democratised gambling and opened an admission-free club for people of all classes. He had also brought prosperity to a barren little principality which, at the time of his death, could boast 19 hotels, scores of handsome villas and furnished apartment houses, together with banks, restaurants and elegant shops.[3] The tax-exempt locals found well-paid employment as gardeners or casino employees and in new industries like the macaroni factory, a model brewery, thriving steam laundries, perfumeries and a pottery started by Madame Blanc.

The Prince of Monaco might affect distaste for the gaming tables but his original 400 SBM shares were now worth £190 each, with 75% dividends paid as regularly as his percentage from the cash lost by an average of 250,000 gamblers every year. Nevertheless, his revenue brought him little solace. His aged mother, on whom he had depended from his early youth and almost entirely since his blindness, died only a few months after Blanc. He was less happy with his rather vinegarish widowed sister, Florestine, and found life at Marchais more congenial, particularly with his little grandson. Louis had been brought up with affection in Baden-Baden but was sent back to Monaco after the annulment of his parents' marriage by the Vatican, soon followed by his mother's second marriage.

His father, Albert, the hereditary prince, had little time for him, having developed a lasting passion for oceanography. He studied under Professor Milne-Edwards, after resigning from the French Navy, and also became interested in the pioneering work of a former American naval officer, Matthew Fontaine Maury, whose logs provided fascinating new material on the mysteries of winds and currents. After the death of Milne-Edwards, Albert decided to continue with independent research in submarine zoology and chemical oceanography.

In England he had bought a 200-ton schooner, renamed

[3] The *Annuaire officiel* de Monaco for 1878 lamented: 'The Condamine, a former bower of oranges, lemons and violets, is now a thriving suburb. A pretty tree-lined avenue is now a road of 20 houses . . . The delightful rococo fountain has been replaced by a pharmacy . . .' Today, almost a century later, local conservationists would almost echo those sentiments!

L'Hirondelle. With a crew of 15 but lacking even a donkey engine, he managed to collect specimens to a depth of nearly 9,000 feet. He crossed the Mediterranean several times and studied Atlantic currents, making surveys of the Gulf Stream at various depths with special floats. A huge shoal of fish, discovered during his soundings to the south-west of the Azores, became the basis of an important trawling centre. The discovery of numerous underwater pits also generated an ambition to prepare a bathymetric map of the oceans. He hoped one day to build a museum in Monaco to house his collection of marine specimens and provide facilities for further research, but his father was unsympathetic to what seemed to him a costly and time-wasting hobby for a future ruler.

Prince Charles had become a figure of pathos in his later years. Blind, helpless and irritable, he suffered prolonged dizzy spells and developed an allergy to dust and the perfume of flowers only relieved by mountain air, but he returned to Monaco for the grand opening of the Casino Theatre on 25 January 1879 when his sister hung the Order of St Charles around Garnier's neck after a pro-logue recited by Sarah Bernhardt.

Madame Blanc had at first expressed misgivings about the architect's extravaganza which seemed more fitting for the Paris Opéra than a small theatre. 'All this vulgar display of gold and gilt will only remind clients how much they have lost at the tables' she once warned her husband, but he was enough of a showman to remind her that, quite apart from the theatre's artistic appeal, the two new tiled and pinnacled towers, visible from the sea, could become a permanent advertisement for the casino.

The cream-coloured façade with its green bulbish domes con-trasted sharply in style with the palace battlements, but it seemed to complement Monte Carlo's flamboyant and bustling vulgarity. The entrance was dominated by gilded statues of Nubian slaves clutching crystal candelabra. The auditorium's accent was on gilt, with a riotous bonus of friezes, garlands and shields. Each of the 540 carved *fauteuils* was upholstered in red plush. Huge mirrors and florid frescoes adorned the walls and the vaulted roof was supported by bronze and gilt Amazons ogling two nude young athletes.

Night performances would be gaslit but large windows allowed perfect daylight for matinées. Admission was free for all seats, and patrons could pass the waiting hours by strolling under the tall palms to admire Madame Blanc's colourful flowerbeds or perhaps gaze on two rather tasteless sculptures planted on the higher terrace outside the theatre. For little apparent reason other than advertisement, Garnier had decided to commission figures by an unlikely couple, Bernhardt and Gustave Doré. The actress's winged girl represented 'Song', a crude effort which only her most ardent admirers would applaud. Doré's attempt was more professional but even his skill as a painter could not compensate for the lack of technique and banal inspiration in 'The Dance', with a dimpled cupid half-heartedly waving his bow and arrow. As they had been hurriedly rushed out for the opening night, there was no time for marble. Without ironworks locally available for bronze, the figures had to be moulded in clay and cast in plaster. Cupid and the songstress would quickly develop bad cases of eczema in the hot Mediterranean sun.

The gala opening on 25 January 1879 was a spectacular success. When Prince Charles entered, the entire audience rose to bow to the royal box and then cheer the flushed architect to his seat. A prologue had been written by some now-forgotten poet from Marseilles whose verses included a stirring call, passionately declaimed by Bernhardt: 'Artists, I have gathered palms to crown your heads. Blessed be you all! You who have awakened the Gods'. Madame Blanc, sabled and bejewelled, dabbed her eyes sentimentally and left the theatre long before the rest of the excited audience.

That night was in a sense a monument to her husband's régime, but she had lost much of her élan and impetus since his death. She had suavely adapted, and often taken the credit for, his bold innovations but now missed his financial acumen. His sons were intelligent and Camille, who had served his years of apprentice management in the casino, now volunteered eagerly, perhaps too eagerly, for more responsibility, but Marie Blanc had never quite trusted him and suspected a threat to her authority. She turned instead to Bertora, her husband's former confidential secretary, who managed the casino efficiently and was such a good son of the Church that the Vatican had made him a papal Count. He was also a very practical man and, within a few months of Blanc's death, proposed marriage to the wealthy and still comely widow. She rejected him gracefully, pleading that her children's welfare was now her only concern.

She had grown disenchanted with the casino and often thought wistfully of retiring to her country house at Moutiers where she liked playing lady bountiful and lavished large sums on a new village church, school and hospital. In Monte Carlo she seldom entered the gaming rooms and spent most of her time supervising the gardens. She always dutifully attended gala performances at the theatre which now seemed to dwarf the casino. As the Salle Mauresque had become too small and shabby-looking, she endorsed Camille's suggestion for a new room designed by Garnier. Its chief feature was a series of rather exuberant murals illustrating popular contemporary sports, including croquet.

Soon afterwards, on 24 April 1880, a bomb hidden under a hat exploded beneath the clock in one of the other rooms, extinguished all the gas jets and blew out every window. It went off when all the tables were crowded after a concert next door. Robbery may have been the motive; if so, it failed completely. Oil lamps were hastily lit to reveal the croupiers still impassively guarding the piles of gold coins and banknotes with poised rakes. Nobody attempted to rush them, but Bertora at once made it a rule that all parcels, hats, coats and valises would have to be checked in the cloakroom. From that time oil lamps were always kept filled and ready for any emergency.

This outrage, following a deluge of begging or blackmailing letters since her husband's death, intensified Madame Blanc's distaste for her gambling empire. Parisian society seemed infinitely more attractive after the engagement of her younger daughter, Marie, to Prince Roland Bonaparte, nephew of the prince who had almost ruined her husband during his early days in Homburg.

This alliance with a Bonaparte was an almost unbelievable social coup for a cobbler's daughter. She was spared the tragic death of her daughter in childbirth but would no doubt have rejoiced in her grandchild, who later married Prince George, son of King George I of Greece. Marie Blanc was only 47 when she died suddenly at Moutiers whose villagers long testified to her piety and philanthropy. Her art treasures alone, auctioned at the Hotel Drouot in Paris, fetched several million francs, and there was spirited bidding for her celebrated five-row pearl necklace and other jewels.

Camille Blanc took over at once, soon demonstrating that he had inherited his father's tactical skills but with the advantage of better health and far more social poise. He camouflaged an ice-cool professionalism by an affable manner which matched his tubby appearance and innocent-looking blue eyes. He was often seen backstage at the theatre where he twirled his flowing blonde moustache at the prettiest young actresses who might be persuaded to sup with him at the Café de Paris followed by a visit to the small villa he had built at La Turbie.

There was nothing of the dilettante in his crisp business style. He had quickly trimmed Bertora's authority and also persuaded his brother to become a sleeping partner. In the year of Mme Blanc's death the SBM's net profits reached a record £700,000, but Camille could not afford complacency. Once the Nice–Menton road was completed in 1881, more visitors arrived by the thousand but, although Monte Carlo's gaming tables now commanded Europe's most distinguished clientèle, they stopped off briefly and continued to spend most of the winter in Cannes, Nice or Menton.

More luxury hotels and restaurants had become as high a priority as the casino's own expansion. Camille also hoped to engage world-famous artists for the theatre but it became more imperative to compete with the elaborate carnivals and sporting attractions of the rival French Riviera resorts. It was a challenge which demanded a far bolder and more contemporary direction than either Blanc *père*, ailing in his last years, or his snobbish widow had achieved. But no significant expansion would be possible without heavier cash reserves and perhaps increased outside investment.

On 14 December 1882 the SBM quietly doubled its capital to £1,200,000, divided into 60,000 shares of £20 each. Apart from a few hundred allocated to the prince, François Blanc's descendants divided 52,000 equally, with most of the remainder taken up by Camille's close friends or his mistresses, past and present, as nominees.

Chapter Two

THE RAILWAY and the newly-completed road from Nice carried half a million visitors a year to Monte Carlo within the next decade. Many franked their letters and picture postcards with the first stamps to carry the ruler's head.[1] The Hotel de Paris soon sprouted another wing and the British-owned Gordon Hotels company opened the stone-built Métropole in 1889. They shared the patronage of the Emperor and Empress of Austria, the Dowager Empress of Russia and the Kings of Sweden, Belgium and Serbia, together with millionaire guests from the United States and the Rand, who now anchored their yachts regularly in the enlarged port.

Fleury, manager of the Hotel de Paris, promised every modern comfort, including lifts and electric light. He also prided himself on the best cellars in Europe, one huge cask of brandy alone being valued at 100,000 francs. His cuisine featured such specialities as *soufflé surprise*, served hot despite a raspberry ice centre, *mousse de loup Bombay* (sea bass with a superb curry sauce) and the hotel's incomparable mandarin ices. But he faced stiff competition from the Grand which had less impressive fittings and décor but a gastronomic edge when César Ritz became general manager. He

[1] This original set was issued in 1885 and has become a valued collector's item. Even rarer are the documents and letter-covers overprinted with 'De Monaco' from the early 18th century. From 1762 letters were marked in an oil-based ink by a linear stamp simply identified as 'Monaco'.

engaged Escoffier, who created kitchen classics like *Timbales de Sole Grimaldi*[2] and celebrated the Prince of Wales's first visit with *Poularde Derby*, a variant of Bernhardt's cherished *Zéphyr de poularde Belle Hélène*, a symphony of chicken's breasts on paté de foie gras, served with asparagus salad.

Even after Richard d'Oyly Carte had enticed the gifted pair to his new Savoy Hotel in London, the Prince of Wales remained faithful to the Grand where his incognito of 'Baron Renshaw' was scrupulously respected. No word ever leaked to journalists concerning Lily Langtry or other charmers in his entourage. He could always rely on his favourite whisky, John Dewar's Black Ball, and the hotel staff was sternly forbidden to turn his bed, a duty performed daily by his personal valet except on Fridays, one of the Prince's firmest superstitions.

He chanced to be staying at the Hotel Esterel in Cannes when the Riviera littoral suffered a severe earthquake shock on the morning of Ash Wednesday, 23 February 1887. He had planned to depart for London that very afternoon but considerately remained for a few more days to avoid starting a panic. He then left to spend a week or two in the Monte Carlo villa of his racing friend, Sir Frederick Johnstone.

The earthquake killed 300 people in a church at San Remo and Nice also suffered many casualties, but Monte Carlo enjoyed the devil's own luck, with only a brief moment of panic when tipsy crowds, returning from a fancy dress ball, knelt hysterically in prayer as the earth heaved and buildings began to creak. The wife of the Banque de France's Governor vowed impulsively to donate all her gambling winnings to the Church if she were spared, but that night settled instead for half-a-dozen thanksgiving candles to the Virgin. Sir Arthur Sullivan lit a cigar nonchalantly as a lady rushed out of the Hotel de Paris in her nightgown, without even time to clap on a wig, and tried to climb a monkey puzzle tree in

[2] Fillets of sole, small crayfish, with truffles, butter, cream, cheese etc. in a pastry case. Among other specialities prepared by Escoffier and leading contemporary chefs are Mousse Monte-Carlo (a meringue and Chantilly cream mould sprinkled with crystallised violets) and Poularde Monte-Carlo (baked chicken stuffed with rice, crayfish and truffles).

the Boulingrins. Other guests also made a hasty exodus but soon returned. Within a few days the Hotel de Paris was again crowded with royalty and most players celebrated their escape with soaring stakes.

The London *Times* had commented righteously, 'There is one place where the earthquake experience will be a matter of special interest – the reprobate but fascinating Monte Carlo. What so appropriate as that on the first morning of Lent that home of wickedness should have suddenly been destroyed by the forces of outraged nature . . . Fortunately or unfortunately, the casino still stands and the course of the roulette wheel is unaltered.' The wages of sin were more than ample. The SBM declared a £790,000 profit for the year.

Queen Victoria, who was holidaying that spring at the Villa Edelweiss in Cannes, endorsed *The Times* with a crushing snub to Prince Charles. He had hurried back from Marchais when told that she would pass through Monaco on her way to Menton. His palace guard was ordered to smarten up their drill and the band practised 'God Save the Queen' with desperate enthusiasm. Camille Blanc took the precaution of sending a huge bouquet to the villa with the SBM's compliments, but Her Majesty got into her landau and drove straight through the principality, tight-lipped and without so much as a glance up at the palace. Two days later Blanc received back his bouquet, still untouched in its handsome casket. He turned sadly to Bertora and sighed, 'It would have been worth at least two million francs in publicity to the Casino had she called on the Prince.' It might also have helped to discourage reports of his 'bloodstained dividends'.

While Monte Carlo's green baize flourished, French hoteliers smarted from a tourist shortage. They joined forces with Europe's leading churchmen, doctors and reforming journalists in condemning the poisoned atmosphere of the casino whose 'sinister roll of suicides' numbered 2,000 since 1860, according to one hysterical over-estimate. Many others joined in the campaign, often for different reasons. Robert Louis Stevenson played a little mild roulette but came away 'nauseated' by the pigeon-shooting, while Karl

Marx, seeking warmth for his shattered lungs, wrote contemptuously of 'Monaco-Gérolstein' (a reference to Offenbach's operetta) in a letter to his daughter. Guy de Maupassant, half mad and afflicted by incurable syphilis, used to find relief in cruising along the coast in his yacht, *Bel Ami*, but he favoured simple fishing villages like St Tropez. In one of his stories he wrote acidly, 'From Cannes, which is full of determined poseurs, to Monaco, which is full of gamblers, hardly a soul comes to this part of the world except to swagger and fling money about and to display, under the glorious sky, in this garden of roses and orange blossom, every form of mean vanity, senseless pretension and vile covetousness and to reveal the soul of man for what it is – abject, arrogant and greedy'.

Some took a more tolerant view. The first Paris edition of the *New York Herald* appeared soon after the earthquake. Its opening issue ran a social column which carried the momentous announcement, 'Mr William C. Vanderbilt will return from London on Wednesday'. Vanderbilt, who had already multiplied his $65 million inheritance, became a regular visitor to Monte Carlo and often put in with his luxury yacht, later replaced by the million-dollar *Valiant*. The paper also welcomed the arrival of J. Pierpont Morgan in his black-hulled *Corsair*. A guzzler of food and wine, constantly chewing black cigars (he had reluctantly cut down to twenty a day), he was an unprepossessing man with his large head, shaggy eyebrows and an inflamed nose which would have dwarfed that of the future W. C. Fields. But his appearance and gruff manner did not deter celebrated actresses like Maxine Elliott or his many paramours whom he used to reward with a standard dowry of $100,000 when they married.[3]

He gave up patronising the casino when the management declined to raise the maximum roulette stake above 12,000 francs (a

[3] Maxine Elliott, *née* Jessie Dermot from Rockland, Maine, was the daughter of an Irish immigrant sea captain. She survived two drunken husbands (she became the fifth of Nat Goodwin's eight wives) to emerge as a celebrated London and Riviera hostess. Apart from J. P. Morgan, whose Wall Street tips netted her an investment fortune, she declined offers of marriage from both Rosebery and Curzon and numbered King Edward VII among her admirers.

paltry $2,400). He retired peevishly to the Hotel de Paris to play his favourite two-pack solitaire and only returned to Monte Carlo when his father, Junius Spencer Morgan, who spent his winters there, died in hospital after his carriage horses had bolted near Eze. Morgan later resumed his short winter visits but grew still more intolerant of the casino. When he took over Carnegie Steel and engaged Charles M. Schwab at a million-dollar salary, he would often lecture him about his wild play at the tables. 'Very undignified in your position' he once growled. 'But I did it openly and not behind closed doors' protested Schwab. 'Well, that's what doors are for', Morgan snapped back.

The ultra-snobbish owner and editor of the *New York Herald*, James Gordon Bennett, who had made journalistic history by sending Stanley in search of Livingstone, hardly missed a single night in Monte Carlo during his regular trips to the Mediterranean. He continued his practice of itemising lists of fellow-American visitors in his Paris edition whose staff had strict orders never to mention bad weather on the Riviera. They zealously charted the yacht movements of the Morgans, Vanderbilts, Astors and Drexels and gave flattering space to well-heeled hostesses like Mrs Ogden Goelet, wife of the real estate and railroad tycoon. She knew everyone from Newport to Cannes, either in her own right or through her family connections (her elder brother married Caroline Astor and her sister, Grace, became Mrs Cornelius Vanderbilt III). The Prince of Wales gorged at her chateau near Antibes but had to sit through endless musical entertainments when he would have preferred baccarat at the Cercle Nautique in Cannes or in Camille Blanc's private salon above the casino.

Bennett's hospitality was legendary, although the dozens of china pekingese and cocker spaniels strewn over his lawn at Beaulieu often tripped Grand Dukes and other festive visitors. But one could pardon a host whose yacht provided a Turkish bath and an Alderney cow in a padded stall to supply passengers with fresh milk and cream. He entertained regally at the Hotel de Paris and used to give flower girls 500 francs for a bunch of violets. He demanded fruits out of season and massive helpings of Beluga caviare with plover's eggs, to which he was addicted, but head waiters quaked when he stalked through a restaurant, tipsily yanking off tablecloths on both sides of the aisle as he crunched china and crystal underfoot. One day he was requested to wait for his usual table at the Café Riche in the Galeries Charles III. He bought the place instead, dismissed the manager and presented the deeds to Ciro, his favourite waiter.

This fat, nut-brown little Neapolitan had served his apprenticeship in America, including a short spell at Delmonico's, before arriving in Monte Carlo to help out in a small bar on the Place du Casino. His broken English amused clients like the Duke and Duchess of Connaught, Sir Arthur Sullivan and Lord Chief Justice Russell, with many rich fellow-Americans following in the wake of James Gordon Bennett. Ciro's, the prototype of similar establishments in Paris, London and Deauville, soon became the principality's most fashionable restaurant for late-night celebrations. Although his prices exceeded those of the Hotel de Paris, his place was so popular that even royalty had to book in advance for the prized terrace tables.

His only serious rival in Monte Carlo was the Café de Paris opposite the Casino and also owned by the SBM. Regular clients included Czar Nicholas I's grandson, the exiled Grand Duke Michael, who used to give elaborate parties and once won a ludicrous-wager by spreading a napkin over a dish of chocolate soufflé and sitting on it throughout a banquet. Another favoured guest was the Prince of Wales, who is said to have made gastronomic history there by first eating Crêpes Suzette, specially prepared for him by Henri Charpentier, then a young *commis de rang*.[4]

He was a special favourite of the Prince, who arrived one day with a party of ten for luncheon and called out cheerfully, '*Bon jour*, Henri, have you something good for us today?' Charpentier handed him the menu, adding brashly that he could perhaps offer a

[4] Others, like Joseph of the Restaurant Marivaux in Paris, the celebrated Savarin and the maître d'hôtel of the Paillard, are each credited with responsibility for this dubious essay in showmanship *flambé*. Yet another theory ascribes the origin to one of Napoleon's chefs who is supposed to have named it in honour of his mistress, Suzette. But the concensus of opinion favours Charpentier.

THE GRIMALDI DYNASTY (Condensed).

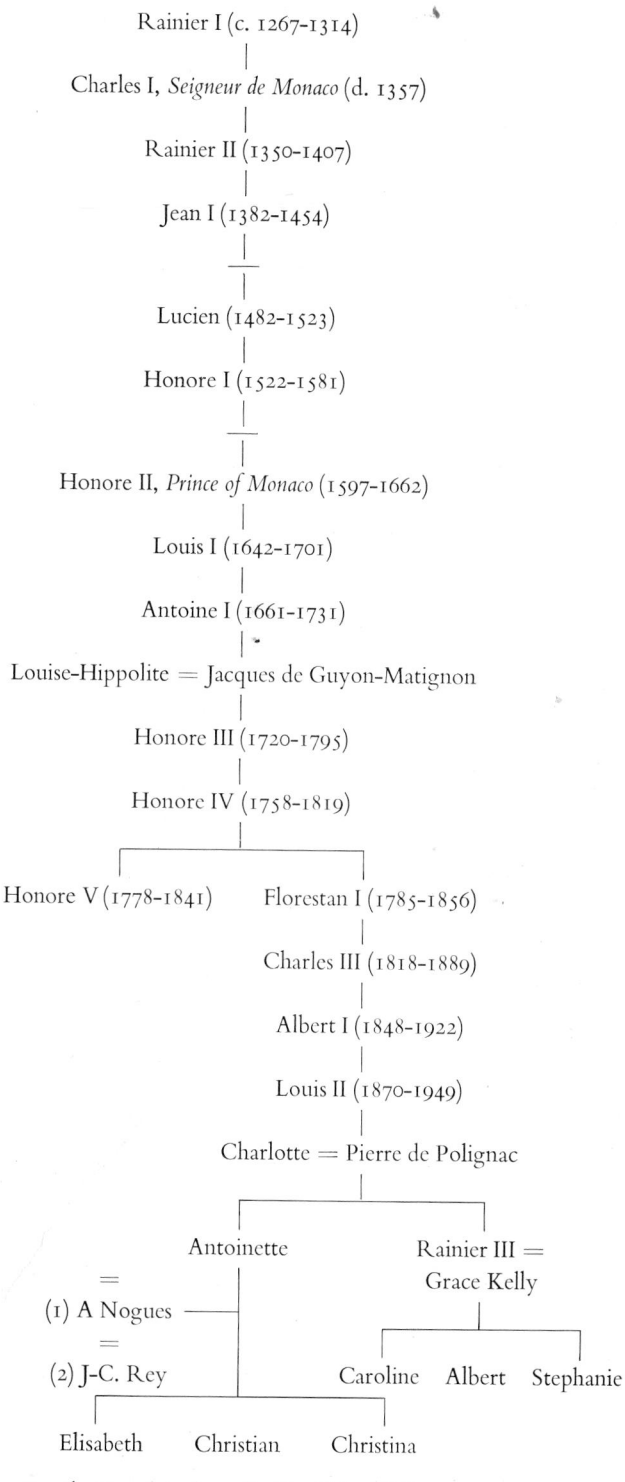

Rainier I (c. 1267-1314)

|

Charles I, *Seigneur de Monaco* (d. 1357)

|

Rainier II (1350-1407)

|

Jean I (1382-1454)

|

Lucien (1482-1523)

|

Honore I (1522-1581)

|

Honore II, *Prince of Monaco* (1597-1662)

|

Louis I (1642-1701)

|

Antoine I (1661-1731)

|

Louise-Hippolite = Jacques de Guyon-Matignon

|

Honore III (1720-1795)

|

Honore IV (1758-1819)

Honore V (1778-1841)   Florestan I (1785-1856)

|

Charles III (1818-1889)

|

Albert I (1848-1922)

|

Louis II (1870-1949)

|

Charlotte = Pierre de Polignac

Antoinette   Rainier III =
                    Grace Kelly

= (1) A Nogues

= (2) J-C. Rey   Caroline   Albert   Stephanie

Elisabeth   Christian   Christina

Family Tree (condensed). *The Grimaldi Dynasty.*

My Lord

Wee having been given to understand, That the Spanyard had some
Designe to attaqe Mardike, did send five Companyes of Colonell
Guibons Regiment from hence, for assisting of the forces there,
but having now understood, that there is an addition of forces of
ffrench and English, which Wee hope (through the blessing of
God) may be able to defend that place, against any attempts of the
Enemy, It is our desire, That your Lordship will please to
cause the returne to England of those five Companies,
of Colonell Guibons Regiment with all possible speed, for whose
transportation Wee have taken care.

yor good freind

Oliver P

Cromwell's letter, dated 30 December 1657, is preserved in the palace archives.
Addressed to Marshal d'Aumont, a Grimaldi kinsman by marriage, it refers to
his support of the French and English armies against Spain.

The first casino, built in the early sixties, was extensively enlarged during the coming boom decades.

The casino's new theatre, opened in 1879, had two pinnacled towers visible from the sea – a permanent advertisement.

Monte Carlo's 'wedding cake' Casino overlooking the Port. Its gaming tables, and terraced gardens continue to attract world tourists of all classes.

François Blanc took over the gaming concession in 1863. Casino profits and land values soared within a few years. He died a multi-millionaire.

Charles Coborn singing 'The Man Who Broke the Bank at Monte Carlo'. It celebrated the phenomenal winning streak of Charles de Ville Wells in 1891.

Princess Alice, wealthy American-born widow of the Duc de Richelieu, married
Albert I in 1889. Their stormy marriage ended in bitterness.

Prince Albert I achieved world recognition for his scientific voyages and as a pioneer in marine research. He inaugurated Monaco's celebrated Museum of Oceanography.

Beauty Queens on display at a 1911 competition in the Palais des Beaux Arts.

Suicides by ruined gamblers brought a crop of hostile cartoons from France, jealous of Monte Carlo's roulette monopoly.

special pancake or *crêpe* as a dessert. The maître d'hôtel, Niccolo, and a furious chef had to stand by while the impudent 16 year-old went into the kitchen and began preparing paper-thin pancakes with a warm fruit sauce which his foster mother used to make. Deciding that it was too homely for royalty, he added curacao, kirchwasser and maraschino but nervously over-poured. The liqueurs caught fire as he was standing too near the chafing dish. The Prince, already sniffing appreciatively, applauded as the coloured flames shot up. The pancakes proved so much to his taste that he called for more, characteristically spooning up the rich syrup. 'What do you call this dish, Henri?' he demanded between mouthfuls. Charpentier thought of replying, 'Crêpes Prince', but as that would have been ungrammatical, blurted out, 'Crêpes Princesse'.

'No, no', laughed H.R.H. with a courtly bow to his host's small daughter. 'You must call it, "Crêpes Suzette".' Next day he rewarded Charpentier with a panama hat and cane, but the young *commis* did not last too long at the Café de Paris. He soon embarked on a successful career which led to the managership of the Rockefeller Center restaurant and finally to his small but exclusive establishment on Redondo Beach.

From Camille Blanc's very first years, Monte Carlo's hotels and restaurants had swiftly won an international reputation among gourmets. Tables glowed with orchids, and elaborate flower arrangements set off the gilt and rich brocades of dining rooms all furnished in the ornate Second Empire style. Carnations were usually avoided in deference to superstitious gamblers who thought this flower had a *malfaisance* or jinx on it. The finest wines, served in Florentine or Venetian crystal goblets, accompanied specialities created by master chefs.

Coquelin and other stage celebrities had dishes named in their honour, and the epoch's most flamboyant cocotte received the fishy accolade of 'Suprèmes de Sole Otéro'. Some were less easily pleased, notably dragons like the Duchess of Devonshire, whose raddled face and passion for bridge won her the nickname of 'Ponte Vecchio'. In the casino she became notorious for 'mistakenly' claiming winning stakes as her own. After her usual substantial lunch she once hurried off to the casino but stumbled down the hotel's marble staircase. Next morning a local journalist reported: 'Yesterday, a lady descending the steps of the Hotel de Paris had an accident. The *fallen woman* (author's italics) proved to be Her Grace the Duchess of Devonshire'. Following a luckless session at trente-et-quarante with the Prince of Wales's banker friend, Sir Ernest Cassel, she was dining alone and even more vile-tempered than usual. A waiter proffered the bill for her signature but his arithmetic happened to be at fault. She called loudly for Fleury, who apologised abjectly and offered to dismiss the culprit. 'Oh, don't bother', said the ogress in a booming voice. 'He may simply be following in the footsteps of Monsieur François Blanc and preparing to found a casino'.

King Leopold II of Belgium was even more autocratic and Monte Carlo's hoteliers murmured heartfelt hosannas when he finally moved into an isolated villa at Cap Ferrat. He liked to take a daily swim with his huge white beard tucked into a rubber envelope, but during his residence in Monte Carlo preferred to have several gallons of hot sea water poured over his head every morning, after which he perused his newspapers all carefully ironed by the staff.

The Emperor Franz Josef always installed a mistress or two at the Hotel de Paris when he arrived to join his wife briefly at Cap Martin where she spent the winter months. She had her own lovers, customarily much younger than herself, but looked remarkably trim and slim-waisted for her years. At the Hotel du Cap, which James Gordon Bennett had saved from collapse by an investment of ten million francs, she had a trapeze-like swing fitted to her bed for strenuous early-morning exercises. She rose at five and bathed in distilled water followed by a vigorous massage before emerging to watch the sunrise. On her daily 15-mile afternoon walk into Monte Carlo she liked the company of a handsome young student from the University of Athens who, among other duties, recited soothingly from the classics when she paused to rest. She used to swim vigorously in a quiet bay near Cap Martin, hiding her jewels in a rock, a secret place known only to her friend, the ex-Empress Eugénie, whom she often joined for tea and pastries at Rumpelmayer's in Monte Carlo.

Eugénie had first come to Cap Martin in 1888. The following year she bought a piece of land and built a villa fronting the sea, with the Rock of Monaco in the background. On the terrace sheltered by a semi-circle of flowering shrubs she entertained Russian Grand Dukes and the Prince of Wales, whose mother never failed to call on her while staying at Cimiez. But no visitors, however exalted, would be received on Sunday, her black day.[5]

She was among the first residents on the coast to install a telephone and electricity, soon abandoning her carriage for the earliest motor cars. She cruised in all weathers in her own small yacht and frequently joined James Gordon Bennett on the *Lysistrata*, striding the bridge with him when most of the other passengers were praying for early deliverance. A beautiful woman even in her late sixties, she used neither rouge nor powder on her pale magnolia skin. For her promenades in Monte Carlo she favoured a large black lace-trimmed hat, long black gloves and invariably a bunch of Parma violets at her waist. Five rings ritually adorned her left hand. In the other she carried either a green silk parasol or a black ebony walking stick, but more for effect than support as she had an elastic step and always slept by an open window, even in England, where she still rode to hounds when most of her contemporaries were in bathchairs.

She seldom visited Monaco at night except to dine with the prince or attend an operatic gala in the Salle Garnier, as everyone now called the theatre. She detested gambling and soon persuaded her young kinsman, Prince Roland Bonaparte, to sell the 4,200 SBM shares he had inherited from his widow, François Blanc's

[5] The Second Empire had collapsed on that 'unlucky' day and her beloved son, the Prince Imperial, had been killed on the Sabbath while serving with the British in the Zulu War. She was destined to die on Sunday, 12 July 1920, in the palace of her nephew, the Duke of Alba, as the bells of Madrid rang for early Mass.

daughter. As a guest one night in Prince Albert's box, she had reluctantly accompanied the others into the casino after a concert and found herself sitting beside Lady Blanche Hozier, Winston Churchill's future mother-in-law. Each had placed five louis *en plein*, but one of the coins happened to slip into the winning slot, paying seventeen times the stake. This started the friendliest of arguments, both graciously insisting that the other had won. The prince good-humouredly agreed to act as judge and decided to place five louis on the next spin, inviting the ladies to nominate a number. The nearest to the winning number would collect the 90 louis in abeyance. The Empress won but never again set foot in the casino.

She could not be persuaded that the Grimaldis had any moral justification for living on the proceeds of gambling, but retained her affection for Prince Albert whose first and disastrous marriage she had so hopefully encouraged. She was far more sanguine about his second wife, although astounded, like everyone else, that the rather dour sailor-scientist should have captured France's richest and most fascinating widow.

Albert had not only broken with the traditional Grimaldi 'marriage of convenience' but his bride would be the first American-born Princess of Monaco.

Chapter Three

PRINCESS ALICE was a native of New Orleans and daughter of Michel Heine, the poet's nephew. Formerly a prominent Hamburg banker, he had spread his operations to the United States to make a killing in real estate and cotton. Alice, the 17 year-old heiress to a huge dollar fortune, had married the Duc de Richelieu, who died in 1880 after only four years of marriage. She had rapidly flowered into the most brilliant hostess in Parisian society. Her salon in the Faubourg St Honoré became a plush-lined nest for France's leading intellectuals and even a waspish chronicler like Proust, who used her as part model for his Princesse de Luxembourg in *A L'Ombre*, paid tribute to 'a woman of the soundest judgment, the warmest heart'. She was gay, witty, cultured and also a dazzling blonde beauty. Her looks inevitably attracted fortune-hunters, but she was coquettish by nature and preferred a succession of bedmates.

She had first met Albert, heir to Monaco, in Funchal, Madeira during one of his scientific expeditions. Like almost every other full-blooded man in European society, he was captivated by her and flattered when she became his mistress or, rather more accurately, enrolled him among her lovers. He was then nudging forty, taciturn and short-tempered, but the vivacious Duchesse, temporarily jaded by Paris, must have found his seriousness refreshing after her dilettantish coterie. Hard-headed and not given to impulse, she had perhaps already decided that the Palace of Monaco might serve as a delightful setting for a social and cultural empire with herself in the rôle of another Catherine de Médici. Albert would no doubt be malleable and undemanding if allowed to pursue his passion for marine specimens, while she would reign in sunny Monaco during the winter months and pass the rest of the year either in her Paris mansion or the Grimaldis' picturesque but rundown Chateau de Marchais on which she proposed spending several million. Her two children, the young Duc de Richelieu and his sister, Odile, seemed to welcome the prospect, while the views of Prince Albert's only son, Louis, could be ignored. After a lonely boyhood he had departed with relief for St Cyr rather than follow his father's naval career. He was now serving in Africa with the Foreign Legion.

Prince Albert's relationship with his own father had been equally cool for many years, but this did not prevent the ruler from sternly vetoing the proposed marriage to a Duchesse whose current liaison with her Jewish doctor, among others, had scandalised Paris. Albert had to acquiesce, under protest, but continued to haunt the Faubourg St Honoré. The situation resolved itself on 10 September 1889 when Charles III died at Marais. He was briefly mourned and soon forgotten in the excitement of proclaiming the new ruler, who revived the ancient patriarchal custom of inviting the heads of all the leading Monegasque families to proclaim their formal allegiance in the Cour d'Honneur. He won more popularity by promising to build a new hospital and also made arrangements for improving the local schools. Within a month his subjects were celebrating his wedding, although some grumbled that the ceremony had been performed in Paris, as the bride insisted, while others did not relish bending the knee to an American Jewess instead of a princess of royal blood.

Her arrival coincided with a peak period in Monaco's affairs. That season, marking the centenary of the French Revolution and the opening of the Paris Exhibition, the principality absorbed a record half-million free-spending visitors. To accommodate them the casino's entrance vestibule was enlarged and a new walnut-panelled gaming room opened, the Salle Touzet, named after an architect whose decorations aped Garnier's florid manner. Camille Blanc seemed quite insensitive to the possibly satirical impact of four huge murals representing Folly, Fortune, Night and Morning. He was enchanted by the princess, who deplored her husband's dependence on the casino (the SBM contributed 95% of Monaco's total revenue) but was practical enough to exploit Blanc's anxiety to change Monte Carlo's frivolous image. He approved her plan to replace his stepmother's cherished hothouses with the new Palais des Beaux Arts whose huge central hall under a vaulted glass roof would give excellent light for exhibitions by artists like Alma-Tadéma, Bartholdi and Burne-Jones.

Prince Alice opened her own purse to build the Tower of Saint-Martin, from which the Grimaldi standard waved above the Rock, and an adjacent three-storeyed edifice with its crenellated turret. Her taste – and cash – also shaped a lavish programme of interior decoration in the Italian Renaissance style. Albert had meantime commissioned a new three-masted schooner of 600 tons from a London shipbuilder. Equipped with a 350 h.p. engine, the vessel had a small laboratory for photography and microscopic examination under the direction of a zoologist, Dr Jules Richard. As a compliment to his wife, who had almost certainly signed the cheque, Albert christened his boat, *Princess Alice*. During the next five years, from 1892 onwards, he made several cruises in the Atlantic and Mediterranean, once trawling for specimens to a depth of 5,530 metres off the coast of Madeira, as he proudly reported to his very bored wife.

The princess, who detested sailing and was invariably seasick, had little taste for squiggly octopi and similar delights. While Albert was away at sea, she offered lavish entertainment at the palace or in the summer at the Chateau de Marais where her guests included Paul Bourget, Duse and Bernhardt, a close friend. Saint-Saëns would be persuaded to sit down at the piano and song recitals were given by visitors from England like the composers

Paolo Tosti and Isidore de Lara, a Sephardic Jew with a rakish reputation as duellist and philanderer. Pierre Loti was another cherished guest. Very small and acrobatic, he would rouge his cheeks like a circus clown, remove his corsets and do back somersaults. He usually walked round the drawing-room on his hands for an encore but amused Prince Albert far more with his racy stories of life in the French Navy.

It was soon an open secret that de Lara had become the princess's lover. She and her husband maintained a polite façade but the cracks widened. While he became more abrupt and ill-at-ease with her friends, she sparkled in their company but still pined for her gay salon. Her collection of pearls and furs excited the envy of every woman in Europe, and she once admitted to owning 1,200 pairs of silk stockings with a permanent stock of over one hundred pairs of handmade boots and shoes.

She was equally bored by flashy gamblers and Monaco's stultifying bureaucrats whom she had to receive at formal receptions as her husband's proxy. Missing the civilised delights of the Paris theatre, she soon convinced Camille Blanc, her doting slave from the first, that some of the casino's profits might usefully be diverted to the 'Salle Garnier' which had lapsed into mediocrity after its early seasons. She argued subtly that a more inspired direction would draw gamblers between their sessions at the tables, apart from the growing number of visitors who had little enthusiasm for roulette but might welcome sophisticated artistic entertainment. Her husband had a keener taste for plankton than Puccini, but even he saw the advantages of bringing culture to his principality, with the SBM of course footing the bill. Camille Blanc gave the princess *carte blanche*, although as yet unaware that he had signed a blank cheque for an impresario, who could spend money faster than any croupier raked it in.

Princess Alice had entrusted Raoul Gunsbourg with the task of transforming Monte Carlo into an operatic capital. He was the descendant of rabbis and had suffered poverty and anti-semitism in his native Bucharest, drifting on to Russia and later Paris where he briefly studied medicine. He returned to St Petersburg to sing in cafés before taking up theatrical management. An ugly dwarf-like figure with a Cyrano nose, he overcame these disadvantages by a caustic wit and quite exceptional vitality, even by Jewish standards. He was a born man of the theatre with an instinct for showmanship which, in a later age, would have made his fortune on Broadway and no doubt in Hollywood. His dynamic personality and high-quality productions had induced artists like Bernhardt to appear in Russia for the first time. Anticipating Benois, Bakst and other masters of design, he had no patience with traditional sombre décor and experimented boldly for elaborate scenic effects. From the late eighties, suffering from weak lungs, he had fled the sub-zero temperatures of St Petersburg to winter in Nice where his superb presentations of opera delighted audiences, including the discriminating Princess of Monaco.

Early in 1892, after petitioning the Czar for formal permission to live abroad, Gunsbourg took over the full-time direction of the Salle Garnier. His régime would last for 60 years. From the first he had demanded a free hand and an almost unlimited budget to engage the world's best singers, dancers and musicians. He had a genius for handling the most awkward performers whom he provided with first-class railway tickets and even arranged for local dignitaries to present bouquets *en route* so that they arrived at Monte Carlo in cheerful spirits and readier for his marathon rehearsals. He rarely signed contracts with artists, who appreciated that his word was worth more than any written document. He gratified their every whim, cosseted them with flower-filled suites at the Hotel de Paris and unhesitatingly paid fees of £400 a performance to Patti, Melba and Jean de Reszke.

He captured the loyalty of his orchestras by offering handsome salaries with pensions for long-term service, but he insisted on the highest standards in return. He had swiftly engaged the musical director of the Théâtre de la Monnaie in Brussels, Léon Jehin, himself a brilliant violinist and composer, who later orchestrated some of Gunsbourg's own operatic scores. Jehin carefully recruited over a hundred first-class instrumentalists from France, Belgium and Italy. One eccentric Englishman, for 20 years the first violin, lived at Cap d'Ail and continued pedalling back and forth on his bicycle long after the advent of automobiles. It was not uncommon to see him in full evening dress repairing a puncture on the roadside and quite unperturbed by jeering motorists.

Gunsbourg also hired some of Europe's most gifted scenic artists. He had fitted out a spacious studio in a long-disused building near the railway station where technicians devoted long hours to perfecting ingenious lighting effects. He would lie, bribe, wheedle and make extravagant promises to get his way, but always with an impish sense of fun.

Elaborate scenery, reflecting Gunsbourg's passion for lush Byzantine décor, was inevitably costly. Blanc had endorsed the payment of huge fees to performers whose names helped to glorify Monte Carlo, but he still blinked at bills for genuine Louis Quinze furniture, Grecian urns and other lavish props. Gunsbourg would scour Paris and Florence for authentic materials demanded by his scenic designer, Visconti, who had a permanent staff of 40. It resulted in Gunsbourg's décor often excelling the Comédie-Française in taste and originality, while his planning genius, backed by inspired team work, enabled him to mount almost any production in two or three weeks compared with the months normally required by the Paris Opéra, Covent Garden or La Scala.

He made an instant impact with *La Damnation de Faust* which Berlioz had originally written as an oratorio for the Comique in 1846. Gunsbourg had personally adapted it for the operatic stage, engaging de Reszke for Faust. He also showed bold enterprise in snapping up two of César Franck's last works for the theatre, *Hulda* and *Ghisèle*, and even charmed Saint-Saëns into writing an opera, *Hélène*, specially for a Monte Carlo première, with Melba in the leading rôle. But his greatest triumph in those early years was to present one of Massenet's most successful operas, *Le Jongleur de Notre Dame*, with Renaud of the Opéra-Comique heading a superb company.

Within a year of taking over he engaged Tamagno, the leading

Italian tenor until Caruso's spectacular advent, for *Otello* at £400 a performance. He was an unfailing box-office draw but impresarios had to pay dearly for the privilege. Notoriously mean, he always supped at the Café de Paris as the guest of lesser members of the company and sycophantic critics. He once shocked Gunsbourg by demanding six free stalls, which he promptly sold, and also insisted on having his carriage fare paid from the nearby Métropole, pocketing the six francs as he always walked!

Gunsbourg had been approached before the opening by the enterprising sales director of Pears Soap, who proposed lightening Othello's complexion by make-up throughout the opera. As the curtain went up for Act Four, a poster would slowly descend and unfold the magic words, 'Pears Soap'. He was prepared to reimburse the management for Tamagno's entire fee and pay him an additional 2,000 francs to co-operate. Gunsbourg angrily showed him the door but refrained from mentioning the offer to Tamagno, who would certainly have jumped at it.

Tamagno was less successful in *Messalina*, in which he sang the gladiator's rôle opposite Calvé as the voluptuous empress. The opera was composed by Isidore de Lara, who based his style on Saint-Saëns and Massenet but lacked their creative spark. It offered Gunsbourg scope for opulent spectacle but he rightly doubted its merit and had long hesitated to stage the première in Monte Carlo. He had to be cajoled by Princess Alice, who secretly contributed 200,000 francs towards the heavy production costs. The gala audience gave the piece an enthusiastic reception, but it had been a night of social, rather than artistic, triumph. *Messalina* was later hissed off the stage at La Scala where it opened and closed after one performance.

Camille Blanc seldom pruned Gunsbourg's enormous budgets. It would have been difficult to cavil at the fees for Tamagno and Melba when the SBM cheerfully spent another £12,000 on building arches on the rocks to improve the pigeon-shooting. Moreover, he was gratified by the aristocratic audiences who flocked to the theatre once he had suspended free admission during the four-month operatic season. Although free entry continued to the gaming rooms he now charged 20 francs for a seat in the theatre, but this was obviously nominal. It did little to reduce a regular yearly deficit which Blanc accepted as a paper loss largely under-written by patrons who trooped into the adjacent casino after a performance.

Evening dress became obligatory for all gala nights, graced by an invited audience of Romanovs and English and French nobility with Her Serene Highness usually gracing the Royal Box. Massenet and Saint-Saëns often attended performances of their works, and Puccini made the journey from his lakeside retreat in Tuscany to assist at rehearsals, since the ebullient Gunsbourg already had a bad reputation for 'improving' scores or even changing parts of a libretto in the composer's absence.

Camille Blanc revelled in this celebrity limelight but without losing his very practical sense of proportion. Dowagers in tiaras might shed a sentimental tear over Melba's soaring arias but even Puccini could not rank as a publicity attraction with the obscure composer of a certain catchy music hall chorus celebrating the exploits of a little Cockney confidence trickster.

Millions, who had never seen a roulette wheel, would soon be whistling, 'The Man Who Broke the Bank at Monte Carlo'.

Blanc had automatically continued his father's promotional gambit of advertising a reward of a million francs for anyone with a fool-proof winning system at roulette. He became confident enough to double the bait but had an uncomfortable moment when a York-shire engineer, Jaggers, pulled off a series of phenomenal coups. Acting on the theory that no roulette wheel could be 100% per-fect, he had engaged a staff of clerks for a solid month to record the winning numbers at half a dozen tables. Having satisfied himself that flaws in a few cylinders accounted for some numbers coming up more often than others, he placed his bets accordingly and won £120,000.

The management had noted his plan of campaign and soon began changing the cylinders from table to table. Jaggers quickly lost £40,000 before he and his sharp-eyed assistants spotted enough distinctive marks on some cylinders to make them identifiable. He won back his £40,000, and more, while all the wheels were being scrutinised by the manufacturers hurriedly summoned from Paris. They agreed that the partitions dividing each number might vary minutely but thought this could be overcome by making a new wheel with movable slots. Thus, if the little receptacle opposite a certain number were placed opposite a different number before play commenced, no system punter could possibly benefit from the flaw in any particular cylinder. Jaggers invested heavily until the casino's counter-attack became painfully clear to him. He stopped playing when still ahead by some £80,000.

It was a costly but valuable lesson for the casino which soon began manufacturing its own wheels in an underground *atelier*. This helped to cut costs and also eliminated the risk of collusion between manufacturers and punters, while minimising possible losses from defective equipment. All wheels would now be spirit-level tested in the presence of the casino directors, every morning at 9.30, half an hour before the popular gaming rooms opened. Precision to one-thousandth of an inch could be guaranteed once the table and wheel were thoroughly tested for perfect balance. A *cylindre* would be withdrawn at the first sign of wear to a spindle or any of the aluminium slots. Even the diameter of the ivory ball, which diminished with constant use, was minutely checked with callipers. Similar attention was paid to croupiers' rakes and the 'shoes' for dealing the cards at chemin-de-fer.

The Jaggers foray was in no way fraudulent but it led to a general tightening of security, with special regard to any unusual activity by teams of punters. A picked squad of plain clothes detectives, nicknamed 'Les Occultes' and known only to Blanc and his closest colleagues, would patrol the rooms and keep an eye on suspicious-looking players as well as other casino employees. More care was now taken to recruit and train croupiers, who could be trusted not to pocket chips or co-operate with patrons. Apart from the essential qualifications of perfect sight, an excellent memory and supple fingers, all had previously served in other capacities on the SBM staff, a safer policy than François Blanc's practice of engaging croupiers from foreign casinos. Their backgrounds would be thoroughly probed with special reference to their friends and such potential weaknesses as nagging or extravagant wives. It also became the custom, in force for many years, to issue them with pocketless suits. This meant keeping handkerchiefs uncomfortably tucked up their sleeves, but they would still be watched by the vigilant *chefs de partie* and inspectors every time they blew their noses. Even so, chips and plaques could sometimes be smuggled out by pressing them against the genitals with adhesive.

Croupiers had to be watchful for cheats, most often women who made false claims or practised *la poussette* by nudging their losing stake towards a winning number after the spin. They also needed steely self-control in handling arrogant and irascible patrons like ex-King Milan of Serbia, who had been deposed by his subjects in 1889. He once became irritated by the presence behind his chair of Prince Stanislas Poniatawski, Napoleon III's Master of Horse and a grand-nephew of the last King of Poland. 'Go away' he snarled. 'You bring me bad luck'. 'Sire, I was not behind you when you lost your throne' the prince reminded him. That night, continuing his bad run, Milan leaned across the table and boxed the croupier's ears. Following a strong hint from the directors that he risked being barred for his conduct, he apologised next day and sent the man 1,000 francs as compensation. The apology was accepted, but not the money, although a croupier's pay was modest at that time for three strenuous two-hour shifts, six days a week. Even with a share in the *tronc* from gratuities, few could afford more than shabby homes in La Turbie or Beausoleil, usually in houses built and owned by Camille Blanc, who had astutely made a corner in low-priced properties.

In addition to charging for admission to the theatre, he had unobtrusively ended the automatic grant of the *viatique* which some punters had abused. One accepted his fare back to Paris and grumbled, 'What about a ticket for my dog?' 'But your dog didn't gamble' Blanc snapped. Players now had to prove a minimum loss of £300 before receiving a railway chit on the authority of two casino directors. The applicant's photograph was also issued to the doormen who would not re-admit without reference to the management. The luxury of free board and lodging at the Hotel de Paris had long since been discontinued, although exceptions would still be made for respected patrons who had been ruined at the tables. Throughout his régime Blanc continued payment of many small pittances, usually 10 or 15 francs a day, some dating from his father's time.

One bearded and beetle-browed Russian, Nicholas Stakaieff, finally gave up after losing eight million louis. Blanc handed him 10,000 francs on his solemn pledge never to re-enter the casino. (By the end of the First War he was destitute and the SBM allowed him 1,000 francs a month on which he lived modestly for another 20 years in a Monte Carlo *pension*. The casino took care of his funeral and even provided luncheon afterwards at the Café de Paris for a handful of mourners.)

Stories of ruined players fuelled Europe's strong anti-gambling lobby. Blanc bribed his way out of much unpleasant publicity but failed to hush up the misfortunes of a world celebrity like Sarah Bernhardt. During the late Eighties she was staying at the Hotel de Paris while studying her part in *La Dame aux Caméllias* for a forthcoming London season. One night she paid her usual visit to the casino and had a disastrous losing sequence. She took a massive dose of veronal in her bedroom where one of her lovers, the Vicomte de Rohan, found her unconscious and called doctors. Thanks to Princess Alice's banker father, who converted her stage earnings into solid investments, Bernhardt was saved from penury and at last cured of her gambling addiction.

All the world's newspapers had run stories of her attempted suicide, but fortunately for Camille Blanc and his fellow-directors, attention switched almost immediately to an astonishing gambling coup. It cost the casino a substantial sum but would be worth countless millions more in free publicity.

★　　★　　★

Charles de Ville Wells, 'The Man Who Broke the Bank of Monte Carlo', was anything but the dashing monocled 'masher' of that rollicking ditty. Shabbily dressed and bald, with a straggly black beard, this brash little 50 year-old Cockney had trained briefly as a naval architect before deciding to live on his wits. Victims credited him with painting sparrows yellow and marketing them as canaries. Among various ventures he had sold sugar in Russia, mined in Spain and tried paper manufacturing in Paris. In 1885, while half-starving on his boat at Plymouth, he turned his nimble brain to inventions and took out nearly 200 patents over the next five years. They included an automatic foghorn, a new sardine tin-opener, a machine for scraping ships' bottoms, an envelope opener and even a musical skipping rope. Money poured in so plentifully from hopeful investors that he opened handsome London offices and bought himself a £20,000 yacht as a mobile showroom.

He was in deep water by the spring of 1891 and turned to the gaming tables in the hope of retrieving his fortunes. In July he sailed into Monte Carlo with his pretty mistress, Jean Burns, a former artist's model. As this was off-season, with only the Hotel de Paris still open but almost empty, so few gamblers patronised the casino that Wells's spectacular coup attracted abnormal attention. Starting with a modest £400, he punted for eleven hours at a stretch and won £40,000 over three days. As each roulette table then carried a float of only £4,000 in cash and plaques, he succeeded in 'breaking the bank' no fewer than six times during this phenomenal run.

Reports of his triumph spread beyond Monte Carlo. Every foreign newspaper carried stories about him and London's penny broadsheets printed daily bulletins of his winnings with extravagant claims for an infallible system which at last threatened to destroy the casino. In fact he did not rely on any system but merely increased his stakes, if winning, and stopped when the luck turned against him or he had lost half his starting capital. Unlike those who relied on the Martingale and were invariably defeated by the bank's maximum, he doubled up to the limit, continued for three more turns of the wheel and, whether successful or not, patiently resumed with his original stake. This so-called 'system' depended on exceptional self-discipline but even more on luck, which certainly favoured him. At the end of his winning roulette streak he whimsically punted at trente-et-quarante with his small change and scooped an extra £6,000 in half an hour.

He paid off some of his most pressing creditors but many more increased their investments, including Miss Catherine Phillimore, the sister of an English judge. She parted rashly with a further £19,000. Like many others, she was intoxicated by reports of his triumph at the tables and exhibited a touching faith in a 'system' which now seemed foolproof.

Wells returned to Monte Carlo that November to win himself another £10,000. The tables were again crêped as bank after bank lost its reserves and punters scrambled to pile their chips on the Englishman's numbers. He was fêted by titled yachtsmen, who not only shared his golden touch at roulette but invested greedily in the musical skipping rope and other alluring patents.

He returned after Christmas aboard his yacht on which he claimed to be testing a new fuel-saving device. He quaffed magnums of champagne and jauntily declared that he had bought SBM shares for £2,500 to help the hard-pressed casino! From January onwards he lost steadily but kept going with funds sent by dupes who had been promised a share of his winnings. Fred Gilbert had meantime jotted down the words and music of a catchy song, 'The Man Who Broke the Bank at Monte Carlo', which Charles Coborn first sang at the Oxford Music Hall in London. Published in April 1892, it was soon being played on barrel organs all over the world.[1]

Wells had lost back several thousands but cannily salted the rest away in annuities, safe from the Official Receiver. Investors started

---

[1] Coborn at first thought the words 'rather too highbrow for an average music hall audience'. He bought performing rights for only a guinea and the publishing rights for £10. He offered the latter to a Leicester Square firm for £30, without success, and later disposed of them for 'a fiver and royalty' which netted him several hundreds of pounds over the years.

clamouring for their dividends and Mr Justice Phillimore, appraised of his sister's stupidity, informed the police. Wells, who continued to plead poverty, was reduced to selling off coal from the bunkers of his yacht in Le Havre where the French police at last handcuffed him.

He stood trial at the Old Bailey for false pretences and received eight years' penal servitude. His subsequent bankruptcy disclosed debts of £50,000. He surfaced again after his term of imprisonment, this time with a bogus Trawling and Fishing Syndicate which netted him another three years in Dartmoor. Still eager to recoup, he was joined by Jean Burns in Paris and opened a 'Banque' which offered depositors a handsome 1% interest *a day*. He soon vanished with the proceeds but was arrested at Falmouth aboard a newly-purchased yacht. The French authorities had him extradited and managed to trace his invested cache of a million francs. He was set free and given a pittance to keep him alive while his victims benefited from the annuities. He survived until 1926, an 85 year-old pauper, croaking a chorus from 'The Man Who Broke the Bank at Monte Carlo' for anyone disposed to part with a few sous.

His brief but spectacular triumph at the tables, celebrated by Gilbert's unforgettable song, handed a publicity bonus of inestimable value to Camille Blanc and his associates. People ignored Wells's subsequent gaming losses and preferred to attribute his downfall to his criminal activities. For many years café bands played the tune night after night, and music hall singers had no difficulty in persuading audiences of every nationality to join in the lilting chorus. It also lured hordes of punters with the pathetic daydream of themselves 'breaking the bank at Monte Carlo'.

Among them was a bearded and egg-bald little Frenchman, who always had a stack of notepaper, covered with numbers, at his elbow while he played roulette for small stakes in the 'Kitchen'. He made no startling coups but would adjourn to the bar after a win for a half-bottle of champagne. He occasionally looked up from his notebook to chat with one of the many *demi-mondaines* prowling for lucky punters. They would later congratulate themselves on not having attracted his serious interest. After he had received the first of several sentences for fraud, the casino inspectors made a careful entry against the name of Henri Désiré Landru. . . .

A run of punters' losses might quickly have taken the gloss off the Wells legend but for the arrival of a Rand magnate, Woolf Joel, who also happened to break the bank. He and his friend, Frank Gardner, an Australian financier, had decided on a walking race from La Turbie to Nice for a wager of £100. The winner agreed to place his stake on the red at Monte Carlo and split any proceeds with his partner. Joel won the bet by seven minutes. He bought a plaque worth £100 and placed it on red which won twelve times in a row, with several spins at the £480 maximum. He also snapped up several winning maximums on '9'. In half an hour he had won £16,000 and the table went 'into mourning'. The couple celebrated with a banquet for exactly 35 guests at the Savoy Hotel in London. The waiters wore red to match the room's décor, and the menu was adorned with a roulette wheel on one side and the lucky '9' on the other. Joel and Gardner sat at each end of the table on raised chairs, like croupiers, and an orchestra repeatedly played 'The Man Who Broke the Bank at Monte Carlo'. Hilarious laughter greeted the arrival of a telegram from Camille Blanc congratulating Woolf Joel and assuring him that he would be welcome to try his luck again. He replied courteously that he would stick to something rather more gilt-edged, such as Kimberley diamonds and his gold mines on the Rand.[2]

The London newspapers soon trumpeted, 'Jersey Lily breaks the bank at Monte Carlo', which was a slight exaggeration. Lily Langtry, for many years the Prince of Wales's mistress, had often accompanied him to Monte Carlo and returned each winter long after they had parted. Her diamonds and clothes (she took 40 trunkfuls of Worth models on a tour of the United States in the Nineties) always made headlines, particularly when she arrived aboard *The White Lady*, a gift from her dissipated lover, 'Squire' George Baird, who had an income of £250,000 a year from his

[2] His luck ran out a few years later when he was shot dead by a blackmailer in his Johannesburg office.

coal mines in Scotland. He gave her a savage beating after surprising her in the arms of a rival, and the yacht, his peace-offering, later became better known as *The Black Eye*.

She bought a house in Jersey and married handsome Hugo ('Suggie') de Bathe, eighteen years her junior. He was a superb raconteur and ladies man, but Lily had little use for him once he had succeeded to his father's baronetcy. The title brought no money and she had to give him £10,000 to pay off his creditors. After one strenuous vaudeville tour of the United States, followed by the British racing season in which her horses won many prizes, she felt very much *en veine* for attacking the casino.

She arrived in Monte Carlo with her usual entourage; Hugo, his valet, her secretary, two maids and two chauffeurs, who took shifts to drive her limousine with its tortoise-shell and gold fittings. She lost £20,000 at trente-et-quarante in one week before Christmas. By the end of February she had barely enough to cover her enormous bill at the Hotel de Paris. On the very last night of her visit, with bags already packed, she decided impulsively to switch to roulette, placing half her chips on '32' and the rest on the same number at the adjacent table. Miraculously, both won. It is said that the croupiers took fully ten minutes to count out her winnings of over £25,000. Sir Hugo almost had a heart seizure in his excitement, but Lily remained perfectly calm as she followed the attendants to the *caisse* with their trays of chips. 'Don't worry, Suggie', she assured her husband with an angelic smile, 'I'll buy you a new set of golf clubs'.

Such coups, heavily publicised by Blanc through his network of tame reporters, tempted less successful patrons. Two contractors from Madrid, sent to buy arms in Essen for the hard-pressed Spanish forces during the war with America, found their £20,000 in German marks inadequate to meet Krupps' prices. On their way home they stopped off in Monaco with the hope of increasing their stock of currency. They lost every mark and disappeared.

Monte Carlo presented other hazards for the unwary. Pickpockets, whores and confidence tricksters could more or less be kept in check by the police, backed by the SBM's own security men, but hotel thieves, usually working in collusion with waiters or chambermaids, became a pest in the Nineties. Visitors, who brought jewels and large amounts of cash for the season, often stayed out until the small hours which made them easy targets. One burglar used to chloroform his victims while they slept.

Richard Polovtsoff, a wealthy Russian financier, had a particularly alarming experience. For two years he had patiently worked out a system at trente-et-quarante, alternating with his secretary to note down all the winning numbers in sequence at a selected table. Starting one night with a stake of 300,000 francs, he lost 14 maximum bets in a row and became even angrier on discovering that his son, Pierre (later director of the Winter Sporting Club), had won 8,000 francs by mockingly backing all the opposite numbers. Polovtsoff Snr. bought himself a last stock of chips which changed his luck. He returned buoyantly to his room at the Hotel de Paris and went to bed after carefully locking his winnings in a metal box.

He woke up, half-throttled, but managed to bite his assailant's wrist. The empty box was later found in the garden. Next day a man with a heavily bandaged hand was arrested on suspicion at the Paris rail terminus as he stepped off the express. He turned out to be a Russian nobleman, the son of General Gurko, and soon confessed to the crime, pleading in defence that he had lost his head after dropping a fortune at the tables. He killed himself with a lethal dose of poison smuggled into his cell by one of his brothers.

The affair started an uproar in the anti-Monaco press, backed by a vicious attack from the English travel writer, Augustus Hare. This vinegary bachelor had been particularly severe on Prince Albert in his latest guide to the Riviera: 'Idler and absentee as he is, he is faithful to the traditions of his House; the merchant sails without dread but a new pirate town has risen on the shores of its bay; it is the pillage of a host of gamblers that maintains the heroic arms of Monaco, that cleanses the streets and fills the exchequer of its Lord'.

At intervals the prince had expressed his personal horror of the casino or *tripot* (den), as he called it, and even threatened to close it down altogether. He now reminded journalists that his father had saddled him with a concession which would, regrettably, run until 1913. Newspaper articles about his righteous disapproval of gambling began to appear, several written or inspired by Frank Harris, who was often a guest at Marchais. A notoriously unreliable reporter at the best of times, he would later complain of having been used as a catspaw by a wily prince who, far from wishing to end the concession, was covertly manoeuvring for better terms from Camille Blanc. This argument was not altogether impartial. Harris had tried without success to secure the prince's patronage for his new hotel in Monte Carlo and always blamed him for its failure.

Even allowing for Harris's venom, the Grimaldis' next moves seem oddly disingenuous. Princess Alice had apparently subdued her private objections to gambling in order to secure a fatter subsidy for Gunsbourg's ambitious programme. And her husband, who needed funds for his projected Oceanographic Museum, had quietly abandoned his plan to close the *tripot*. Instead, he invited Blanc to scrap the existing concession for another to run 50 years. Blanc had no option but to agree the ruler's new terms, drafted no doubt by his very business-like consort.

By the covenant signed in April 1898 the Casino Company undertook to pay £400,000 for public utilities, with the promise of a further £600,000 in 1913 when the previous concession would normally have expired. £200,000 would at once be allocated to deepen the harbour and build two new quays with improved facilities for commercial navigation and pleasure yachts. Gunsbourg was not forgotten. Blanc agreed to contribute £1,000 towards the cost of staging each play or opera produced, up to 24 a year. The SBM would continue its responsibility for the supply of below-cost gas, water and electricity, together with other public utility services like sewage and street cleaning. The prince's income was hoisted to £50,000 per annum, with 3% on the first £1 million of the casino's turnover and 5% thereafter. With takings running high, he could expect an average contribution of almost £150,000 a year towards his budget.

Monte Carlo's booming prosperity justified Blanc's confidence in the future. The Café de Paris was rebuilt and luxuriously equipped. The commune could now boast 600 apartment houses, a dozen florists, 15 jewellers, 85 wine merchants, plus some of the best-equipped hotels in Europe, headed by the Hotel de Paris, the Grand and the Métropole. Two more, the Swiss-owned Victoria and the Prince de Galles, were smaller but competed with the others in opulence. Later that year the top three would be joined by a new palace, the Hermitage, built by a syndicate from Bordeaux. It had two wings, 200 yards separating the residential section from the luxurious restaurant, with carriages provided for the convenience of lazy guests in transit!

Prince Albert could now afford to indulge in a new yacht, *Princesse Alice II*, a two-master rigged as a schooner and built at Laird's of Birkenhead. A magnificent craft of 1,420 tons with three 1,000 h.p. engines and a speed of 13 knots, she was equipped with drums and windlasses to operate nets, and thousands of metres of galvanised steel cable to drag weights of up to seven tons without snapping. Two laboratories, one on deck towards the stern and an inner one with four cabins and a photographic studio, ensured the most up-to-date facilities for oceanography.

The new vessel consoled Prince Albert for disquieting reports about his son and heir. Louis had fought two desert campaigns with the Foreign Legion and won a medal for a daring raid, but his private life was distinctly less creditable. He had formed a liaison with a pretty laundress, Jeanne Louvet, by whom he had a daughter, Charlotte, born in Constantine on 30 September 1898. Marriage to such a lowly commoner was out of the question, but he had acknowledged the child and shrugged off all hints from his father urging him to abandon his mistress and seek a wife suited to his station as hereditary prince. A fine horseman and excellent shot, he was also fond of amateur acting and much preferred to spend his leaves theatre-going in Algiers or Paris rather than in Monaco with his gloomy sire whose own luckless marriage had made him even more short-tempered. He and his wife had long found it mutually agreeable to avoid meeting, whenever possible, the princess usually leaving for Paris or Marchais as soon as he returned from his cruises. After his departure she would promptly re-instal herself in the palace with her Parisian coterie, headed by Isidore de Lara whose presence always fanned local gossip.

The Dreyfus affaire was one of the very few matters on which she and her husband saw eye to eye. Prince Albert befriended the Abbé Pinchon, who had lost his chair as Professor of Mathematics in Paris for speaking in favour of Dreyfus. He was given the living of Ste Dévote in Monaco to keep him from starvation. When the new trial was arranged Prince Albert had written to Madame Dreyfus inviting her and her husband to stay at Marchais after his 'inevitable' acquittal. This brought a spate of abuse from the Dreyfusards, led by Boni de Castellane, whose three-masted luxury schooner with its 100-strong crew had often anchored at Monaco. The sybaritic marquis had married an American heiress, Anna Gould, and squandered her millions on his pink marble palace in the Avenue du Bois. During his visits to the Riviera he never dipped a toe in the sea until a footman had cleared his path of pebbles and ceremoniously taken the water temperature with a thermometer. Escorted by a second lackey, who carried his master's poodle and an elaborate peignoir, Boni would take a leisurely bathe followed by a session with the hotel's Chinese pedicurist, who painted his toenails a delicate shell-pink.

Hitherto he had been cordially received at the Grimaldi palace, and the socially-conscious princess, who had now married off her daughter, Odile, to Comte Gabriel de Rochefoucauld, also welcomed him to her Paris salon.[3] It did not preserve her from Boni's rabid anti-semitism exacerbated by her husband's letter to Madame Dreyfus which appeared in all the newspapers. He sneered at the ruler of Monaco: 'You meddle in a matter that is none of your affair, Your Most Serene Highness. You are a relative by alliance of Captain Dreyfus, but in their case it is premature for you to triumph.' Events justified his prophecy; Dreyfus, white-haired and pitifully shrunken, was brought back from Devil's Island to be tried before a new court-martial at Rennes.

[3] Her son-in-law, one of Proust's decadent circle, later appeared in *A L'Ombre* as 'Saint-Loup'.

Prince Albert's championship of Dreyfus and his friendship with President Félix Faure led to his appointment on a diplomatic mission of some delicacy. He was asked to convey the Kaiser's assurance that Dreyfus had never spied for Germany together with a strong but unofficial hint that his acquittal on the trumped-up charges might ease Franco–German tension. Prince Albert was received by Faure at 5 p.m. on 16 February 1899 and they had a 20-minute talk. The President had a fatal stroke shortly before six. It was afterwards said that Prince Albert's forceful views had brought on an apoplectic fit, but Faure was already a very sick man and seemed half-dazed throughout the interview. He had then tottered off for a rendezvous with his waiting mistress, who proved too much for his arteries. The hysterical woman, terrified by the corpse in her arms, was swiftly bundled out of the Elysée by a side-door only minutes before the arrival of Faure's grief-stricken family.

The new President, Emile Loubet, an anti-clerical and staunch republican, pardoned Dreyfus after a second court martial had again convicted him of treachery. Whether or not he had innocently accelerated Faure's death, Prince Albert earned the Kaiser's grateful consideration. Two months later the German Emperor was represented by his ambassador to France when the prince laid the foundation stone of his Oceanographic Museum in Monaco. Count von Munster praised him effusively 'for contributing to the good fellowship and closer relations of all nations.'

It stimulated the cynical Emperor to exploit Prince Albert's high-minded internationalism to which he had been converted by Professor Charles Richet, the French physiologist and an ardent pacifist. He persuaded the prince to sponsor a Peace Congress in Monaco, soon followed by the foundation of an International Institute of Peace which distributed earnest appeals to Europe's prickly chancelleries. Prince Albert regularly despatched batches of charts and oceanographic reports to the Kaiser whom he praised naïvely for his 'legitimate pride in the great promise that scientific advances give for the peace of the world'.

The Crown Prince often used to return to Berlin boasting of his success at the tables and with the girls. His father had discounted these stories until a far more reliable witness, Erich Ludendorff, then a Colonel of Uhlans, paid his first visit to the casino and won 150,000 francs. While in Nice the following year, the Kaiser heard that a certain Dr Schott, Professor of Mathematics at Heidelberg, had perfected an 'invincible' scientific method for winning at roulette. The Kaiser sent for him and insisted on buying the exclusive rights.

He arrived at the Monte Carlo casino one night and hurried upstairs to the Salon Privé. Within an hour the Schott system had collapsed, like so many others. The Kaiser stalked out, the poorer by 5,000 louis and with his ego so bruised that he would later accuse some imposter of having impersonated him.

Prince Albert's long absences, either on cruises or dabbling with pacifist missions, gave his wife plenty of scope to cuckold him even in his own principality. Isidore de Lara became such a regular visitor that a waggish punster once chalked on the palace walls, '*Ici dort de Lara*'. It was of course erased long before the prince's return but the whispers may have reached his ears. However, he remained surprisingly unconvinced of de Lara's guilt and began nursing a quite mistaken jealousy of Léon Jehin.

Matters came to the boil at an operatic gala performance in April 1901. Wearing the full-dress uniform of a French general and bristling with medals, including a new decoration from the Kaiser, Albert entered the theatre with his wife. During the interval he summoned the conductor, who had expected compliments but was harshly rebuked instead for undue familiarity with Princess Alice. According to some accounts, Jehin retreated in confusion after the prince had slapped his wife's face. The ruler no doubt realised too late that he had picked the wrong man. Jehin remained for many years in charge of his orchestra, but Princess Alice packed her bags and left for Paris next morning. The marriage ended officially in a legal separation on 30 May 1902, Prince Albert having meantime sternly prohibited his wife from ever re-entering Monaco.[4]

Her departure went almost unremarked in the bustling, money-hungry principality whose population had soared from a mere 1,200 in 1861 to over 20,000, although with only 1,400 Monegasques by birth or naturalisation. Apart from tradesmen, most of the residents were wealthy expatriates living in hotels or their own villas except in the hot summer months when they migrated to London for the Season or sought diversion at the German spas and Biarritz which King Edward VII had made fashionable.

Camille Blanc had opened his new 50-year concession with an impressive programme of entertainment. He had already launched the Lawn Tennis Championship of Monaco with a handsome cup presented by the ruler. The excellent hard courts near the casino attracted the world's crack players, notably the Doherty brothers, who carried off the trophy in alternate years for an entire decade. The popular Tir aux Pigeons received a publicity boost when the American jockey, Tod Sloan, who had lost his licence for crooked riding in 1901, took the first prize two years later. After a bad gambling run he had borrowed the entrance fee of 200 francs for the pigeon shoot, backing himself at odds of fifty to one. He won the Grand Prix du Littoral by killing all thirteen birds with successive shots. Collecting the prize of £400 and his winnings, he went off to the casino and picked up another £4,000 at roulette.

Blanc attempted without success to copy Nice's Battle of Flowers. He also misfired by staging a prize fight for a purse of £1,500 on the Condamine tennis courts. It captured the headlines but Monte Carlo's residents and snobbish visitors wrinkled their noses. The experiment was not repeated. Blanc fared better with his fencing competitions, regattas and bicycle races. He copied the

---

[4] It was no hardship. She relished her freedom and entertained even more lavishly in her magnificent Paris mansion or at her London base, Claridge's, where the faithful de Lara also occupied a permanent suite. After her sudden death in 1925 at the Crillon in Paris, he inherited a million francs together with valuable furniture and books. He was named executor as 'my friend for forty years whose friendship and devotion have been the joy and consolation of my life'. De Lara's own will provided a sum of money for fresh flowers to be placed on her grave every month.

example of Spa in Belgium which had recently staged the first Concours de Beauté with a prize of 5,000 francs won by a Creole girl. But he achieved a major publicity coup in 1898 by inaugurating the first International Concours d'Elégance for 'horseless carriages'. Competitors included some of the world's richest men, with their wives or mistresses beside them. Prizes also went to the best-dressed women, but Blanc was too much of a showman to offend jealous losers. *All* competitors received a first prize of some sort from an endless list of individual awards, even including one for the most graceful parasol. Competitors and spectators were thoughtfully protected from dust by an Italian contractor, who provided Monte Carlo's roads with the first tarred surface in Europe.

William K. Vanderbilt II was one of the earliest winners of the Concours d'Elégance. He gave mammoth parties at the Café de Paris and lost cheerfully at the tables, but even his geniality was severely tested by an unpleasant experience in 1903. While speeding at night in his 60 h.p. Mors, he was arrested by an officious gendarme for driving without lights. At the police station he patiently demonstrated his still warm headlamps but was locked up in a bare cell with only a candle stuck in a beer bottle. The Chief of Police soon arrived with profuse apologies, followed by an invitation to lunch with Prince Albert.

Gunsbourg missed Princess Alice, his most loyal supporter, but he could not complain of any budget skimping by Camille Blanc. In 1903 he staged an elaborate revival of Massenet's *Hérodiade*, following an even more spectacular coup in the previous season, when the little-known Caruso was engaged for *La Bohème* with Melba, but at one-third of her fee. The little Neapolitan had already conquered Italian audiences, but had so far only appeared outside his own country on two short Russian tours. His magnificent performances, partnering Melba and later Geraldine Farrar, brought offers from Covent Garden and the Metropolitan, New York, launching him as the world's leading international tenor.

At the time of his Monte Carlo début he was still very nervous but Gunsbourg encouraged him with a star's suite at the Hotel de Paris and did not allow Melba to upstage him or take her usual curtain calls alone. Caruso never forgot his kindness which would be repaid with interest.

Gunsbourg always boasted of having 'discovered' him, but his risk had been minimal. The Czar Nicholas II had presented the tenor with a pair of gold cufflinks set in diamonds after a concert at the palace in St Petersburg. Such Romanov approval, as Gunsbourg well knew, would automatically be endorsed by the principality's corps of Grand Dukes whose cachet far outweighed that of Prince Albert.

Chapter Four

THE ROMANOVS dominated Monte Carlo's social scene throughout the two prewar decades. They presented the most valuable prizes for sporting events and ensured the success of any gala performance by grandly filling the theatre with their guests. Their patronage could make any restaurant instantly fashionable or demolish it overnight with an imperial thumbs-down. It was no passing whim but practical commonsense for the new Hermitage to name itself after St Petersburg's fashionable establishment.

The Hotel de Paris had never failed to serve dishes like *aspic d'homard à la Russe* and *zrazi Caucasienne*, a rare fillet steak served with lemon, paprika, mushrooms and klouskis, but its decision to advertise for a special Russian chef was a mistake. A feckless tenor named Proferice, who sometimes sang in Gunsbourg's chorus, had brazenly offered his services. He ordered vast quantities of caviare and also demanded a supply of bear's paws, a delicacy much favoured by discriminating Muscovites, according to him. The job lasted one frantic week until Fleury's entire kitchen staff threatened to walk out.

The Russian nobility stayed on the Mediterranean coast for two or three months every winter. Nobody could mistake their spanking carriages in Nice, Cannes or Monaco. The coachmen all wore cockaded hats sideways and drove with the white reins exclusively reserved to those of imperial rank. Several Romanovs owned villas in Cannes but the majority preferred to take entire floors at the Hotel de Paris, the Métropole and the Hermitage which were more convenient for gambling or the theatre. They arrived by private wagons-lits with retinues of mistresses, valets and even soothsayers.

The Czar's reactionary uncle, Grand Duke Vladimir, had so many enemies bent on his assassination that an inspector from the Sûreté was specially assigned as bodyguard. Hearing a suspicious sound late one night, Vladimir picked up a heavy candlestick and crashed it down on the skull of 'the intruder'. His victim turned out to be the unlucky policeman whose widow collected heavy compensation to hush up the story.

Grand Dukes were almost a kopeck a dozen in that era. All related to the Czar – brothers, uncles, nephews and cousins – they owned huge estates and commanded high rank in crack imperial regiments. Apart from their private fortunes, each enjoyed an annual allowance of $100,000 from the Czar, with an automatic dowry of $500,000 for Grand Duchesses. They transcended the most snobbish English or German gentry in arrogant self-indulgence. One of them, addicted to the perfume of crushed strawberries, had a dozen baskets delivered to his hotel suite every morning, in or out of season. He would fork the fruit into a pulp, inhale deeply and then have it removed by a servant. Another had the flowerbeds outside his villa changed nightly to feast his eyes on a new arrangement every morning.

The Grand Duchess Constantine (a Lord High Admiral's relict) invariably travelled abroad with her own chamberpot to avoid the indignity of entering a station toilet or the home of some commoner, even *in extremis*. After wintering at her Riviera villa she once refused to sail for Italy by ordinary steamer with her grand piano and other possessions. The French government sent a frigate, but at Genoa she declined to entrust either her person or her baggage to the waiting pinnace. She stepped ashore a fortnight later only after a special pier had been built.

The Grand Duke Michael Nicolaivitch, Czar Nicholas I's only

surviving son, owned most of Tiflis together with a valuable spring providing mineral waters for home consumption and export. His sons and their families lived in a St Petersburg palace so vast that they cycled or roller-skated between the various wings. He would arrive in state at his Villa Valletta in Cannes with four ADCs, two doctors and a corps of flunkeys. His Santa Claus beard matched a patriarchal manner but he grew more demanding after suffering a stroke. All local railway schedules had to be adjusted as his private six-coached train crawled across Germany, Belgium and France at the maximum speed of 24 m.p.h. prescribed by his doctors.

His eldest son, Nicholas, tall and ramrod-straight, had a passion for roulette. As he was more courteous than some of the others, the casino staff respected his idiosyncracies. He would plaster the baize with gold louis, moving restlessly between tables. He never sat down and used to turn his back as the wheel span since he could not endure seeing his stakes raked away. After making his usual spread of bets he once asked a bystander to double any winning stakes on his behalf as he had to catch the night train for Paris. Two of the numbers won and the young man, Pierre Polovtsoff, successfully doubled and redoubled up to the maximum. He turned to the *chef de partie* and suggested handing the winnings to Nicholas's sister, the Grand Duchess Anastasia Michaelovna, but the official very prudently advised him to remit the cash to Nicholas's account in the Paris branch of the Crédit Lyonnais.

Anastasia was haughty and unreliable. A green-eyed statuesque beauty, with a helmet of black hair tightly coiffed on her narrow head, she had a fanciful belief that the croupiers could be hypnotised into directing the wheel in her favour. Several became her lovers without noticeably changing her usual bad luck at the tables. She and her husband, the Grand Duke of Mecklenberg, drove over to Monte Carlo almost every night from their Cannes villa where he was killed, possibly by accident, by toppling over a garden parapet. She married off her daughter to the German Crown Prince and gambled even more feverishly, apart from developing an insatiable taste for young waiters and bellhops.[1]

[1] She died in 1922 at her Cap d'Ail villa which a handsome young croupier in-

Almost all her clan died violently, with the notable exception of her brother, the Grand Duke Michael Mikhailovitch, who had luckily been exiled by his cousin, Nicholas II. He became infatuated with a St Petersburg beauty, a grand-daughter of Pushkin, but the Czar refused to accept a commoner in the family. They fled to San Remo, where they married in 1891 and later set up house in the luxurious Villa Kasbeck overlooking Cannes, with eight footmen in wigs and satin breeches. Although stripped of his army rank and other privileges, Michael had ample means and even more after his father's death in 1910. He and his wife gave many parties at one of which the Prince of Wales met the last of his long line of mistresses, the beautiful Mrs Alice Keppel.

Michael, tall and slender with a trimmed beard dyed black, had charming manners. As leader of Cannes society, he built and endowed the local Russian church and also became a guiding light of the Polo Club. He formed the Cercle Nautique on the Croisette (now replaced by the hideous Palais des Festivals), where flunkeys in breeches, powdered wigs and white gloves served caviare and champagne to the Duke of Westminster and other millionaire yachtsmen. He also inaugurated the golf club at Mandelieu and presented tournament winners with Fabergé teasets of inlaid red enamel.

During the disastrous war with Japan, and still denied re-admission to the Imperial Army, he opened his villa to Russian wounded soldiers, some of them very rough Caucasians who stole most of his crested cutlery and plate. He particularly missed his unique gold cigarette case which lit up when opened and then automatically snuffed itself out. He finally called his guests together and offered them medals in return for his property.

He was extravagantly good-natured but had the Romanov dis-like of losing. He once argued violently with the Prince of Wales over a doubtful decision at croquet although they were playing for a mere sovereign a side. At Monte Carlo he took his roulette even more seriously. He used to sit at one end of the table, never in the

---

herited. She had apparently taken an overdose of sleeping tablets but had made enough enemies to support alternative theories.

middle which he considered unlucky, and would order croupiers to turn the wheel very slowly for his special benefit.

He had no liking for his Uncle Sergei, the tyrannical Governor-General of Moscow, whose unfortunate wife was forbidden to read *Anna Karenina* because it might excite 'unhealthy curiosity'. Sergei made few friends in Monte Carlo where he treated casino officials and hotel managers like moujiks. Nobody wept there when he was blown up by a bomb in February 1905 while entering his carriage outside the Kremlin.

The Grand Duke Michael's young brother, George, could have served as the prototype for his entire clan. Handsome, over-perfumed and quarrelsome, he half-expected the staffs of the Hotel de Paris and the casino to kiss the ground when he made an entrance with his wife, a daughter of King George I of Greece. At his palace in St Petersburg he had 300 servants several of whom, including chefs and footmen, accompanied him each winter to the Villa Valletta which he had inherited from his father. His wife always blazed with jewels, many later bought by Queen Mary of England after George's murder at the hands of the Bolsheviks.

Another future victim, still enjoying Riviera frivolities to the full, was the Grand Duke Paul, who had married a commoner and divorcée. Unfortunately for him, he was not banished by the Czar whom he would later warn against Rasputin and fruitlessly urge to grant overdue reforms. He visited Monte Carlo every winter and succeeded in breaking the bank one night at trente-et-quarante. With three of his aides also playing maximums, he won over £25,000 in a single session, although the *chef de partie* tried to disrupt the winning sequence by changing croupiers for alternate deals.

His son, Dmitri, one of Rasputin's assassins, was already a dissipated spendthrift even in his teens and gave an historic dinner party at the Hotel Hermitage for half a dozen guests. He ordered 60 bottles of champagne of which they consumed only 15, smashing the rest against the marble pillars and mirrors in the dining-room. They then started taking pot revolver shots at the crystal chandeliers. The courtesan, Augustine de Lierre, once received

from George a 20 million franc pearl necklace on a platter of
oysters for a dancing performance. She was luckier than other
entertainers, who often had their breasts pronged with sharp forks
by the playful Romanovs.

Among the grand ducal mistresses pride of place went to
Mathilde Kschessinska, the vivacious prima ballerina assoluta of the
Imperial Ballet. She had first enslaved the Czarevitch (later,
Nicholas II), who lavished jewels on her and installed her in a St
Petersburg mansion owned by Rimsky-Korsakov. He abandoned
her to marry the golden-haired Princess Alix of Hesse-Darmstadt,
a grand-daughter of Queen Victoria. She then consoled herself
with the Czar's cousin, yet another Grand Duke Serge, who
bought her a *dacha* with a garden by the sea, but she soon turned
to his younger kinsman, André. Their son was born in Cannes in
1902. Diaghilev had once teased her by remarking, 'Ah, Matil-
doshka, you deserve all your success, even to the two Grand Dukes
at your feet'. 'Why not?' she replied airily. 'After all, I have two
feet.'

Her diamonds, though magnificent, were rivalled by many
others in the opulent and ostentatious Nineties. Years later the
Aga Khan would still recall the jewellers' windows on the Boulevard des Moulins: 'Sparkling diamonds, pearls, rubies, emeralds
and sapphires, winking and gleaming in the bright winter sun.' As
spiritual leader of the Ismaili sect, whose tithes made him one of the
world's wealthiest men, he had already cultivated a taste for
western pleasures and rarely missed a few weeks at Monte Carlo
in the season. Dressed in a white silk suit, with a flower in his
buttonhole and his little waxed moustache glistening, he left the
Hotel de Paris every morning for a ritual call at Lloyds Bank. He
would emerge with £2,000 in banknotes, wrapped in a newspaper,
for his daily session of roulette and usually celebrated his wins with
supper *à deux* at Ciro's. The cocottes gladly overlooked his squat
body and short legs for the almost statutory reward of a ring or
necklace.

The Grand Dukes left their exquisite footprints on all Europe's prewar playgrounds, but La Belle Epoque belongs even more emphatically to the glittering courtesans who found Monte Carlo the perfect showcase for their talents. 'Les Grandes Horizontales', as the Paris boulevard wits called them, rated endless newspaper columns of gossip about their lovers and diamonds. Few disputed the leadership of Caroline Otéro, a voluptuous Spanish gypsy dancer whose splendid breasts, usually separated by a sparkling jewel, inspired the architect of the Carlton Hotel in Cannes. Its twin cupolas are still known locally as 'Les boîtes à lait de la Belle Otéro.'

She had no respect for men, however exalted. After being ordered to give up her box at the Comédie-Française to the Czar Nicholas, she paused at the exit to scream, 'All right, I'll leave, but from this day on I'll never again eat caviare!' This could not be taken too seriously. Like all these substantially built *courtesans de marque*, she enjoyed a splendid appetite. In that guzzling era almost every bedtime story demanded a 10-course banquet as prologue. However, Otéro is known to have made a rare exception for the Prince of Wales. One evening, while tucking away with his friends, he scribbled a crude drawing of a clock face on the back of the menu to confirm his proposed rendezvous with Otéro. A true professional, she managed to expedite a previous engagement and was stripped for action when His Royal Highness tapped on her door.

Her first husband had been an Italian opera singer, ruined by his weakness for Monte Carlo. She became similarly addicted and often lost money at the tables, but managed to re-stock her jewel cases from a succession of husbands and lovers. 'No man with an account at Cartier's can be called really ugly' she once declared after a romp with the crippled Kaiser. At one wild supper party in St Petersburg she was served up as dessert, stark naked in a huge silver tureen. Each of the grateful guests presented her with a diamond souvenir.

The management of the Hotel de Paris respected her every whim. One of her lovers, Count Michael Pirievski, was obsessed by a manic fear of burglars and used to keep a small arsenal of firearms handy. Late one night, still tipsy and irritable after an unlucky gaming session, he accused her of infidelity with the Grand Duke Gregory. She picked up one of his revolvers and fired at him. The bullet penetrated the wall, narrowly missing a next-door guest, who summoned the police. Fleury somehow explained it all away but, prompted by Otéro, ordered the count to leave.

Otéro had the born actress's flair for publicity and always treasured a piece in *La Vie Parisienne* which extolled her 'blood-red lips and blue black hair, with jewels blazing from chest, hair, ears, arms, wrists, hands and ankles'. Stung by such praise, one of her jealous rivals, Diane de Chandel, decided one night to wear her entire collection at the Monte Carlo casino in an effort literally to outshine Otéro. It was a formidable threat as she had a vast hoard, including even a ruby-studded coat for her poodle. But Otéro had learned of the plan through a chambermaid and timed her own entrance with devastating effect. She sailed in wearing a simple black dress, revealingly décolletée as usual but without a single ornament. Her very plain maid followed, resplendent in her mistress's five-roped pearls, once the property of the Empress of Austria, as well as a dazzling assortment of rubies, emeralds and sapphires. Round her waist was a diamond corselet valued by Cartier at 2,275,000 gold francs. All the players stood up to applaud as Otéro took her favourite place at the tables without more than a glance at de Chandel.

Her only serious rival was Liane de Pougy, whose classic features and white magnolia skin had once inspired the connoisseur, d'Annunzio, to sprinkle rose petals at her feet from a gold chasuble. She often alternated with Otéro at the Folies Bergère, their carriages sometimes crossing in the Bois, but the Spaniard's earthy gibes could never penetrate Liane's frosty dignity. She ran through a series of romances and survived a few cautious attempts at suicide before marrying Prince Ghika of Moldavia. Unlike Otéro, who gloried in her gutter coarseness, she had an endearing charm of manner. One night at the casino she stepped aside for an attendant laden with a heavy tray of drinks. 'Non, Madame la Princesse,' he objected deferentially, 'I am but a waiter'. She gave him a ravishing smile and murmured, 'Pass, *mon ami*. You know quite well I am only a cocotte'. After her husband's death she entered a convent in Lausanne under the name of 'Sister Mary Magdalene of the Penitence.'[2]

Blanc continued to reap expanding dividends from the tables. He now owned a magnificent hillside villa overlooking Cap Martin, lavishly appointed with parquet floors and marble. He took justifiable pride in its luxurious gardens and had also continued his stepmother's policy of beautifying the Boulingrins. These sloping green lawns, palm-lined and studded with colourful blooms, became a floral carpet to the casino. They enchanted most visitors but not the eccentric baronet, Sir George Sitwell. He despised Monte Carlo's over-formal flowerbeds which had to be wrapped in sacking at night and with never so much as a blade of grass awry. From his window in the Hotel de Paris he would rake the Boulingrins with binoculars and compare them adversely with the far more tasteful creations of Montegufoni, his estate near Siena. 'Such a pity not to have consulted *me*', he once snorted. He also nursed an enduring hatred for the sugar-loaf casino which had ruined several of his kinsmen. 'These buildings have a most *objectionable* gaiety about them' he informed his son, Osbert, who nevertheless used to sneak in for a few spins of roulette.

Other English visitors shared Sir George's horror of the gaming rooms. Daisy Cornwallis-West, whose mother had been one of Edward VII's favourites, inherited beauty, taste and elegance. After marrying Prince Henry of Pless in 1891 she would visit the Riviera

[2] Otéro died many years later, very fat and relying on a faulty memory periodically refreshed by gossip-hungry journalists. She had long since lost all at the gaming tables. Her portrait, commissioned by the Kaiser, adorned a wall in her one-roomed apartment in Nice until it too vanished with the rest of the souvenirs from the old caviare and champagne days. For years the Monte Carlo casino paid her a very small allowance.

every year, usually renting a house in Monte Carlo to accommodate her circle of friends and relations. (Her brother, George, married Lady Randolph Churchill and her sister, Sheila, became Duchess of Westminster.) She also stayed often at the Villa Kasbeck with the Grand Duke Michael and his wife, much preferring Cannes to the raffish principality but quite unable to wean her husband from roulette. One of her diary entries describes Monte Carlo as 'dusty, horrid, with its tainted men and women. Personally, I think it is a boring place as there is nothing to do but gamble, gossip and eat'. Returning from a party at Ciro's, which ended in the guests pelting each other with rose petals, she wrote off her host as 'a loud fat German and a snob – his wife is an American, longs for social success and copies all I wear'. She aimed another poisoned dart at the ruler after a palace dinner: 'The worst use the Emperor (Wilhelm II) ever made of the Order of the Black Eagle was to give it to the Prince of Monaco'. Her diary records that her sister-in-law, Jennie, and the Duke of Marlborough (Consuelo Vanderbilt's husband) had hit a storm while motoring back to Monte Carlo: 'They ran out of essence or whatever the stuff is called that makes the motor go. I think essence is a most inappropriate name for a substance that smells so horribly'.

Her contempt for Monaco was viciously echoed in Sabine Baring-Gould's *Book of the Riviera*, published in 1905. This Devon cleric, who wrote 'Onward, Christian Soldiers' and 'Now the Day is Over', liked the fleshpots but a nagging moral conscience turned his tastebuds to bile when he addressed himself to Monte Carlo: 'The pity of it is that one of the fairest spots in Europe, this earthly paradise, should be given over to harlots and thieves and Jew moneylenders, to rogues and fools of every description. The entire Principality lives on the tables; the prince, the bishop, the canons, the soldiers, the police, those who have villas, the cab drivers, the waiters, the boatmen, all are bound together by a common interest – the plunder of such as come to Monte Carlo to lose their money'. He thought both the casino and theatre 'vulgar and displaying no token of genius or sense of beauty but appropriate to a gambling hell'.

Some, however, found romance in the scented starlit principality. While everyone was discussing Baring-Gould's bitter attack, a socially ambitious English matron, Mrs Cooper, arrived that Easter with her daughter. They were soon followed by a briefless young barrister, John Galsworthy, who had become infatuated with Ada Cooper, his cousin's wife. Their snatched moments of happiness in Monte Carlo directly inspired his first novel, while her wretched marriage, followed by divorce and social ostracism, undoubtedly inspired several of Irene's experiences in *The Forsyte Saga*.

The resident British colony, reinforced by a regular crop of titled visitors, cultivated its own aura of wealth and distinction, but some preserved an upper crust on painfully stretched incomes. They always wore full evening dress at the theatre and casino, gambling for small stakes with quite pathetic enthusiasm. Others sponged on acquaintances when their remittances ran dry. One well-dressed couple, apparently English although the woman had a strong French accent, arrived in Marseilles from Monte Carlo on 6 August 1907. They deposited a trunk in the station cloakroom, giving a local hotel as their overnight address. A receipt was issued to them in the name of 'Jervis'. Within a few hours the cloakroom attendant noticed blood oozing from the trunk. He called the police, who found a woman's torso and arrested the couple as they were paying their hotel bill. 'Mr Jervis' had the rest of the body in his suitcase, and his wife was wearing some of the dead woman's jewellery.

He turned out to be Vere Goold, younger brother of an Irish baronet. A London man-about-town and sportsman (he had competed at Wimbledon), his heavy drinking and the gambling losses of his wife, a former dressmaker, had brought them down in the world until they depended mainly on the pickings from rich men attracted by Mrs Goold's pretty niece. Their victim was a Swedish widow, Emma Liven, with whom they had struck up an acquaintance. She was not wealthy and had an unfortunate taste for wearing flashy jewellery, most of it paste. One afternoon over tea in their apartment, they had lost their tempers when she refused to lend them any more money. Although Goold gallantly took the sole blame, the real truth emerged after detectives had re-enacted the murder in their presence. In a fit of blind rage Mrs Goold had struck their guest over the head with a mallet. Her husband had then stabbed her to death and cut up the body.

Extradited to Monaco, they stood trial there in December. Mrs Goold continued to protest her innocence and swore that her husband, insane from chronic alcoholism, had committed the crime single-handed. She was sentenced to death and Goold to life imprisonment. She demanded to be guillotined in the Place du Casino as a dramatic warning to others of the danger of gambling, but the authorities, alarmed by so much ugly publicity, hurriedly commuted her death sentence. The couple returned for the last time to Marseilles on their way to serve a life term on Devil's Island where both died within two years.

The gruesome story touched off more criticism of the wicked principality. A letter in *The Times* demanded, 'How long are the nations of Europe going to tolerate the continuance of this plague-spot in their midst? Gilded youth are ruined annually in scores, for they flock thither in ever-increasing numbers because of the gambling facilities, made more seductive by the beauty of the place, its gardens and the unrivalled Casino band. The profits from the tables, which average 30 million francs, are divided between the shareholders, the municipality, and the Prince of Monaco . . . The Governments of Europe should stamp out this blot on our civilisation. President Roosevelt might well assume the initiative in this righteous crusade, for the American plutocrats are as prominent at the tables as the aristocracy of Europe'.

The governments ignored this plea but France's very practical hoteliers, long jealous of Monaco, now grasped their chance. Although Monte Carlo would still retain its exclusive grip on roulette and trente-et-quarante, 'games of skill' like baccarat and chemin-de-fer might now be played publicly in France. But the French casinos made a point of prohibiting no-limit baccarat, and the SBM entered into a gentleman's agreement to the same effect.[3]

[3] The essential difference between baccarat and 'chemmy' is that in the former game the bank is put up to auction to the highest bidder, who deals the whole time

The concession was wildly welcomed in France but it came as such a surprise that at first only a few small gaming rooms were hastily opened in the leading hotels. Some time would pass before Nice, Cannes and Biarritz ventured to build casinos, and Monte Carlo still retained the advantages of a long-established clientèle and its monopoly of roulette, easily the most popular of all contemporary gambling attractions. Camille Blanc had nevertheless sensed the dangers of over-complacency. The Carlton in Cannes, like Nice's Ruhl, opened by an enterprising Swiss in 1905, already offered stiff competition to the Hotel de Paris. Within a very few years Nice would flaunt the even more luxurious Negresco, which took its name from a Roumanian, formerly maître d'hotel at Monte Carlo's Helder. He had the backing of the French industrialist, Alexandre Darracq, to build the Riviera's most elegant hotel, with marble pillars and a crystal chandelier weighing over a ton. Blanc clearly saw the possibility of the Hotel de Paris, with its rococo nymphs and cherubs, becoming a vulgar anachronism. He therefore decided to invest heavily in amenities and entertainment on a scale which would outdazzle Cannes, always his most serious competitor. His first significant step was to accommodate patrons who did not care to rub shoulders with lesser breeds.

The SBM showed a profit of £1 million for 1910. A million and a half people crowded into the principality for the short winter season, with at least 10% patronising the casino. 'The democracy has permeated even Monte Carlo', a contemporary historian noted in disgust after an uncomfortable tour of the 'Kitchen'. From 10 a.m. onwards, eager gamblers, many laden with talismans, jammed the public rooms. Apart from backing birthday dates,

---

and limits his losses to the amount of his bid. The casino takes a fee from each 'shoe', the deal box from which the cards are dealt out to both sides of the table. At chemin-de-fer the bank is held in turn by punters playing against a single opponent, the deal passing around the table after a losing hand. The casino normally takes 5% from every winning bank after the first. This cut, known as the *cagnotte*, takes its name from the slit in the table into which the percentage is dropped. It can be very lucrative after a long session.

numbers on cloakroom tickets and 'lucky' colours, some also brought locks of hair, jade monkeys, toy elephants and even bits of alleged hangmen's rope, sold in every souvenir store. One woman had a spider in a matchbox, divided into red and black sections, and staked her money according to its movements. Others carried spoonfuls of salt in their pockets or handbags. A slightly senile lady, unable to afford a tip for the *personnel*, would hand croupiers two sticky sweets if her colour or number won. Another was knocked down by a car and paid a croupier generously for a transfusion of his 'lucky' blood. And everyone, rich or poor, would dart into the lobby of the Hotel de Paris to rub a coin on the left hock of Louis XIV's equestrian statue before entering the casino.

Hunchbacks paraded outside and charged a fee for having their humps patted. Soothsayers made a fortune and a Roumanian half-gipsy woman amassed enough in a few years to retire to a splendid villa overlooking Eze. Pawnbrokers flourished. One English resident used to pledge his gold-banded umbrella for exactly 125 francs every morning, not trusting himself in the casino with a centime more. Many others never returned. Monte Carlo's most thriving pawnbroker, Isaac, started his business in 1905 and over the years accumulated 750 violins, 1,000 evening dress suits, 40 baby carriages, riding boots by the dozen, and even a large boa constrictor left by a celebrated snake charmer, who needed cash for one more night's play!

Blanc and his fellow-directors did not despise francs from the 'Kitchen', but the whole future of Monte Carlo depended on the aristocracy, who played far more heavily and also gave 'the wedding cake on the Rock' its elegant hallmark. They courted patrons like Count von Zernsdorf, who often lit his cigars with *mille* notes, and Arthur de Rothschild, whose yacht anchored in the bay each winter. He was also a motoring enthusiast and one of the first residents to add a garage to his villa. At roulette he regularly staked on '17', playing for precisely one hour when he would go out on the terrace to smoke a Havana and then return for a further hour to the very minute.

English patrons enjoyed a reputation for good manners and exceptional calm even in a losing streak. King Edward's racing friend, Sir Frederick Johnstone, happened to drop something as he was leaving the tables. A passing attendant begged him not to look for 'the louis' and asked obsequiously, 'Where do you wish it placed, milord?' Sir Frederick replied absent-mindedly, *'Rouge, toujours le rouge'*. The croupier promptly laid a louis on red which won a maximum. Sir Frederick walked off, refusing to accept the winnings as he could not recall placing a stake. The inspectors insisted on paying him; otherwise, they explained, the play could not proceed. Hours later, when undressing in his hotel bedroom, Johnstone missed a gilt button from his yachting blazer. He at once guessed the truth but the management stubbornly declined his offer to return the money.

They were far less generous to a Nice Chef de Police who plunged disastrously at roulette. It had long been an unwritten rule to exclude officials of the Alpes-Maritimes, but this only applied in practice to petty functionaries. Far from being discouraged, he was escorted to the bar by a director and regaled with drinks before proceeding to the gaming rooms. Earlier that day he had lunched rather well at the Hermitage as the guest of a Lyons silk manufacturer, who jokingly passed on his 'unbeatable' roulette system. The police chief, heavily in debt at the time, hastened to his office and withdrew the entire weekly staff payroll from his safe. He drove back to Monte Carlo and lost the last franc before midnight. He then went home and blew out his brains. The municipality demanded reinbursement, but the casino disclaimed all responsibility.

The Nice police soon returned good for evil by alerting their colleagues to an American, who had entertained flashily at the Ruhl but appeared to be living on his wits. Joseph Simard, Monaco's Directeur de la Sûreté, found an excuse to hold him on suspicion of some passport irregularity while his hotel room was dry-bathed. His bags disclosed a complete burglar's kit, together with two trick roulette wheels and several packs of marked cards.

Such episodes sharpened Blanc's determination to protect his distinguished clientèle from undesirables, while also guaranteeing them far more privacy and comfort than could be expected in the ordinary rooms. In 1910 he linked the former Salle Touzet with a new wing designed by a local architect, Médécin. The lofty gaming hall was decorated in the Empire style with green and gold dominant. A French painter, Sagaud, contributed the flamboyant ceiling and panels. Showily furnished with satin and velvet seats, crimson curtains and pile carpets, it also had the advantage of the latest ventilation and a system of ozonized air.

Admitted from 4 p.m., patrons could gamble until dawn and for much higher maximums than in the public rooms, but they had to pay a heavy entrance fee for the privilege. Admission to the Salle Médécin or 'Salon Privé', as it came to be known, was most strictly scrutinised, and players had to wear evening dress. Royalty expected, and received, courtlike obeisance. When the Queen of Sweden entered for a little flutter after dining in the downstairs restaurant, play stopped at once and all present stood respectfully as she made her way to a table, followed by her six ladies-in-waiting. Winston Churchill was one of those to pay an early visit, interrupting a Mediterranean cruise in Baron de Forest's yacht with his wife and brother, Jack. 'I went to the Gambling Hell of Monte Carlo four times and came away with £160', he reported gleefully to his private secretary, Edward Marsh.

The Salle Médécin became so popular that Blanc opened a still more exclusive haunt, the Sporting Club, in the nearby Avénue d'Ostende. Candidates were proposed by two members, seconded, and had to pay a stiff subscription on election. Ex-King Manoel of Portugal was once turned away because he had not troubled about these formalities. He never played again in Monte Carlo which spared him the embarrassment of meeting his former mistress, Gaby Deslys, whose extravagance had helped to lose him his throne.

She arrived with her American dance partner, Harry Pilcer, who had appeared with her in the Ziegfeld Follies. They gave performances in Beausoleil but Gaby braced her stage earnings with several 'love affairs'. Wearing rose tattoos on her breasts, she entertained suitors at the Hotel de Paris for a minimum tariff of

£100 a night, with diamonds as a frequent bonus. At the casino she made spectacular entrances in Worth gowns adorned with a 17-string pearl necklace, said to be a gift from King Manoel but in fact an offering from an Argentine lover, who had followed her to Monte Carlo. He disdained routine bouquets or orchids and announced himself with a wine cask brimful of 20-dollar gold pieces.

Monaco seemed to be swimming in so much money that Gunsbourg insisted on even huger allocations. Early in 1910 he and Camille Blanc had visited Paris for the Russian company's second season of opera and ballet at the Théâtre Châtelet. While Diaghilev demanded more time to consider an engagement in Monte Carlo, Gunsbourg engaged Chaliapin for the première of *Don Quichotte*. It was not one of Massenet's happiest inspirations, although the basso gave a dominating performance. He commanded the record fee of £1,000 a night but automatically lost most of it at the tables.

Soon after Chaliapin's début, Monaco inaugurated Prince Albert's majestic Oceanographic Museum. It had taken eleven years to build at a cost of over £500,000, mostly contributed by the SBM. Camille Blanc, now also Mayor of Beausoleil most of which he owned, naturally took his place among the civic dignitaries at the opening ceremony on the brow of the Rock facing east. Former President Loubet attended with the French Foreign Minister and representatives of many other governments. The Salle Garnier's chorus and orchestra, under Léon Jehin, interpreted celebratory verses set to music by Massenet. Gunsbourg also put on a gala concert for which he had composed an Ode recited by an actress from the Comédie-Française as the prince entered his box. A nautical fête was staged on the following night with an antique galley as the centrepiece. Titta Ruffo sang the rôle of Hercules in a re-enactment of Monaco's discovery and thousands on the shore watched the realistic battle scenes rounded off by a firework display. Guests enjoyed a short cruise in the *Princesse Alice*, picknicked at La Turbie, and attended a final reception at the palace where arrangements were announced for opening the

Oceanographic Institute in Paris established with an endowment of four million francs in Prince Albert's name.

The marble museum in Monaco presented models of Prince Albert's yachts, harpoons, instruments and charts. They combined with stained glass windows portraying marine life to offer a graphic visual history of oceanography. Visitors could now pass through the magnificent laboratories with the latest photographic equipment and movable dissection tables. A white marble statue of the founder dominated the entrance. It had been commissioned by eminent admirers, local and foreign, the latter headed by Emperor Wilhelm II. Showcases in the Salon d'Honneur glittered with the prince's gold medals awarded by numerous universities and learned societies.

He had meantime turned to ambitious schemes for building a modern port and deepening the harbour. He also sponsored plans to link the port by tunnel with Fontvieille, a new industrial quarter on land partially reclaimed from the sea. Here an electrical plant and a brewery would be set up but without disfiguring a beautiful corner of the principality. Perched on a cliff face, where the Middle Corniche came in from the west, a 'Hanging Garden' (later renamed the Jardin Exotique) had been tastefully laid out. Rising to a height of 450 feet and landscaped in tiers, it displayed hundreds of rare species from Mexico and South America, with giant cacti and euphorbia transplanted from Abyssinia.

But once the locals had goggled at the Museum and the new gardens, they began grumbling at their high cost and saw even less profit from the prince's latest enterprise, a new meteorological station. This seemed to them as useless as the Museum of Pre-historic Anthropology which he had lovingly filled, during the past decade, with ancient relics discovered in local caves, including rare coins left behind by the Phoenicians and Romans.

Radicals were taking a closer and less enchanted view of their 'tax-free paradise' which seemed to benefit only the prince, the SBM shareholders and the foreign colony, who represented 85% of the population and enjoyed a virtual monopoly of trade and business. For all but a minority of Monegasques incomes had remained low, while the cost of living had soared. It was also being whispered that the whole economy, based on gambling and seasonal tourism, could be in jeopardy if France continued opening rival casinos.

Monaco's figures for 1910 did not justify such scare-mongering. The 'gross national product' was valued at £16,640,000, the casino accounting for £15 million and the hotel industry most of the balance. The receipts for Nice's three casinos amounted to only £320,000, while the tables at Cannes brought in a paltry £44,000 which the French Government taxed at 15%. But the best posts in the Monte Carlo casino went to Frenchmen, with only menial posts as doormen, attendants and croupiers (far from overpaid at £17 a month) open to the locals. And only French or Swiss managers and chefs seemed to have any chance of employment in the luxury hotels. Land ownership showed similar inequalities. Most real estate had fallen into the hands of Frenchmen and Italians, who had also taken options on the choicest sites for sea reclamation schemes.

The prince's subjects, prodded by liberal propagandists, suddenly became aware that they had no voice in the affairs of their country and could expect little sympathy from an absentee ruler, who pocketed his SBM percentages and seemed preoccupied with taking soundings in the Azores or lecturing abroad on the mysteries of marine biology. Angry over rising prices charged by foreign profiteers who drove them to shop as far afield as Nice, they finally decided to force the issue. In October 1910 a noisy affray started on the palace ramparts. Although some of the rioters flourished revolvers, nobody was hurt, but Prince Albert took the threat of further demonstrations seriously enough to send for his son. He was granted special leave from the Foreign Legion to act as his father's delegate in investigating local grievances. The sovereign ruler had panicked. He urged the French troops in Menton to hold themselves ready to restore law and order and even arranged for an English man-of-war at Villefranche to send in a number of sailors, ostensibly on 'holiday leave' but ready to protect British lives and property. According to local rumour, a large consignment of wine cases, containing rifles and ammunition, had been delivered to the Hotel de Paris by order of Monaco's very nervous Governor-General. These weapons were to be seized by the British sailors as soon as a banner hoisted on the hotel's flagpole signalled the start of the 'revolution'.

The truth of this unlikely story was never tested. Nobody fired a shot on either side and the young prince impressed the now-sheepish rioters with his amiability and good sense. A face-saving new Constitution was formulated. The former Governor-General, who had taken the brunt of Prince Albert's unpopular policies, would be replaced by a Minister of State and three Councillors appointed by the ruler. Legislation became the responsibility of a 21-strong General Council, meeting twice yearly and elected by universal suffrage for four years. The prince agreed vaguely to consult the Council on any new laws 'and matters of general welfare', but since he could dissolve it at will and personally appointed the Chairman and Vice-Chairman, only paper liberties had been won. The prince remained an autocrat and his Council timidly side-stepped any suggestion to tax the rich foreigners.[4]

Prince Louis returned cheerfully enough to North Africa. He had welcomed the chance of seeing his illegitimate daughter, Charlotte, who had won her lonely grandfather's heart and was being brought up at the palace with all the advantages of a princess. Prince Albert celebrated the end of the constitutional 'crisis' by ordering a new and larger yacht, the *Hirondelle II*, a 1,600-tonner, with two 2,200 h.p. engines, a speed of 15 knots, and the most modern laboratories aboard for examining marine samples. His researches, extensively covered by the world's press, brought thousands of visitors to the Oceanographic Museum which exhibited specimens collected during each cruise. But Camille Blanc needed more worldly tourist attractions to give him an edge over the rival French resorts.

[4] Monaco's eagerness to placate the French government, long anxious to obviate the principality's economic and fiscal advantages, was exemplified by the agreement of 1912. The principality henceforth forfeited all customs dues in consideration of a payment by France of 400,000 gold francs a year.

Returning from Cannes after a round of golf at Mandelieu, the British political leader, Bonar Law, remarked that Monte Carlo might benefit from a good course. Blanc took the hint but, as no land was available in the principality, the SBM had to pay the French Government £320,000 for 56 hectares near rocky La Turbie. In 1910 workmen started laying a course at Mont Agel, 2,625 feet above sea level. It took two years to clear the pebbles and rocks under the direction of Willie Park, who mixed English seed with various other specimens from Germany, North America and New Zealand to provide a perfect surface. The view was spectacular, with nine holes overlooking the blue sea and the rest facing a majestic alpine skyline. Harry Vardon, in tight knee-breeches, led an impressive group of the world's top professionals in the opening season, but Andrew Kirkaldy took one look at the slopes and declared grumpily, 'I'm no bleeding goat'. However, once the adventurous holes had been mastered, enthusiasts flocked to Mont Agel, ready to pay costly membership subscriptions or green fees for the best club staff in Europe and a cuisine up to Hotel de Paris standards.

Blanc had meanwhile approved an idea for a motoring rally proposed by Alexander Noghues, President of Le Sport Automobile et Vélocipedique de Monaco. The first Grand Tournoi Routier, held in January 1911, offered a cup and a £400 prize for the best run from various starting points in France, Germany, Austria and Switzerland. It attracted 23 competitors, who raced along rough and uneven roads at the required minimum average speed of 10 kms an hour in what a contemporary reporter described as 'noisy monsters whose hoods hid mysterious motors of explosive and capricious humour'. The Rally was won by Henri Rougier, starting from Paris in a 25 h.p. Turcat-Méry. He covered the 570 miles in a blistering 28 hours 10 minutes, followed by a 40 h.p. Gobron tourer and a 38 h.p. Martini from Berlin, with the Daimler, Fiat and Mercedes each doing creditably.

The more leisurely were not forgotten. 'Sea baths' in warm salt water could at last be enjoyed in a building near the casino almost half a century after the creation of the Société des Bains de Mer.

The premises were luxuriously appointed and supervised by a resident physician with trained attendants in charge of Turkish and vapour baths, underwater massage and the dispensing of mineral spa waters. Of all Blanc's prewar attractions, however, and second only in tourist appeal to the casino itself, none won Monte Carlo more prestige and approval than the Ballet Russe. In retrospect the creation of Diaghilev's first independent company, with Monte Carlo as its headquarters, has an air of inevitability. Yet it had come about almost by chance and, literally, for the flimsiest of reasons.

Gunsbourg owed his most spectacular artistic triumph to a pair of Nijinsky's too-revealing silk tights.

Chapter Five

GUNSBOURG'S VISIT to Paris in 1910 had not only finalised Chaliapin's first engagement at Monte Carlo but led to his offering Diaghilev a contract for a minimum guarantee of 8,000 gold francs a performance, with a percentage of the proceeds. Blanc had hesitated but Gunsbourg, entranced by graceful Tamara Karsavina and Nijinsky's electrifying *entrechats*, was irresistible. He raved over Bakst's exotic décors and the barbaric splendour of Benois' costumes for *Cléopâtre* and *Schéhérazade*. However, Diaghilev had delayed signing the agreement and left with Nijinsky to holiday in Karlsbad and on the Lido before returning to St Petersburg.

The autumn season at the Mariinsky had opened without hint of coming squalls. Diaghilev was already preparing the repertoire for a return visit to Paris and hoped to include *Petrushka* which Stravinsky had expanded into a full-length ballet from a short poem. The Imperial Company seemed to be running smoothly, although Diaghilev often snapped his fingers in irritation when Kschessinska showed open jealousy of Karsavina, her nearest rival. But trouble came from another and quite unexpected quarter.

Giselle, an established favourite in court circles, was chosen for a gala performance with the costumes and scenery used for the Paris production. Nijinsky went on stage in the close-fitting white silk tights and black velvet gilet designed by Benois but without the small slip obligatory for all male dancers at the Mariinsky. The Dowager Empress took one scandalised look and swept from her box, followed by the Czar's young daughters, the Grand Duchesses Olga and Tatiana.

Nijinsky was suspended but would not apologise. He had the support of Diaghilev and most of the dancers apart from Kchessinskaya, whose liaison with the Grand Duke André prompted her to take the official line and simultaneously strike at Karsavina, Nijinsky's partner. Since the authorities would not climb down, Nijinsky resigned, encouraged by Diaghilev's pledge to star him in the company which would open at Monte Carlo following its winter season of opera. Nijinsky left Russia, never to return.

Diaghilev and several of the Mariinsky's leading dancers, with the exception of Kschessinska, arrived in the principality in March. The company included Bakst, Benois and the *maître de ballet*, Fokine. They were later joined by the martinet coach, Enrico Cecchetti, at the insistence of Nijinsky, who declined to rehearse without him. Diaghilev had turned down Gunsbourg's offer of a suite at the Hotel de Paris to avoid Kschessinska, already installed there with her Grand Duke. He preferred to stay in Beausoleil and made the half-hour journey with Nijinsky every day on the zig-zagging road. It was also more convenient for consultations with Stravinsky, then busily completing the *Petrushka* score in his nearby villa.

The monocled Diaghilev, nicknamed 'Chinchilla' from the single white streak in his hair, held regular court on the Café de Paris terrace. Even in the warm sunshine he had a fur-collared coat draped over his shoulders and used to whack the table with his heavy walking stick to command silence. Beside him sat Nijinsky whose hair cut in a fringe gave him the look of a sultry faun. Bakst, dapper and heavily perfumed, would be squinting through his pincenez at a sketch-pad on his knee, while Chaliapin, who had cancelled several engagements to welcome his compatriots, tossed off beakers of wine. The Aga Khan often joined them, particularly if Karsavina happened to be present. He made his intentions very plain and embarrassed her with a barrage of bouquets and jewels. Diaghilev sympathised but thought it tactful to humour a multi-millionaire who might underwrite the company's future tours. He had to coax her not to return a huge rope of pearls. 'Accept them, Tamarochka, as you would a bouquet from anyone else,' he advised.

The Aga Khan soon turned to another and more accommodating member of the company, Josefina Kovalevska. He invited Diaghilev to India with the entire company, including of course Kovalevska. Nijinsky was enthusiastic – Karsavina, predictably less so – but Diaghilev thought it impractical after a strenuous series of engagements in Europe. He had been deluged with offers from the moment of his arrival in Monte Carlo when he announced his plans to extend the tour beyond the previous eight weeks. The company was booked for the International Exhibition in Rome, then Berlin for a première in the Kaiser's presence, followed by Paris and a first season at Covent Garden, with a gala performance to celebrate King George V's Coronation.

The London engagement had come about through the Marchioness of Ripon, half-Russian on her Woronzow mother's side and a former mistress of the Grand Duke Michael. A wealthy patroness of the arts (Oscar Wilde had gratefully dedicated the printed edition of *A Woman of No Importance* to her), she was for years the real power of Covent Garden and had sponsored the early careers of Melba, de Reszke and Caruso. Lady Randolph Churchill once described her cattily as 'a luxurious woman with perfect manners, a kind disposition and a moderate sense of duty', but none disputed her dedication to ballet and opera. She and her daughter, Lady Juliet Duff, both so tall and emphatic that they almost resembled exclamation marks, assured Diaghilev that the London season would have influential backing from Lady Ripon's intimate friend, Alexandra the Queen Mother, a sister of the Dowager Empress of Russia.

The company rehearsed cheerfully every morning in the Palais du Soleil, now a disused theatre, until an accident completely unnerved the always superstitious Diaghilev. The dancers had been practising a routine for *Le Pavillon d'Armide* when the stage manager fell to his death through an open trap door. The company, with a Slavic capacity to oscillate from the deepest gloom to hysterical high spirits, was soon back to the harsh routine of rehearsals under Diaghilev.

Other ballets in the repertoire were acclaimed but Le Spectre de la Rose, based on Théophile Gautier's verses and superbly choreographed by Fokine, created the true sensation of that memorable season. Bakst's sets had a breathtaking beauty and the audience was stunned when Nijinsky took the stage in a startling costume of silk rose petals, with his face made up to personify a rose, the mouth like an open petal and the eyebrows resembling a beetle. The theatre practically erupted as he made his astounding final leap across the stage. This ballet, originally planned as a 'filler' between more serious items, became a classic overnight. By the time the company arrived in Paris, the newspapers were still wildly enthusing over Nijinsky's extraordinary agility, and women admirers clamoured so hysterically for rose-petals from his costume that the dancer was tempted to snip them off and sell them as souvenirs after each performance.

The troupe repeated its triumphs in Paris, Berlin and London before disbanding. Karsavina and several others returned to the Mariinsky eager to take part in another tour. Even Kschessinska, hearing that Karsavina would be required in St Petersburg until the end of the season, suddenly announced herself available to join the company in Hungary. Diaghilev recognised her drawing power and gladly accepted the olive branch. Nijinsky also welcomed the chance of dancing with her again, but although she nursed him through a high temperature in Budapest and lovingly prepared his tea in her own gold samovar, he could not be cajoled into making his peace with the Mariinsky.

In March, 1912 the troupe arrived in Monte Carlo for a second season, preceded by reports of their triumphant reception in Prague, Vienna and Budapest. Every performance seemed a gala night. The patronage of the Grand Dukes was of course assured by

Kschessinska's return, but other celebrities appeared in force. Lady Ripon and her daughter brought parties; Lord Curzon, the Grand Duke Michael's house guest, drove over with him from the Villa Kasbeck; Lord and Lady Dunsany joined their hosts, the Jerseys, together with Mr and Mrs Joseph Chamberlain; and Puccini, newly arrived to rehearse his *La Fanciulla*, with Martinelli in Caruso's old part, slipped shyly into a seat after the lights went down.

The opening night on 8 April offered *Carnival*, *Le Spectre de la Rose*, *Prince Igor* and *Schéhérazade* to an enraptured audience. Kschessinska danced impeccably and did not seem to resent Karsavina's arrival from Russia to partner Nijinsky in Stravinsky's *L'Oiseau de Feu*, the first ballet for which Diaghilev had specially commissioned a score.

The *corps de ballet*, weary of packing trunks and shuttling between cities, took their ease in Monte Carlo's gardens or enjoyed drives over the Corniche with wealthy admirers who entertained them to supper at the Café de Paris and, like the Aga Khan, often distributed handsome presents or even gaming chips.

When Nijinsky's mother came for a visit – her first trip outside Russia – she seemed dazed by the luxury and adoration which enveloped the company. Her son and Diaghilev escorted her everywhere. As Gunsbourg's guest she dined almost every night at the Hotel de Paris before attending the ballet. The company made much of her and bravely masked their feelings when she returned from shopping sprees in Nice with too-youthful silk dresses and absurdly feathered bonnets. She had some qualms over her son's 'gypsy' life and thought it a mistake to abandon the security and prestige of the Imperial Theatre, but still had no suspicion of his relationship with Diaghilev.

Nijinsky had never felt more relaxed or so confident. Fêted and admired for his performances, he was now busily working on his first venture in choreography, *L'Après-midi d'un Faune*, which he had outlined to Diaghilev while they were staying in Karlsbad during the previous summer. Debussy had composed the music back in 1891 and gladly gave his consent without restricting the adaptation in any way.

Nijinsky insisted on no fewer than 120 rehearsals from which he excluded even Diaghilev and Bakst until satisfied that the production was ready for the Paris opening. Both were enthusiastic. Fokine, then occupied with his own novelties, seemed unaware of any threat to his own position as chief choreographer when Diaghilev mentioned, with studied casualness, that Nijinsky had almost completed his work on *L'Après-midi*. It opened at the Châtelet to a storm of boos and cheers on 29 May 1912. Some critics denounced its obscenity but the majority agreed with Rodin and other eminent intellectuals in acclaiming it a masterpiece of originality. Nobody talked of anything else in the repertoire, least of all *Daphnis et Chlöe* choreographed by Fokine, who resigned in a fit of pique.

Nijinsky had become an international idol. He posed in the nude for a Rodin sculpture and Lady Ripon commissioned two portraits from Sargent. He danced for an enormous fee at the opening of a new casino at Deauville and the Aga Khan paid him 15,000 gold francs to prance for four minutes at a London garden party attended by King George and Queen Mary. But Diaghilev became so obsessively jealous and possessive that he put a stop to the sittings for Rodin's sculpture which was never completed. However, all seemed harmonious when the company arrived in Monte Carlo for the 1913 season. Nijinsky stayed at the recently opened Hotel Riviera Palace in Beausoleil and anxiously awaited Diaghilev's return from Russia. He needed his encouragement while working on the choreography of a new ballet, *Le Sacré du Printemps*, with a score by Stravinsky. One of his assistants was a Russo-Polish girl, Miriam Ramberg (later known as Marie Rambert), who had joined the company in Budapest the previous Christmas. They flirted mildly and sipped chocolate on the terrace at Pasquier's, both amused by the clumsy spying of Diaghilev's valet.

Nijinsky also fascinated a young Hungarian dancer, Romola de Pulszky, who had studied drama in Paris before becoming a pupil of Enrico Cecchetti. He had secured her a minor place in the company, together with another recent recruit from England, 17 year-old Hilda Munnings (later, Sokolova), but Romola was far more sophisticated and also had the private means to dress elegantly. She was resourceful enough to attract Nijinsky's attention. One day she sprained her ankle during a lesson and clutched at him for support. He massaged her foot and remained solicitous until she had recovered. The acquaintance blossomed into friendship but Romola acted so demurely that Diaghilev suspected nothing when he returned from St Petersburg with Karsavina.

The ballet enchanted full houses at every performance, but it was only one of a round of brilliant tourist attractions. The Mont Agel golf club already boasted a full membership, apart from visitors like Winston Churchill, who disdained knickerbockers and wore a lounge suit with a spotted bow tie. He sometimes played a round with the still beautiful Maxine Elliott, sporting a huge hat which could not have improved her swing.

Encouraged by the success of his international car rally, Blanc had decided in 1913 to launch the first aeroplane races, with a competition for the Schneider Trophy as the star attraction. The main event was preceded by a Hydro-Aeroplane Grand Prix for a race from Monaco to Beaulieu, on to San Remo and back to the principality. The competitors, mostly French and headed by Roland Garros, flew light monoplanes or big tractor biplanes which skimmed the waves. Nobody completed the course but Moineau reached San Remo before crashing and received a consolation prize of 13,000 francs (£520). Next day Prévost won the Schneider Trophy, covering 28 laps of the 10 km course in 2 hours, 50 minutes, 47 seconds.

The races pulled even more enormous crowds in the following year. Apart from the main event, interest centred on a rally from various parts of Europe. This time Roland Garros took the first prize of £1,200 by flying from Paris to Monaco in 12 hours 14 minutes. The Schneider Trophy race attracted eight top international pilots, with Lord Carbery leading a strong British contingent, including Howard Pixton, who won in a 100 h.p. Sopwith Float Seaplane. He flew the 172-mile course in 2 hours 13 seconds, cracking the world speed record with 92.1 m.p.h.

These races stimulated a craze for flying schools. Alfred Agostinelli, a former Monegasque taxi driver, was among those who enrolled at Antibes. He had become Proust's chauffeur, secretary-companion and the most cherished of all his bedmates. 'His black rubber cape and the hooded helmet which enclosed the fullness of his young beardless face made him resemble a pilgrim or, rather, a nun of speed' Proust later recalled. On his second solo flight in a monoplane Agostinelli rashly headed out to sea, stalled and crashed. A non-swimmer, he lost his life.

From Monte Carlo Diaghilev and Bakst wrote tender letters of consolation to the stricken novelist whose grief had brought on another acute attack of asthma. Although a devotee of the Russian ballet, he never took to Nijinsky whose 'rejection' of Diaghilev had been the most hotly-debated subject in Paris salons for many months. Proust's sympathy, like that of most other homosexuals, went out to the impresario, but Monte Carlo audiences mourned the missing dancer when the season opened in April 1914.

The company had sailed for a South American tour in the previous August without Diaghilev, who had a premonition of dying 'on water'. A last-minute decision to cancel his booking enabled Romola de Pulszky to further a tender shipboard romance with Nijinsky. They were in love by the time they landed at Rio where they exchanged betrothal rings. They married in Buenos Aires and Nijinsky quickly wrote a letter of explanation to Diaghilev. Weeks passed before he received a curt reply in Budapest just before Christmas: 'Your services with the Russian Ballet are no more required. Don't join us. Sergey de Diaghilev'.

The first performance of *Les Papillons* starred Karsavina, with costumes by Bakst. It launched a repertory of the highest technical standard but lacked Nijinsky's magic. Fokine was reinstated as chief choreographer and Diaghilev had replaced his faithless faun with Leonide Massine, who soon experienced the impresario's rabid jealously. He once entered Massine's hotel room, ripped the telephone from the wall and smashed up all the furniture before dissolving into tears.

The capacity audiences included several distinguished foreign visitors who had arrived to celebrate Prince Albert's silver jubilee as ruler. He attended various gala dinners in his honour but took distinctly more interest in welcoming senior detectives, magistrates and jurists to discuss international police co-operation. This congress, the seed of Interpol, was the direct result of the prince's personal initiative in canvassing leading officials from 24 countries to discuss extradition procedures and the possible establishment of a central office for exchanging statistics and other forensic information. The prince then sailed off in the *Hirondelle II* but interrupted his cruise to attend the Kiel Regatta in June 1914. He was aboard the Kaiser's yacht *Meteor* when a launch drew alongside. Admiral Müller was observed to fold a note into his cigarette case which he tossed to an officer on deck. The Kaiser read the message and turned away, obviously much agitated. 'Now I must begin all over again', he exclaimed. Within minutes all his guests had learned of the Archduke Ferdinand's assassination at Sarajevo.

The prince resumed his cruise but returned to Monaco when war had become inevitable. He proclaimed a state of neutrality, which did not please Paris, although some French newspapers noted with approval that Prince Louis had at once rejoined his old regiment.

All Frenchmen in the reserve and others of military age had quickly crossed the frontier. The depleted casino staff now took turns at traffic duty in place of policemen called to the colours. Some of the Monegasques, tasting power after many years of French bureaucracy, became so arrogant that Prince Albert once again over-reacted to vague 'revolutionary' threats. He brusquely suspended the Constitution on 8 October but set an example of self-denial by closing the palace to live aboard the *Hirondelle II* with his grand-daughter, Charlotte. His enemies preferred to assume that he was taking precautions for a quick getaway if the Germans broke through. However, he relaxed his neutrality by opening hospitals and convalescent homes for French casualties.

The casino closed for a short time and was back in business by New Year's Day. Gunsbourg had meantime been frantically adjusting to a wartime schedule. Most of the leading dancers had returned to Russia, while Diaghilev, with Massine as dancer/choreographer and Cecchetti coaching a handful of artists exempt from military service, established his headquarters in Lausanne to be near Stravinsky with whom he discussed future productions. Nijinsky had sired a baby girl, Kyra, and dreamed of forming his own company, assisted by his sister, Bronia, but he would spend the first two wartime years under 'house arrest' in Vienna as an enemy alien.

In the early months of the war, while Italy stayed neutral, Gunsbourg was still hopeful of staging operas. In mid-October, before Caruso sailed back to New York, Gunsbourg hastened to meet him in Paris. He declared over dinner, 'I'll open the season in Monte Carlo, even if nobody comes.' Caruso grasped his hand and said warmly, 'I will come. You can announce that I shall open for you next March. On that you have my word.' They embraced emotionally as Caruso boarded the Rome express.

Although the Metropolitan management threatened to sue him for $100,000, he sang for a month at Monte Carlo and gave superlative performances in *Aïda*, *I Pagliacci* and *Lucia*. Before leaving, Caruso was visited at the Hotel de Paris by an impresario who asked him to name his own fee for a Latin-American tour. Half in jest Caruso demanded 3,500 francs in gold ($7,000) a performance. It was agreed on the spot and he sailed for Buenos Aires within a week. He never again visited Monte Carlo but Gunsbourg would always pay tribute to 'le gentilhomme tenor', who had saved his first wartime season from certain disaster.

The casino's £1,500,000 income for 1912 dropped by two-thirds within two years. Foreign residents, Allied soldiers on leave and a number of wartime profiteers kept the wheels spinning, but Camille Blanc had to meet heavy overheads on a reduced intake. Employees in the French forces remained on the payroll and the

SBM was still responsible for the prince's guaranteed minimum income.

Blanc co-operated loyally with the authorities in reporting activity by possible enemy agents. Spy mania became rampant. It was freely rumoured in the early months that neutral-owned steam yachts received radio messages about French troop or ship movements and transmitted them to the Wilhelmstrasse through a secret base in the principality. The arrest of a suspected spy even led to a close watch being kept on anyone feeding pigeons outside the casino!

One of his Gunsbourg's was Puccini's *La Rondine*, an operetta originally commissioned by two over-hopeful Viennese impresarios. The war had held up its production in enemy countries and nobody else seemed interested in a piece which an Italian manager dismissed as 'bad Lehar'. But Gunsbourg, in no position to be over-critical, shrewdly decided that the lightweight confection, with Puccini's name as ballast, might make ideal escapist entertainment for his war-bored audiences. He mounted the production with taste and engaged the beautiful soprano, Gilda Dalla Rizza, one of Puccini's favourites, to partner Tito Schipa. In March 1917 the composer arrived from Tuscany with his wife and stepdaughter. Gunsbourg gave them two suites at the Hotel de Paris and staged a gala première on the old magnificent scale. The final curtain came down to thunderous applause.

The Constitution was re-established later that year. The three Communes would be administered by a single municipal council and the General Council reduced in size. Since only Monegasques could be elected, this meant excluding the foreign business colony from all representation. Three years would pass before a Chamber of Commerce was set up to safeguard their interests. The new Constitution also failed to satisfy the prince's more democratic-minded subjects, who grumbled that Monaco was still the only completely autocratic monarchy in Europe, not excluding even the Romanovs, Hapsburgs and Hohenzollerns.

But the consequences of the Grimaldi line becoming extinct were now all too apparent. Prince Albert was nearing 70. If his soldier son, a 48 year-old bachelor, were killed, the succession would technically pass to German cousins, the Urach-Wurtembergs, whom no French government could possibly accept. It was soon being rumoured that the principality might have to be taken under French protection, if not directly annexed.

The Monegasques, already nervous of losing their gaming monopoly, tax privileges and exemption from military service, would have been even more alarmed had they known of a treaty, signed in Paris between the two countries on 17 July 1918 but not made public until the Peace Conference a year later. France had confirmed the independence and sovereignty of Monaco, subject to an agreement by the prince to exercise his rights 'in conformity with the political, military, naval and economic interests of France'. Furthermore, if the Grimaldi throne fell vacant through lack of an heir, *direct or adopted*, Monaco was to become a protectorate although remaining autonomous. But on 7 November Prince Albert proclaimed that, in the absence of a legitimate direct heir, the reigning prince and his heir apparent could adopt a child with full succession rights and prerogatives. This was promptly followed by the formal adoption of Charlotte by her father, Prince Louis, at a ceremony attended by President Poincaré.

The move to abolish the old 1882 law of succession, linked with Prince Albert's anxiety to conclude a secret treaty with France while his country was still technically neutral, was no sudden whim on his part. It dovetailed rather too neatly with a certain other private arrangement initiated early that summer by his Minister, Count Balny d'Avricourt, who had called at the Ritz Hotel in Paris to sound out Sir Basil Zaharoff on the prospects of taking over the administration of the SBM. He was given a most sympathetic audience by a man seldom associated with comparatively minor deals and, still less, disinterested gestures of generosity.

La Belle Otero, Spanish gypsy
dancer and international courtesan,
whose jewels and extravagance
enlivened the Nineties.

Cocteau's celebrated
poster for Nijinsky's
Le Spectre de la Rose.

THÉÂTRE DE MONTE-CARLO

SAISON DE BALLETS RUSSES

Organisée par M. SERGE DE DIAGHILEW.
Directeur Chorégraphique : M. MICHEL FOKINE.
Directeur Artistique : M. BENOIS.

SOIRÉE du 19 Avril 1911

CARNAVAL

Pantomime-Ballet en 1 acte de M. FOKINE et M. L. BAKST
Musique de ROBERT SCHUMANN
Orchestré par RIMSKY-KORSAKOW, LIADOFF, TCHÉREPNINE et GLAZOUNOFF

Groupes et Danses réglés par M. FOKINE, **Maître de Ballet des Théâtres Impériaux de Saint-Pétersbourg**
Décors et Costumes dessinés par L. BAKST
Décor exécuté par ANISFELD — Costumes de Mlle MUELLE de Paris

Colombine	Mmes KARSAVINA	Pierrot	MM. BOLM
Chiarina	FOKINA	Arlequin	NIJINSKY
Estrella	SCHOLLAR	Pantalon	CECCHETTI
Papillon	NIJINSKA	Eusébius	SERGUEIEFF
		Florestan	SEMENOFF

SHÉHÉRAZADE

Drame chorégraphique en 1 acte de MM L. BAKST et M. FOKINE
Musique de RIMSKY-KORSAKOW

Danses et Scènes de M. MICHEL FOKINE
Décor et Costumes dessinés par L. BAKST.
Décor exécuté par MM. BAKST, ANISFELD, ALLEGRI.
Costumes de Mlle MUELLE de Paris.

LE SPECTRE DE LA ROSE

(CRÉATION)

Tableau chorégraphique, Poème de TH. GAUTIER, Musique de C. M. WEBER
Scènes et Danses de M. FOKINE — Décor et Costumes de L. BAKST

La jeune fille .... Mme KARSAVINA
La Rose .... M. NIJINSKY

LE FESTIN

Danses Polovtsiennes du « PRINCE IGOR » — Musique de BORODINE
Danses composées et réglées par M. FOKINE

The gala opening of Diaghilev's first season was graced by stars
like Nijinsky and Karsavina, with choreography by Fokine and
Bakst's superb decor.

The Churchills and the Duchess of Sutherland (right) promenade at Monte Carlo, February 1913. Sir Winston became a regular visitor for the next half-century.

The first Monte Carlo Rally in 1911 attracted 23 competitors. The winning Bugatti covered 570 miles from Paris in 28 hours 10 mins.

Prince Louis II with his daughter, Charlotte, who gave up her accession rights in favour of her son, Rainier, when he came of age.

Sir Basil Zaharoff, the armaments king, ousted the Blancs in 1923 by secretly paying a million sterling for the Casino concession. He sold out after two years for £3,400,000.

Superstitious gamblers often rub the left fetlock of Louis XIV's equestrian bronze in the Hotel de Paris lobby.

The twin Dolly Sisters, music hall stars of the Twenties, won and lost fortunes at the tables. Gordon Selfridge ruined himself through his infatuation for extravagant Jenny.

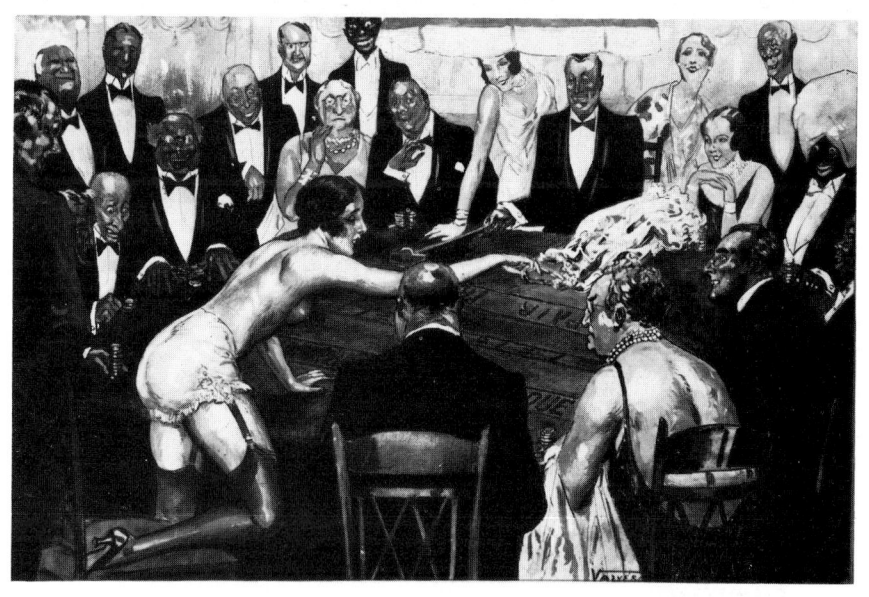

How to lose one's chemise in the pre-Second War decade of feverish gambling.

The Monaco Grand Prix, a 200-mile race round Monte Carlo's corkscrew twists, started in May 1929. Every year, watched by huge crowds, it attracts the world's crack drivers.

Cocteau (left), who wrote the libretti for *Le Train Bleu* and other original works, with Diaghilev, brilliant impresario of Monte Carlo's historic Ballet Russe.

Part Two

FROM
ZAHAROFF TO ONASSIS

Chapter Six

Prince Albert had already begun to lose patience with the SBM months before the war ended. Embittered by his two broken marriages and never the most amenable of men – few Grimaldis less deserved the honorific 'Serene Highness' – his years of enforced anchorage aboard *Hirondelle II* had left him thrashing about like a harpooned whale. He had aged rapidly without the tonic of his cruises. Stooping, gaunt and with his wispy moustache and beard as dun-coloured as the rumpled tweeds he always wore, he ate little and only seemed to revive in his Museum or when poring over blueprints for a new model fort on which work had been interrupted in 1914.

When he requested a substantial advance against the casino's 'future profits', Camille Blanc had lamented the drop in gaming receipts and also sidestepped all demands for funds to restock the Oceanographic Museum or provide new uniforms for the Palace Guard. He reminded the prince that tourists would only be lured back by reviving the car rally, the Russian ballet, the regattas and other high-priority attractions. Such essential expenditure, he explained, when added to the salaries for demobilised employees, would drain the company's reserve fund of barely £1 million. He had even hinted pointedly that the ruler might show his goodwill by accepting a cut in his £90,000 a year.

Prince Albert bit his lips and decided to seek a wealthier and more co-operative backer than this over-cautious paymaster, who was evidently more eager to serve his shareholders than the principality. He was already acquainted with Zaharoff, who for many years had spent part of each winter at the Hotel de Paris with his mistress, the Duchess of Villafranca, wife of a mentally deranged Spanish nobleman. Nevertheless, he seemed a surprising candidate, with nothing in his background to indicate the remotest interest in casino affairs.

Born in Anatolia of poor Greek parentage, Zaharoff had started as a money-changer before working for an uncle, who discharged him for embezzlement. He soon met Nordenfeldt, the Swedish gun designer, and became his agent for the Balkans, later master-minding the absorption of Hiram Maxim's business by a typical stroke of duplicity. The firm's subsequent amalgamation with Vickers established him as a master technician in the field of international finance. During the war years he had added to his already colossal personal fortune by selling guns and submarines to all comers. He simultaneously acquired major interests in ship-building and oil, together with numerous directorships of banks, railways, hotels and factories. With an ability to lie fluently in eight languages, and insulated from unwelcome publicity by his own corps of nominees, tame journalists and venal officials, he became outstandingly successful in manipulating governments through trusted confidants like Lloyd George and Clemenceau.

Following the visit of Count Balny, he began dining *à deux* with Prince Albert at 53 Avenue Hoche, his Paris mansion. Subtle politicking of any kind was congenial to him, but the sunny little principality must have offered a special spice. He later confided to his friend, Sir Charles Mendl, Press Attaché at the British Embassy, 'Monaco is a territory one can control easily; one could make it overnight into a true fairyland.' But his underlying motive was probably far more sordid and characteristic. He had formerly owned brothels in Paris and on the Riviera with obvious scope for compromising influential statesmen and bureaucrats. The casino's unique security files, almost a miniature global rogues gallery, had presumably tempted this ruthless wheeler-dealer, who always believed in holding a fistful of blackmailing trumps. Little else, certainly not the relatively modest profits to be expected from the SBM, could have induced him to bale out a needy princeling.

Zaharoff moved fast. Subject to their arrangement being kept a close secret, he agreed to place a million sterling at the ruler's future disposal for an option to take over the Casino Company. But he knew that this investment would become almost valueless if France incorporated her neighbour into the Alpes-Maritimes after the war. Since that would automatically end the principality's monopoly of roulette and its unique fiscal advantages, Zaharoff saw the need to safeguard Monaco's sovereignty.

Prince Albert had no objection to a treaty which would protect his dynasty and help to reassure his subjects. Prodded by Clemenceau, Zaharoff's good friend, France had also signed readily enough once the stipulations securing her 'vital interests' were incorporated. The treaty aroused little overt opposition in Monaco when its contents finally became known, but the SBM option would remain under wraps for almost four years during which the unsuspecting Blanc sat on a time bomb. Surprisingly, no whisper reached his ears while he continued spending effort and cash to take Monte Carlo into the precarious post-war era.

The situation had obvious appeal for a sadistic monster like Zaharoff, but he had other good reasons to delay exercising his option. He had become heavily preoccupied behind the scenes at the Peace Conference and helped to foment the bloody Greco-Turkish War, one of his few unsuccessful ventures. It cost him several million sterling, but he had wisely avoided involving himself in another Balkan intrigue which, as it happened, ended ingloriously in the Monte Carlo casino.

The ex-Emperor Karl, chafing in Swiss exile with his beautiful wife, Zita, hoped to return to Hungary, then ruled by Admiral Horthy as Regent. Several monarchists and other members of the old nobility had subscribed half a million Swiss francs to the cause, but their funds were hopelessly inadequate even though supplemented by the sale of the Empress's jewels. The conspirators, headed by two former cavalry officers and a forceful Austrian countess, rashly planned to swell their bankroll with a sure-fire roulette system. They lost their entire capital in a month's feverish play. Karl and his wife, still pathetically certain of a rapturous welcome, decided to fly to Budapest. Their aircraft made a forced landing and the couple fled back to Switzerland whose government, weary of these embarrassing intrigues, ordered them to leave. Karl died in Madeira within a few months.

The Monegasque dynasty was more fortunate in resolving its own succession problem through an alliance warmly welcomed by the French. Early in 1920 Prince Albert had received the new President, Paul Deschanel, on a State Visit. Soon afterwards Princess Charlotte married a member of the long-distinguished Polignac clan, who assumed the title of Prince Pierre Grimaldi. Their first child, Antoinette, was born in Paris shortly after Christmas.

Prince Pierre, a cosmopolitan socialite and boulevardier, was equally at home on the polo field and in a set dominated by intellectuals like Princesse Bibesco, Cocteau and Paul Morand. He had also become friendly during the war years with Proust, who arranged to spend a holiday that first summer in Monaco but angrily cancelled his visit when Prince Pierre neglected to order the de luxe edition of *A L'Ombre*. Proust took revenge by caricaturing him as the Comte de Nassau, who announces pompously to the Duchesse de Guermantes, 'I make a point of getting up when my wife passes'. The Duchesse snaps back, 'Well, that makes a change from her grandmother, because she expected the men to lie down'. The Paris salons chuckled over this gibe at playful Princess Alice, and Proust was never again asked to Monte Carlo.

Prince Pierre enjoyed greater camaraderie with Diaghilev, whom Gunsbourg had invited back to provide dancers for his 1920 opera season, with the promise of a future short annual ballet season to precede the company's regular engagement in Paris. Gunsbourg's resources were still too meagre for a return to the old budget, but Diaghilev was in no position to bicker. Without Nijinsky, now hopelessly insane, he had endured several thin war years, followed by none too successful seasons in England and France. His situation became even more precarious after the defection of Massine whose 'disloyal' marriage he could not forgive. He had arrived in Paris owing money in London and elsewhere, and had even sold his most cherished possession, a black pearl stud given him by Lady Ripon during his first Monte Carlo season. 'Coco' Chanel, whose establishment in the Rue Cambon was already a temple of haute couture, came to his rescue with a cheque for 200,000 francs. She also took as her lover the tall and handsome Grand Duke Dmitri, appointing him publicity officer to promote her new perfume, 'Chanel Cinq'. He had escaped the Red holocaust through being banished to Persia for participating in Rasputin's murder. He soon fell on his feet in Biarritz by marrying Audrey Emery, daughter of the American leather magnate.

He was luckier than most of his clan. Camille Blanc, checking a prewar list of patrons, discovered that over two-thirds of his former Russian clientèle had met with violent deaths. But the Grand Duke Nicholas escaped from the Crimea in a British battleship with the Dowager Empress and died ten years later in Antibes. The Czar's first cousin, Cyril, proclaimed himself 'Czar of All the Russias' and established something of a court in a Breton village where he pompously reviewed a few Cossack ex-officers. The Romanov heyday was over. Apart from the wealthy and long-exiled Grand Duke Michael, who returned from England to his Cannes villa, few of the emigrés could have survived without the generosity of better-placed relations. King George V of England rescued his 'dear Aunt Minnie' (the Dowager Empress) with a pension of £10,000 a year and Queen Mary bought up many jewels, including the Grand Duchess Vladimir's tiara, which she bequeathed to her grand-daughter, the present Queen.

The exiles usually made their way to Paris or the Riviera. Attended by a handful of loyal retainers, they insisted on the niceties of precedence and would gather in force for sentimental reunions, particularly at Easter, when tables were loaded with *pashka*, multi-coloured eggs and other traditional cold table dishes.

Gunsbourg's supper guests after the ballet were almost

exclusively compatriots, including Diaghilev, Pavlova and the former rival ballerinas, Karsavina and Mathilde Kschessinska, who had at last married the Grand Duke André. Her mansion in St Petersburg had been sacked by a mob who chopped up the grand piano and looted her other treasures while she was holidaying in the Crimea with André and their son, Vova. They reached France almost penniless but the Grand Duke had left his elegant clothes in the custody of the Hotel de Paris, and 7,000 francs still stood to his credit in a Monte Carlo bank. They were soon forced to mortgage their fine villa to pay the wartime caretakers and other creditors.

Their financial situation improved from André's inherited share of his Aunt Marie's jewels, but they entertained beyond their means and Kschessinska could not resist gambling. She was often partnered at the tables by Pavlova, who habitually forgot where she had placed her stakes and caused havoc by knocking over other players' plaques with her long fringed shawl. She had to borrow from her friend after one losing session, but returned the cash next day in an elegant silk purse with a gold fastening worth far more than the loan of 1,000 francs. Kschessinska also had a sense of style, in victory or defeat, but heavy losses finally forced her to give up gambling. She departed for Paris to open a ballet studio where she trained Margot Fonteyn among many other future stars.

Camille Blanc accorded these fallen Romanovs undiminished deference but his anxiety to restore the casino's former aristocratic image had made him rather too unwary of a fast-changing clientèle. Many of the English and French nobility, like the Grand Dukes, had come under financial strain. Monte Carlo was now being invaded by a free-spending bourgeoisie, war-rich profiteers and many confidence tricksters with bogus titles. In 1920 the casino cashed over £100,000 in bad cheques and the Hotel de Paris had more than its share of unpaid bills including one from an English company which had optimistically embarked on a film, 'The Man Who Broke the Bank at Monte Carlo', with Charles Coburn cast in the rôle of Wells.

The unit arrived with a flurry of advance publicity but soon ran into difficulties when the SBM stubbornly adhered to its rule of prohibiting all photography inside the casino. The script was hastily adjusted and shooting restricted to the steps of the casino and the gardens.

The picture was never completed as the company ran out of cash and the directors quarrelled bitterly among themselves. Coborn paid £50 out of his own pocket towards the hotel bill and, as a gesture, offered to give a free performance for patrons of the Café de Paris. To his astonishment, the management banned him from singing 'The Man Who Broke the Bank' and explained that it was an SBM rule to exclude any allusion to gambling by entertainers in all their establishments. Coborn could not budge them and instead sang 'Two Lovely Black Eyes' and other popular favourites from his repertoire.

Casino security had been tightened up but criminals slipped through more easily than in the past. One victim was the Hohenzollern Baroness Groner, who used to gamble for maximum stakes. A stately brunette, her jewels and very low-cut elegant gowns won admiration whenever she swept into the Salon Privé with her ostrich-feathered bag stuffed with banknotes. One night, playing with her pile of 5,000 franc plaques, she won so heavily that the bank ran out of currency. Blanc sent in a dozen magnums of champagne for the baroness and her friends before she moved across to an adjacent table and again 'broke the bank'. This time she cashed her chips and left for the Hotel de Paris by way of one of the casino's long ante-rooms. From behind some ferns two hands reached out to grasp her throat while an accomplice snatched her handbag. She collapsed and had to be attended by doctors.

An hour later, supping with sympathetic friends in the Salle Empire, she glanced at a nearby table where a handsome couple seemed to be in high spirits. She noticed a sliver of ostrich feather on the man's trouser leg and hastily pencilled a warning message to the casino's Commissaire, who arrived with three detectives. They searched the suspects and found an ostrich bag in the man's possession. Round the girl's slender waist was a bulging money belt. Both had police records and went to prison for three years. This episode, together with an unseemly scramble for places even in the Salons Privés, persuaded Blanc to open a new International Sporting Club whose members could play for high stakes in plushy seclusion, and with additional facilities available for gala banquets or dances.

In June 1922 Prince Albert was about to remind Zaharoff of his option when he caught a severe cold while out shooting in the Pyrenees. Pneumonia set in and he had to be brought down to the valley by ambulance. He died before the end of the month. His son, Prince Louis, was summoned to Monaco while supervising the plebiscite in Upper Silesia on General La Rond's staff. An easy-going bachelor of 52, but every inch the colonel with his bushy moustache and bootbrush crop of hair, he had been far too long out of the country to understand its cross-currents. He soon sold *Hirondelle II* to an English yachtsman although he dutifully persuaded the Council to expand his father's research laboratories at the Museum. He briskly re-equipped the Palace Guard with over-due new uniforms and personally smartened up their drill, but he still preferred shooting parties at Marchais. He also began to leave his son-in-law, Prince Pierre, a free hand to sponsor sporting or artistic events in his name.

Prince Louis, who had had some experience of engineering in his Legion days, took an interest in the projected harbour improve-ments which Blanc found every excuse to delay. But their first open clash was over the long-dormant scheme to drive a tunnel under the Rock to the industrial suburb of Fontvieille, now slowly rising on land reclaimed from the sea. The ruler was far too ac-customed to barrack discipline to tolerate Blanc's polite evasions and his penny-pinching arguments for economy. Within a few months of his accession he began to ponder wistfully on the pend-ing casino option with its inviting cheque for a million sterling. His reminder reached 53 Avenue Hoche precisely when Zaharoff, still bruised from his ill-fated Greek adventure and the eclipse of Lloyd George, Clemenceau and Venizelos, needed some outlet, however minor, to gratify his power hunger. Once decided, he guillotined Camille Blanc with surgical efficiency.

In May 1923, with the Monegasques still joyfully celebrating the birth of a chubby baby son, Rainier, to Princess Charlotte, Zaharoff made his move. He soon bought a majority of SBM shares at slump prices through nominees. While Blanc was absent on business, Zaharoff sat on the terrace of the Hotel de Paris, an admirable vantage point for viewing the execution. A note was occasionally passed out to him from the casino opposite. He would stroke his white imperial beard, snap an order and sit back with his panama tilted over slate-grey eyes colder than any croupier's.

In the company's panelled head office the Board of Control, infiltrated by his henchmen, was powerless to oppose the *coup d'état*. The prince made it even more decisive with a resolution insisting on all future measures being countersigned by a Zaharoff nominee. Blanc returned to find himself out-gunned and out-manoeuvred. It was futile to appeal either to the sovereign or to François Blanc's grandson, Prince Léon Radziwill, a big shareholder, who would continue serving on the board but without any real administrative control. Blanc resigned 'for reasons of health', followed by his single faithful supporter, Louis Brun, manager of the casino.

The new president, Alfred Delpierre, had controlled France's wartime mercantile services without any disadvantage to Zaharoff. A directorship went to another tried ally, the brother of Louis Barthou, a former Prime Minister, but they were merely pilot fish for a shark like Zaharoff. He still needed a super-efficient manager to run the casino which had never quite recovered its pre-war momentum. René Léon proved an inspired appointment. A spry little bachelor, he was a university graduate in mathematics with a brilliant technical brain behind the suavely disarming manner of a maître d'hôtel. He was practically teetotal, yet the most delightful of hosts and always receptive to reporters, unlike his brusque employer.

Léon had a sense of irony and liked recalling the night he had walked into the Salon Privé with a friend, General Pierre Polovtsoff, just before his appointment was officially announced. They punted modestly and were on the point of leaving when Léon stepped on a 20-franc chip. He placed it on '29', *à cheval*, which had previously evaded him. This time it won and within a few minutes he had cleared over £100. He squared his conscience by solemnly handing over a 20-franc chip to the *chef de partie*!

One of his first innovations was to abolish 'zero' for half an hour each night in the hope of attracting more punters on pair, impair and colours, but this misfired as too many players still favoured zero. He was more successful in doubling the minimum on all stakes at roulette and trente-et-quarante. 'Why not offer a 100-franc minimum for soixante-neuf?' Zaharoff suggested coarsely.

A Roumanian punter was an early victim of the higher stakes. Frenzied by heavy losses, he poured a bottle of petrol over the green baize and attempted to set fire to it with a match. He also took a revolver from his pocket and fired up at a crystal chandelier. He then jumped through a window, fracturing his leg. The shock brought on a heart attack to which he succumbed in hospital. When five bullets were found in the ceiling, superstitious gamblers rushed to the same table and enthusiastically backed 'cinq', but without any success.

Zaharoff at once initiated a security check and simultaneously took steps to improve the quality of his croupiers, who had been recruited rather too haphazardly in the past and sometimes supplemented their salaries by stealing counters or shaving the odds for accomplices. He soon instituted a closer watch by *chefs de partie* and inspectors.

He kept a very tight rein on the casino's administration, although rarely entering the gaming rooms himself. Within a fortnight of his arrival he had scrapped the traditional free admission and also charged a higher entrance fee to the Salons Privés. He dismissed many employees, who had inherited jobs for generations, and ruthlessly eliminated the sinecures which Camille Blanc had weakly condoned. Scores of pensioners were removed from the budget or paid off with small lump sums.

But Zaharoff was too canny to economise on prestige attractions. He voluntarily increased the subsidy for the Oceanographic Museum and spent liberally on the gardens and parks, with a special allocation to the Jardin Exotique. Above all, he encouraged better harbour facilities to attract back the millionaire yachtsmen who had begun drifting off to Cannes. Their vessels soon began anchoring again in Monte Carlo's harbour. Lit up at night, they glittered like a necklace in Cartier's window and equally beyond the reach of those who gawped on shore or from passing ships. Shortly after Zaharoff took control, another Levantine crowded to a ship's rail for his first glimpse of the principality. He was one of many Greek refugees travelling steerage from Turkish-occupied Smyrna to start a new life in South America. He lacked a passport but his travel document, valid for a single one-way trip to Buenos Aires, identified him as Aristotle Socrates Onassis, aged 17.

Baron Henri de Rothschild was among many now wintering regularly in Monte Carlo. A qualified physician, who also wrote plays under his pseudonym of 'André Pascal', he gave magnificent parties aboard his yacht, aptly named *Eros*. He smoked Caporals and ate fresh peaches while playing, much to the distaste of Bendor ('Benny'), Duke of Westminster, whose arrogance paralleled that of any Romanov. A valued free-spending patron of Monte Carlo since pre-war days, he was rated the third richest man in the world in 1923 after Henry Ford and John D. Rockefeller. He always carried a full complement of passengers when he sailed into harbour in his *Cutty Sark*, a half-completed war destroyer which he converted into a fast 883-ton steam yacht. A procession of chauffeur-driven Rolls-Royces picked up his guests when they chose to come ashore. He gambled with fistfuls of *mille* notes, sometimes playing three or four tables at once and leaving it to the attendants to scoop up any winnings.

Another millionaire yachtsman, Solly Joel, had the same capacity to stop playing when the cards or wheel turned against him. Equipped with nerveless self-control, reinforced by a shrewd assessment of the odds, he seldom lost. Like Westminster, he was notoriously short-tempered with fools and any others who trespassed on his privacy. One day he was sunning himself on the hotel terrace with Zaharoff slumped in the next chair. Neither liked chatter but their peace was disturbed by a young man, who approached the Rand magnate and brashly invited him to join a game of chemin-de-fer in the Sporting Club. Solly chomped his Havana and snapped, 'What's the good? If I win a thousand pounds it makes no difference. If I lose it, I'm miserable for the rest of the day. However, if you're so keen on wasting your father's money, I'll be happy to toss a coin for £10,000'. The youth retreated in a hurry, followed by a derisive Zaharoff chuckle like the crackling of dried leaves.

Joel's yacht, *Eileen II*, with its miniature putting green on the quarter deck, had a gleaming white pine promenade on which passengers and crew were forbidden to walk except barefoot or when wearing rubber-soled shoes. On the main deck he provided stabling for his children's ponies and a miniature basket-weave victoria. His guests enjoyed superb meals prepared by a chef from London's Embassy Club. The men smoked fat Corona Coronas and drank Veuve Clicquot but had to endure their host's practical jokes. He liked to wager that nobody could climb ashore on one of the taut hawsers. Those who accepted the challenge discovered that Solly had fixed the line so that it suddenly dropped and gave the victim an unwelcome sea bath. He would also provide his shapelier guests with chic-looking bathing costumes made from a synthetic material which dissolved on contact with water.

Lily Langtry had long since given up her yacht but had retired to Monaco to escape the severe winters of London or New York. She bought and modernised a croupier's villa, Le Lys, and settled in with a widowed friend from her stage days. She had wearied of Sir Hugo but continued his allowance, small yet sufficient to maintain his mistresses and even a modest house in Nice. At Le Lys she liked entertaining royalty like King Alfonso and his wife, Ena, and maintained two cars, a chauffeur, cook, maids and an English butler. With her bobbed hair dyed auburn and Paris gowns shortened to flapper length, she paid twice-weekly visits to the casino but now seemed keener to display her diamonds and greet old friends than to break the bank.

Up at Eze above Beaulieu, Douglas Fairbanks, Mary Pickford, Chaplin and Gloria Swanson, then the Marquise de la Falaise, were fêted by the former Consuelo Vanderbilt, who had divorced her duke to marry the French aviator, Jacques Balsan. Their villa, Lou Sueil, encircled by giant cypresses, became a celebrated rendezvous for Riviera visitors from the early twenties onwards. One of their guests, Lord Curzon, the former Viceroy of India and British Foreign Secretary, arrived one year in acute physical distress. Although badly crippled and forced to wear a cruel steel corset, he could not refuse an invitation to dine at the palace but had to stand about, leaning heavily on his stick, until the prince entered. In fairness to the ruler, he did not care for formality and everyone knew that his good humour could be ensured at any official banquet or reception by simply ordering the orchestra to play his favourite 'March of the Foreign Legion' at frequent intervals. Recalling the Curzon incident, Madame Balsan commented graciously, 'Prince Louis was a simple man who enjoyed talking about his years with the Legion in the nineties', but she had no word of praise for his palace; 'instead of creating a court like that of the Medici or Valois where men of genius were honoured and artists encouraged, it is merely the showplace of a garish pleasure-loving place that takes its advantages of scenery and climate for granted and allows the corrupt Casino to pick up the bill for all the amenities'.

But Madame Balsan was generous in her praise of the artistic perfection of the Diaghilev troupe in Zaharoff's very first year at Monaco. Although without Nijinsky and Massine, and with the manic-depressive Bakst soon to die alone in a locked Paris studio, the Ballets Russes enjoyed an astonishing second flowering with exciting scores from Stravinsky, Prokofiev and Poulenc interpreted by such talented newcomers as Anton Dolin and Serge Lifar. The latter, whom Chanel used to call 'my godson' because her money had enabled Diaghilev to get him out of Russia, came to Monte Carlo in January 1923.

Lifar recalls that he used to rehearse all day, often alone, and sometimes practised for hours to strengthen his take-off and other movements. He would suffer from attacks of dizziness and stage-fright, particularly if the Prince and Princess of Monaco looked in at rehearsals, although both were kindly and often revived the company with champagne. Diaghilev could be terrifying, alternating between excessive affection (he would always kiss Lifar and make the sign of the cross over him before a performance) and sadistic humiliations calculated to keep him insecure. It was standard procedure for Diaghilev to strengthen his own position by fomenting rivalries. He played off Stravinsky against Prokofiev and tormented Lifar by simulating a preference for the young Anglo-Irishman, Patrick Healey-Kay (renamed, Anton Dolin), who had been engaged just after the start of the 1923-4 season. Sitting one morning outside the Café de Paris with Dolin, he roughly ordered Lifar not to join them. 'You should be working and not wasting your time' he jeered.

Always mindful of his 'betrayal' by Nijinsky and Massine, he would station himself at his bedroom window in the Hotel de Paris and keep a lookout for Lifar with his powerful binoculars. After midnight service in the Russian church at Menton, forty guests once assembled for Easter breakfast in Kschessinska's villa. Lifar was a little tipsy and staggered slightly as he danced the traditional polonaise with his hostess. He began flirting innocently with Karsavina behind a sofa until Diaghilev, black as thunder, curtly sent him back to Monte Carlo.

Lifar would often be placed in the back row of the corps de ballet until ready to abase himself. He was far more brittle than Dolin, who used to relieve his tensions by doing handstands and cartwheels in the wings. It gave Cocteau the idea for a one-act beach ballet, *Le Train Bleu*. Diaghilev quickly commissioned him to write the libretto for a score by Milhaud. Nijinska, the dancer's sister, handled the choreography and Chanel designed the bathing costumes.

Lifar had slowly established himself in the company although sometimes unnerved at rehearsals by critical onlookers like Stravinsky and Picasso, a close friend of Diaghilev's since a war-time Paris season when he had designed the scenery and costumes for *Parade* by Cocteau. The latter had recently been shattered by the sudden death of his paramour, Raymond Radiguet. Almost insane with grief, he lapsed into melancholia and soon turned to opium. Waiters at the Hotel de Paris used to sniff the odour seeping beneath the doors of his suite where he smoked in the company of the more experienced Poulenc and Georges Auric. Their behaviour drew a rebuke from the *Paris-Journal* which also took a swipe at Gunsbourg's rather mediocre festival of French music: 'The audiences are sub-subtle, sub-urbane, sub-sophisticated. No wonder musical lemonade is in such demand. Monte Carlo is a mixture of sex, un-sex and emetics . . .'

Perched on his box-office receipts, Gunsbourg could afford to disregard such outbursts. He delighted patrons by engaging Kreisler at stupendous fees which, like Chaliapin, he would too often fritter away at the tables. He also welcomed the then almost unknown pianist, Vladimir Horowitz, who had left his native Kiev in 1924 to capture a wider public. And Ravel, who had still not recovered from his wartime ambulance-driving, gratefully accepted an invitation to spend several months of semi-convalescence in Monaco while working on *L'Enfant et les Sortilèges* for which Colette wrote the libretto.

Gunsbourg always remained grateful to Zaharoff for his generous support of the Salle Garnier. The end of his short three-year régime would also be mourned by the SBM shareholders, but not Prince Louis II of Monaco, who had found several thorns in his million-pound cheque.

Chapter Seven

IN NOVEMBER 1923, only a few months after his casino coup, Zaharoff had rejoiced at the long-awaited demise of his mistress's husband. They married in the following September. He was then 75 and his beloved duchess in her early sixties. They spent their summers at the palatial Chateau Balincourt, near Paris, and occupied the largest suite in the Hotel de Paris during the winter months. They ate off gold plate among other treasures from Balincourt and the Avenue Hoche, seldom dining in the hotel's Salle Empire except to entertain Vickers' directors and other business associates.

Zaharoff's devotion to his wife, perhaps the only human being for whom he ever felt the smallest spark of affection, grew obsessive when her health began to fail after their marriage and she became reluctant to leave Monte Carlo's warmth. His uxorious anxiety must have tilted him into megalomania. No rational argument could justify his ambition to place the crown of Monaco on her white head.

To such a power-drunk man, who had so often manipulated Prime Ministers and once declined to visit the Queen of Roumania until she had sent her private train to Paris, the dethronement of Prince Louis must have seemed both simple and practicable. His wife had outstanding qualities of charm, culture, goodness and charity, quite apart from her royal ties with the Spanish Bourbons. For the rôle of Consort he could parade his own British title, the Grand Cross of the Legion of Honour and countless other foreign decorations. Among his well-advertised benefactions he had endowed the Prix Balzac for Literature and also promoted French aviation and sport.

Since his wife had no hope of issue and the end of the Grimaldi dynasty would justify invoking the 1918 Treaty, he felt confident of France's support for a move which would ultimately lead to the principality's absorption.

Zaharoff moved with all the familiar guile. A Nice scandal sheet had reopened the old attack on Monte Carlo's roulette monopoly, followed by articles vilifying the prince for his youthful dissipations, his illegitimate daughter and an extravagant palace ménage maintained at the expense of his helpless subjects. Other hacks spread alarmist rumours of his impending abdication in favour of Princess Charlotte and her husband.

After a lifetime of professional military service, Prince Louis particularly disliked being accused of anti-French bias, but he kept a dignified silence even when gossip revived about the still-resented secret treaty with France and the £1 million cheque which had changed hands for the SBM. Significantly, Zaharoff was never cited as the sinister hand behind these manoeuvres. Reporters praised him instead for boosting the casino company's revenues to a record 110 million francs a year, with 100% dividends for shareholders.

But all his sunbeams turned into worms on 25 February 1926, when his wife died in Monte Carlo. At the funeral he lapsed into self-pity and bleakly remarked to Sir Charles Mendl, 'eighteen months of marriage after waiting forty years – a meagre dividend for a man who has invested so much in one passion'. Within a few weeks he had sufficiently mastered his grief to drive a very hard bargain for the sale of his interests to a consortium headed by Dreyfus et Cie., the French banking firm. They paid him £3,400,000, a thumping return on his original investment.

It was some time before he resumed his favourite place on the hotel terrace, wrapped in rugs and wheeling angrily away in his electrically-propelled bathchair when reporters dared to quiz him on the investigations of both a Senate committee and a British Royal Commission into the international arms trade. In his last years he took to hiring young whores for his priapic frolics which came to a sudden end in November 1936. He died of a heart attack at the Hotel de Paris in the arms of a dry-eyed valet.

The Dreyfus transfer had been handled, on Zaharoff's behalf, by René Léon. He had served in the same regiment as the new president, Prince Radziwill, through whom the Blanc dynasty again came into its own, although only nominally, since Léon now became the effective boss. He at once placed General Pierre Polovtsoff in charge of the International Sporting Club.

Both had quickly sensed the danger of increased competition from the French Riviera resorts. After Henri Negresco's death in 1920, his luxurious Nice hotel had been taken over by a Belgian syndicate whose millions made it more than a match for Monte Carlo's opulent but dated palaces. Even without roulette, Cannes was drawing some of Europe's heaviest gamblers to its casino and the highly exclusive Cercle Nautique, under the Grand Duke Michael's patronage. The harbour accommodated as many luxury yachts as Monaco; the tennis tournaments on the Carlton Hotel's courts attracted the same international stars, headed by Suzanne Lenglen's bandeau. Only Mont Agel's unique scenic beauty gave it any advantage over Mandelieu or the club at Mougins which snobbishly insisted on a £200 entrance fee and an impeccable pedigree.

But Léon, backed by the ruler's son-in-law, Prince Pierre, now Monaco's social kingpin, was even more perturbed by the phenomenal postwar vogue for sunbathing which had transformed fishing villages like Antibes and Juan-les-Pins into flourishing summer resorts and also established Deauville as the favoured playground of wealthy yachtsmen and gamblers. Monte Carlo, without a beach and with almost all its hotels firmly shuttered from April to November, unwisely ignored this challenge. It had been lulled by its reputation, the roulette wheels and a kind of financial gastritis during Zaharoff's looming regime.

Russian and English nobility could jointly claim credit for Monte Carlo's genteel hegemony in the last years of the century. American expatriates and other refugees from Prohibition, seduced by excellent food, wine and almost limitless sunshine at 50 francs to the dollar, pioneered the postwar Riviera's off-season delights. The French had traditionally trooped off to Normandy in the summer months or spent September on the Basque coast, the ladies always screened by parasol and sunshade against a bronzed skin, then the vulgar tradesmark of peasants or fisherman. By the early twenties social distinction suddenly demanded a year-round cigar-leaf brown. The Côte d'Azur became the world's headquarters for sun-worshippers far more numerous than the privileged few who had previously migrated south only in winter.

The revolution had started inconspicuously at Antibes in the summer of 1922 when the rose-coloured Hotel du Cap normally closed down. An American couple, Sara and Gerald Murphy, who had made their home in Paris (he was a talented amateur painter and had designed sets for Diaghilev), persuaded the hotel proprietor, André Sella, to let them the whole of the first floor. They cleared the seaweed from a few hundred yards of beach at La Garoupe, doused themselves with banana oil and astonished the natives by exposing their skins to the broiling sun. Sara Murphy, a bronzed nymph who swam with a pearl necklace round her neck, and her husband, still elegant even in fisherman's trousers, espadrilles and a sombrero, became infatuated enough with their summer retreat to build themselves the Villa America, furnished in the latest tubular aluminium and with a fine view of Golfe Juan and the Estérels. They provided an excellent cuisine and non-stop supplies of liquor. Murphy would pile guests into his Renault to dine or gamble in Monte Carlo, paying in advance even for their cloakroom tickets.

In the summer of 1925 they received Scott Fitzgerald, then flushed with the success of *The Great Gatsby*. He looked healthy when sober and frolicked with his chubby daughter, Scottie, while Zelda swam about for hours and dived like a professional. One night he was refused admission to the Monte Carlo casino because he could not produce his passport. '*Très bien*, you son of a bitch', he shouted, taking a wild swing at the doorman. He missed and passed out. During dinner at the Hotel de Paris he once amused himself by bombarding the bare back of a French countess with iced figs.

Thanks to the Murphys, Antibes became fashionable with other Americans, but a far more formidable challenge came from Frank Jay Gould, who had inherited a railroad fortune of over £3 million and commanded a reputed income of £250,000 a year. Tall, bulbous-nosed, jowly and dour, he wore an old-fashioned high collar even in the warm sunshine. Having found Cannes too noisy for a honeymoon, he arrived in Juan-les-Pins in 1923 and quickly sized up its potential. He took over the small casino, opened by a local hotelier, and built the elegant Hotel Provencal, soon followed by the acquisition of others in Nice and Cannes.

He almost emptied Nice's two municipal gambling houses by spending £800,000 on the new marble Casino de la Méditerranée. His tall half-French wife, Florence Lacaze, formerly of the Folies Bergère, was chic, elegant and had enough style to put Juan-les-Pins firmly on the social map. The Prince of Wales played golf nearby and occasionally joined her parties. She was never short of house guests like Chaplin, Gould's close friend, Lillian Gish and Peggy Hopkins Joyce, the barber's daughter and ex-Ziegfeld chorine who amassed a hoard of jewels and a huge bankroll from five millionaire husbands, one of whom had to slip a $500,000 cheque under her bedroom door as his entrance fee for the honeymoon first night.

René Léon kept a vigilant eye on the Goulds but took them less seriously than post-war Deauville's astonishing popularity with summertime gamblers. Its revival had been master-minded by two brilliant impresarios; Eugène Cornuché and François André. The former, once a *commis*, had joined forces with Maxim to make his Paris restaurant the most fashionable in Europe. He took over the casino at Deauville after selling his shares in Maxim's.

André had started as a dishwasher and later delivered beer barrels from a donkey cart. He then turned professional pallbearer, resourcefully selling cut-price wreaths on commission as a sideline. He married a pretty milliner whom he rashly persuaded to invest her savings in a roulette system. He lost every sou in Monte Carlo and moved back to Paris where he worked as a part-time croupier in small gaming clubs. Finally, he pooled his own resources with the proceeds from the sale of his wife's shop and acquired the gambling concession for Ostend. He returned there after the war but could not resist an offer from Cornuché of a partnership to run the chemmy and baccarat tables at Deauville.

They were soon joined by a professional gambler, Nico Zographos, whose Greek Syndicate took on all comers at baccarat from the summer of 1922. As he and his colleagues were an independent group, they operated without paying the government tax on proceeds at source and, more important, could also evade the rule prohibiting French casinos from running no-limit (*tout va*) baccarat. André and Cornuché soon became under-cover sleeping partners. From the normal percentage to the house, plus their tax-free 20% share in the profits made by the Syndicate, they quickly reaped millions of francs which went shrewdly into two new luxury hotels, bathing facilities and improved access by boat and 'plane.

Quite apart from the small but appreciable odds in the Syndicate's favour (an estimated 80%), its success hinged on two factors; enough capital to withstand the world's richest gamblers and, equally important, the most brilliant card-player of all time. Within a short time Zographos had started making his annual and very profitable circuit; six summer weeks at Deauville, followed in September by three months at Cannes which, after Cornuché's death in 1925, André had incorporated into his gambling empire, lavishly commissioning artists like Dufy and Domergue to paint the scenery for his stage shows.

Deauville was an irritant but the SBM still tended to under-rate it as an upstart without even a golf course and subject to variable weather. Snug in its monopoly of roulette, the company also saw little danger from the Greek Syndicate's no-limit baccarat which Monte Carlo was precluded from operating by the 1907 agreement with the French. Moreover, money was still so plentiful in the feverishly gay years before the Depression that most gamblers automatically came on from Cannes for a longer stay in Monte Carlo. Typical of these regular visitors, ready to stake upwards of a million francs almost any night, were the Dolly Sisters, who ruined Gordon Selfridge.

A small-town boy from Jackson, Michigan, he had begun his working life at ten dollars a week in the Chicago department store of Marshall Field and soon became his right-hand man. While making a tour of Europe, which included his first visit to Monte Carlo, he opened his own department store in London's Oxford Street with a capital of £900,000. He was a power-house of energy and his dazzling advertising ideas turned Selfridge's into a national institution.

Sensitive about his lack of inches (he used to bar six-footers from all executive posts!), he would square his shoulders to give him extra height and habitually wore high stiff collars, a polished silk hat, a white vest slip, pearl tiepin and an orchid in his buttonhole. A handsome man, with rimless pince-nez and thick white hair parted in the middle, he had the look of a dignified Supreme Court judge, but certain weaknesses of character incubated among his quick millions. He developed sybaritic tastes, acquiring a baronial seat, Highcliffe Castle, as well as renting Lansdowne House in London. After the death of his adored mother, followed by the loss of his wife in May 1918 (she lay in state at Highcliffe under a pall of 3,000 roses), he began his fatal pursuit of cocottes.

His first unlucky choice was Gaby Deslys, whom he set up in a house in Kensington Gore, complete with an immense bed which stood on a dais under an arch of black marble. Her retinue included a gigantic Negro chauffeur in a tight-fitting cream uniform to match her Mercedes. On Sundays, with only the firemen on duty, she would arrive at the Oxford Street store with her besotted lover. Cocooned in chinchilla, short and rather plump with pink and white colouring, ('her vacantly-parted lips like a split plum', recalls Norman Hartnell), she would plunder each department like a greedy child at its first Christmas tree.

But even Gaby could not compete in extravagance with her successors, the diamond-digging Dolly Sisters. These petite red-headed twins, born of poor Hungarian parents, had first charmed audiences in the Ziegfeld Follies of 1911. They repeated their triumphs in post-war London revues and were appearing at the Kit-Kat Club in the Haymarket when Gordon Selfridge saw their cabaret act and became infatuated with Jenny Dolly. As she and her sister, Rosie, were inseparable and shared the same appetite for jewels and gambling, it proved an expensive attachment. They cost him an estimated two million sterling in a seven-year spree of Diamond Jim Brady proportions.

The trio travelled about like monarchs, cavorting by Rolls-Royce, Blue Train, chartered air flights and in Selfridge's fine steam yacht, *Conqueror*, which cost him £10,000 a year to maintain. The young ladies would bet in maximums, with Selfridge's credit or cheque book at the ready if their luck ran out. He bought Jenny a chateau at Fontainebleau and would airfreight daily supplies of her favourite ice-cream sodas, never forgetting a chicken breast for her lapdog. At Deauville and Cannes she won or lost as much as £100,000 at a baccarat session, but never missed a winter visit to Monte Carlo because Rosie preferred roulette and both found Van Cleef et Arpels and other jewellers irresistible – with Mr Selfridge in tow.

Arriving one night from Cannes, where she had dropped a small fortune to the Greek Syndicate, Jenny sailed into the International Sporting Club in her chinchilla cape covering a black sequinned gown, the statutory corsage of orchids, and her usual armour of jewelled bracelets up to her elbows, a seven-string pearl necklace and a ring with a walnut-sized emerald which Solly Joel judged to be around 50 carats. His sixth sense had warned him against joining that particular session of chemin-de-fer. Instead he took a seat beside Gordon Selfridge, who looked on benignly when the cards were dealt. The other players included the Aga Khan and Prince Esterhazy, an autocratic voluptuary who often ordered dinner for a hundred guests at the Hotel de Paris. As he always demanded gold plate, the management had to supplement its own stock from other Riviera hotels, sometimes even sending special messengers to Paris.

That night Jenny was on such a winning streak that all the other players dropped out except Esterhazy. He also yielded after she had relieved him of 10 million francs (then worth over £90,000). She gave each of the flunkeys a £100 tip for emptying her ashtrays and, while others loaded the stacks of plaques on a trolley, broke the club's unwritten law by openly crowing over Esterhazy. Whitefaced with anger, he bowed to her in exaggerated deference and stumped out. 'I'm glad I whipped him,' she confided to Selfridge in a stage whisper. 'My grandfather was lashed often enough on his family estate in Hungary'.

It was newsworthy but rated far less column space than a mammoth Fourth of July party in 1926 for which Sella had specially opened. The sixty guests included Grace Moore, the Scott Fitzgeralds, Hemingway, Woolcott, Sir Hugo de Bathe, Noel Coward and, inevitably, Elsa Maxwell, who was invited over to Monaco shortly afterwards for a serious talk with Prince Pierre.

Shaped like a cottage loaf with currant eyes, this former honkytonk pianist from Keokuk, Iowa, had first thrust herself under the lorgnettes of the Four Hundred at charity shows. She was soon holding ladders for social climbers, launching nervous but well-heeled debutantes and supplying titled free-loaders to ambitious hostesses, who valued her undoubted talents as a party arranger. Quite unsnubbable herself, she developed her own brand of snobbery, feuding with duchesses and dowagers who sometimes took exception to her mischief-making intrigues. Her name-dropping became legendary ('he's Augustus *Jack* to me', she once assured a relative of the painter's). Cole Porter, whom she adored even more than Noel Coward and Aly Khan, once wrote a song which ended with, 'I'm dining with Elsa and her ninety-nine most intimate friends!' She sang it *ad nauseam* at parties, oblivious to the implied sarcasm. But she had a genius for organising charity beanfeasts and freak parties for the rich, sophisticated and frivolous members of the Anglo–American social circus. By the mid-Twenties her dynamic personality and contacts had placed a high reserve on her services as a press agent.

Prince Pierre was sufficiently impressed by her recent success in promoting the Venetian Lido to invite her to boost the potentia summer charms of Monte Carlo. The SBM agreed a retainer of $6,000 a year, plus a generous expense account. A luxurious blue-tiled pool, adjacent to the new coffee-coloured Summer Sporting Club, was built and Elsa succeeded in persuading the Société to open the pink stucco Beach Hotel, located on a site leased from the French near Cap Martin. It was blue-printed by her friend, Addison Mizner, whose grandiose Spanish-style architecture had already transformed Florida's Palm Beach.[1]

At the gala opening of 'Le Sporting', the entertainment was led by Grace Moore, who would always remain sentimentally attached to Monte Carlo. After her Broadway success in the Music Box Revue, she had ignored Irving Berlin's advice and taken up an operatic career. She arrived in France with her modest savings to study under Caruso's old teacher, Barthélemy. Her money had almost run out when her friends, the Louis G. Kaufmans, invited her to the Hotel de Paris for dinner. She had no taste for gambling but Kaufman insisted on lending her 1,000 francs to tempt beginner's luck. She won several times on 'cinq' at roulette which netted her a profit of 43,000 francs (then £5,375) and helped to finance her studies.

The Summer Casino, open from July to the end of September, was an immediate success, particularly the Friday night galas initiated by Elsa Maxwell, who regularly signed the dinner bills for two or three dozen influential celebrities. 500 guests often dined on the

---

[1] Princess Alice's son, the Duc de Richelieu, was prominent in the consortium which developed Florida.

terraces with coloured lanterns among the giant palms and a view of the numerous yachts sparkling at anchor.

£500,000 had been spent on the Country Club, also located in France, by the time it was opened by the Duke of Connaught in 1928. Cochet won the men's singles and again in the following year. Members could entertain their guests in the moorish-style club house, embowered in rambler roses, with a restaurant and bar staffed by the Hotel de Paris. The first-class tennis courts, backed by the plushiest dressing-rooms in Europe, catered for all the crack tournament players and celebrity enthusiasts like the lanky – and cranky – King of Sweden, who often partnered Alvarez in mixed doubles. He was not the most popular of visitors as he hated losing and hotly disputed all unfavourable decisions. Obsequious officials made allowances for his astigmatism which did not altogether excuse his gamesmanship at tennis or his weakness for sneaking glances at his opponents' cards at the bridge table.

Despite an enormous outlay of nearly £2 million on 'Le Sporting', the Country Club, Beach Hotel and its recent acquisition of the Hermitage, the SBM's £5 shares stood at a record £120 in 1928 when the directors felt confident enough to inaugurate another summer attraction, the Grand Prix de Monaco. Antony Noghues, supported by Prince Pierre, René Léon and the local champion driver, Louis Chiron, proposed a motor race of 200 miles round the town's corkscrew twists. With so many houses on the route and hazards like the steps of a *tabac* opposite the Church of Ste Dévote, quite apart from the tramway tracks which would not be scrapped for five years, the numbers had to be kept down for safety reasons. Even so, the first competition in May 1929 was like a Roman chariot race with 16 cars, never designed for such an event, hurtling a hundred times round the circuit. Williams in a Bugatti won in 3 hours 56', averaging 80 kms. 194, with another Bugatti nosing Caracciola's Mercedes into third place. Until the outbreak of war the Monaco circuit attracted the world's most powerful racing cars driven by international aces like Nuvolari, Fagioli, Earl Howe and Whitney Straight.

*   *   *

Although the SBM was anxious to promote a summer programme, it had wisely maintained the high-season attractions.
Gunsbourg still delighted his faithful balletomanes but the creative
spark had gone out of Diaghilev, who now seemed far more
interested in cataloguing books and musical manuscripts for his
projected Russian Library in Europe. However, he boldly encouraged Prokofiev to work on *Le Pas d'Acier*, with its 'factory'
music and novel dissonances glorifying Soviet industrialisation. It
was composed and rehearsed in Monte Carlo before the Paris
première in the summer of 1927. Diaghilev, dressed in white
flannels and a blue double-breasted coat with a huge rose in his
lapel, presided as always at the Café de Paris, with Lifar at his side,
but their relationship often neared breaking point.

Bloated and tetchy, Diaghilev was incensed by Lifar's many
women admirers and one, in particular, a German blonde of
excellent family who pursued him round Europe with flowers and
passionate notes. One night she smuggled herself into his bed at the
Hotel de Paris, threatening to scream when he tried to escape. He
managed to push her into the corridor and lock his door. Diaghilev
heard the noise and became hysterical on sniffing an unfamiliar
perfume, but Lifar somehow persuaded him of his complete innocence.

Diaghilev re-engaged Dolin for the 1929 season but he had
tactfully appeased Lifar by appointing him choreographer of
Stravinsky's new ballet, *Le Renard*, with sets and costumes by
Rouault. It earned many curtain calls but Diaghilev had lost his
old first-night exuberance. Within a few months his strange premonition of dying 'on water' was fulfilled in Venice. Too weak
even to slip into the sleeves of his pyjamas, he died wrapped in his
dinner-jacket, with Lifar weeping at his bedside.

Gunsbourg remained hopeful of maintaining the company with
its fine repertoire, costumes and scenery still intact, but Diaghilev's
death was soon followed by the departure of his most loyal and
always generous patron, whose marriage to Princess Charlotte had
collapsed. Four years later, the Supreme Court of Monaco, sitting
in camera on 18 February 1933, adjudged Prince Pierre the guilty

party but made him responsible for his children's education, subject to the ruler's approval.

The nine year-old Rainier now faced uncomfortably divided loyalties to his parents, further complicated by the well-meaning if erratic tutelage of his grandfather, who had angrily banished Prince Pierre from Monaco.

Chapter Eight

IN NOËL COWARD's *Private Lives* Amanda stands at the window of a Monte Carlo villa and asks, 'Whose yacht is that?' Elyot replies languidly, 'The Duke of Westminster's, I expect. It always is.' The quip was more than an ironic half-truth. Before the end of the Twenties, 'Benny' had added the slow but very picturesque *Flying Cloud* to his fleet. Built at Leghorn, she was a 1,200 ton four-master with panelled cabins and exquisite small-scale Queen Anne furniture.

He usually shared his silk-curtained four-poster with 'Coco' Chanel, who had helped to pioneer the Côte d'Azur's summer vogue. Her jumper suits, bell-bottomed beach pyjamas and costume jewellery became standard equipment for all the chic flappers. They paraded like a musical comedy chorus, almost indistinguishable with their plucked eyebrows and long cigarette holders. Rubens gave way to Modigliani. Otéro's opulent curves had been replaced by leggy flat-chested giraffes, who relieved the monotony of their 'banting' charts by swilling cocktails or pink champagne. Weaned on Michael Arlen, Coward and early Waugh, rounded off in a finishing school of night clubs and shrill fancy-dress parties or treasure hunts, they headed dizzily for Monte Carlo's swimming pools, with the pick of sumptuous yachts and villas for their bed-hopping.

Few of them wore as well as Chanel, although her successor, Loelia, the third Duchess of Westminster, uncharitably wrote her off as 'small, dark and simian'. In her early forties 'Coco' was still a fascinating brunette whose droll wit could resurrect the most tiresome party. Customarily wearing white silk pyjamas, she would enter the Monte Carlo casino on the duke's arm, her bobbed hair tucked into a turban sparkling with a single diamond star. Beside her the Dolly Sisters looked vulgar and overdressed, but she had more competition from Jay Gould's wife, 'Queen Flo', who often favoured the rival creations of Captain Edward Molyneux. He had lost an eye and won the M.C. in the war, soon afterwards borrowing the capital to open his fashion house in the rue Royale, next to Maxim's. In 1925 he set up another establishment in Monte Carlo, where his pearl grey and gold-labelled hat boxes, carried by Gertrude Lawrence and other clients, became passports of elegance. He also bought himself a villa at Cap d'Ail, and 'Coco' later followed suit, as a result of a gift from the duke, with her 40-roomed 'La Pansa' among the olives and jasmine above Monte Carlo. She served elaborate cold buffets on the terrace to Cocteau, Dali, Lifar and a corps of admirers including her former lover, the Grand Duke Dmitri, who had first introduced her to Westminster.

They were soon hopelessly infatuated, despite jealous quarrels. While cruising in *Flying Cloud*, Chanel resented the duke's attentions to a beautiful French painter and had her put ashore at Villefranche. As a peace offering he bought her a huge emerald which 'Coco' examined indifferently and then tossed overboard. The Spanish gilt-iron bed in her villa was hung with fertility charms and she often took hopeful exercises to stimulate pregnancy. In the end, despairing of giving her lover an heir, she finally rejected his offer of marriage and they parted.[1]

The duke was the despair of most Riviera hostesses whom he snubbed brutally, preferring the company of his own friends for

---

[1] Winston Churchill, an old polo-playing friend, was best man at the duke's third marriage which ended in divorce. He married for a fourth time and died in 1953, still without an heir to replace his only son who had died at the age of six. A cousin succeeded to the title.

lightning swoops on the casinos of Monte Carlo and Cannes. He condescended to call occasionally on Maxine Elliott and Consuelo Balsan, but had no trouble in repelling the advances of such an obvious lion-hunter as Mrs Laura Corrigan. This former telephone switchboard girl from Cleveland, Ohio, had launched her bizarre social career by marrying a drunken steel magnate after a truly 'blind' date. He died within a few months, in 1927, leaving her nearly $100 million for a most determined assault on London society. She managed to have herself presented at Court without Elsa Maxwell's help and rented a mansion from Mrs Keppel, who threw in her invaluable guest list with the fittings. She was soon giving enormous parties in Grosvenor Street, which she called her *ventre à terre*, and ecstatically stood on her head when Prince George arrived for one of her birthday celebrations. She presented his bride, Princess Marina, with a $5,000 mink coat. Few of her other guests, almost always titled, went unrewarded at her tombolas when she started handing out gold cigarette cases and diamond bracelets as prizes. She once bought Constance Talmadge's husband, Captain Ali Mackintosh, a triple-sized shaving brush at Asprey's for £100, but only Primo Carnera could have found it usable.

Guests less fastidious than Bendor Westminster put up with her painted face, bright auburn wigs and frequent malapropisms. Asked her opinion of Milan's cathedral, she declared solemnly that 'the flying buttocks were magnificent'. The showy prewar Riviera mirrored her flamboyance. In addition to her villa behind Cannes she maintained a permanent suite at the Hotel de Paris where guests had strict orders to charge all drinks, meals and tips to her account. Her chartered yacht never lacked a full complement of passengers, who could rely on an envelope of pocket money, $500 minimum, whenever they went ashore.

Her rival hostess, Maxine Elliott, was quite as generous but infinitely more dignified, although grossly fat and weighing in at over 230 pounds. She would never quite lose her aura of Edwardian grandeur with its memories of Hartsbourne Manor, her English country house where she had fêted Rosebery, Asquith,

Curzon and the like. The Wall Street crash had been costly but she could still afford to spend $300,000 on the Chateau de l'Horizon, overlooking the Bay of Cannes. Guests either swam in the dazzling white pool or used a chute to shuttle them into the sea, but Johnny Weissmuller preferred showy dives from the top terrace. On dark nights an artificial moon was switched on among the trees and Miss Elliott had obviated the nuisance of a nearby railway by obligingly throwing a bridge over the tracks to connect the house with the main road. Winston Churchill, then still in the political wilderness, arrived each year for his painting holiday, and the Prince of Wales used to motor over with Mrs Simpson for a swim and tea.

Maxine Elliott adored a rubber of bridge but always gave in graciously when house guests wished to go over *en masse* to the Sporting Club to dine, dance and gamble. In her later years she had become a figure of pathos, white-haired and still elegant but with her enormous frame teetering on tiny geisha-sized feet. She never quite recovered from Tony Wilding's death at Ypres. She took to food in preference to drink or drugs, rather like a bereaved widow committing *suttee* on a pyre of chocolate creams. A pet lemur, Kiki, shared her addiction to corn bread, chocolate cake and vegetables cooked in cream. Her eating neurosis dictated even the style of her bathrooms, each of which was shaped like a slice of cake.

Another American-born châtelaine, Lady Cunard, widow of the elderly shipping magnate, preferred artistic celebrities to Maxine Elliott's political heavyweights. Blue-eyed and with a deceptively Fragonard daintiness, she had a sharp tongue which spared neither friend nor foe. She once gave a party for Michael Arlen, whom she introduced as 'the only Armenian who hasn't been massacred'. He had made a fortune from his best-seller, *The Green Hat*, but wrote himself out and retired gracefully to enjoy what he called, 'all the enchantments of disenchantment'. They included a canary yellow Rolls, a mahogany Gar Wood speedboat, with his Portuguese chauffeur at the wheel, a beautiful wife (the former Countess Mercati) and a sleek villa near Cannes where they entertained grandly. Scott Fitzgerald came over one night, wearing a striped blazer and white flannels, with everyone else in formal evening rig. He looked round the candlelit dining-room, commented thickly, 'this is how I want to live' and fell asleep over his soup. Next day, soured by a hangover, he dismissed his host as 'a finished second-rater who's jealous of a coming first-rater'.

Arlen was short and slender, with dark crinkly hair and a bristly moustache. He wore a pearl pin even in his Old School tie. He also favoured Hawes and Curtis backless waistcoats, platinum watch chains and a fur-collared topcoat ('per ardua ad astrakhan', he once explained lightly). Dressed in sky-blue plus fours and a Fair Isle sweater, he occasionally played golf at Mont Agel with Maugham but preferred the company of his closest friend, playwright Freddie Lonsdale, with whom he often had amusing tiffs. After one expensive night's gambling, they met for some healing Bollinger in the Hotel de Paris bar. 'Well, how are you, Michael?' Lonsdale asked sympathetically. 'I decline to tell you' responded Arlen with exquisite hauteur.

For years Lonsdale coined £1,000 a week in royalties from *The Last of Mrs. Cheyney*, *Maid of the Mountains* and many other hits in London's West End and on Broadway before going out to Hollywood as a top-priced screen writer. Like Arlen he revelled in gambling, fast cars and luxury hotels. They made the rounds together of the fashionable villas, specially favouring Lady Cunard's and the Chateau de l'Horizon, often accompanied by E. Phillips Oppenheim, who used the Riviera as a background for many of his melodramatic thrillers. His florid face, with the bulging eyes of a hooked fish, testified to a love of the fleshpots. He had a villa at Cagnes-sur-Mer and a small yacht, *Echo*, previously owned by Stavisky. He called it his 'double bed', as the salon had room for only a large divan on which he entertained legions of women.

Echo was tied up at La Garoupe when Oppenheim, glancing through the porthole, spotted an attractive girl sunning herself on the beach. He was spinning a yarn into his dictaphone which he then abandoned for the blonde. An hour or so later they checked into the Hotel de Paris for ten strenuous nights, an achievement for one already in his early sixties but possibly assisted by his friendship with Dr Voronoff. On returning to his yacht he greeted his wife, Elsie, with affection and went down to the cabin to resume dictating his story in mid-sentence.

They stayed a month each year at the Hotel de Paris where he would be massaged and barbered every day, before swaggering forth, his monocle clipped under a bristling white eyebrow and with a clove carnation in his lapel. He adored being addressed as 'Sir Phillips Oppenheim' by head waiters and casino attendants.

Maugham often invited Arlen, Lonsdale and Oppenheim for a swim and cocktails at his villa, near St Jean-Cap Ferrat, which he had bought in 1928. But gambling bored him and he did not share their affability to autograph hunters. On his infrequent visits to the Monte Carlo casino he would sit in the pale green bar waiting impatiently for his secretary-companion, Gerald Haxton, to come away from the tables. This fair-haired and handsome American, whom he had met during the First War and taken with him on his tours of the Far East and South Seas, had been deported from England as an undesirable alien in 1916 following a charge of gross indecency. After dinner at the Villa Mauresque he would drive over to the Sporting Club where, flushed with drink, he regularly squandered his master's royalties at roulette.

Maugham often had to forego the pleasures of bridge to avoid offending Haxton. He once accepted an invitation to dine at Lady Cunard's but was fidgety throughout the meal and announced over coffee that he would have to leave. Lady Cunard had looked forward to a few rubbers of bridge and tried to persuade him to stay, but he was adamant. 'I must get back to bed if I want to keep my youth', he stammered. 'Well, why didn't you bring him with you?' she murmured, giving him a disapproving peck at the door. 'We would have loved having him'.

The hard-drinking and fun-loving Americans made their summer headquarters at Antibes or Juan-les-Pins, but most of them enjoyed a night's gambling after the floor show at 'Le Sporting' where René Léon had enterprisingly started top cabaret entertainment. 'Les Girls', a troupe of leggy Broadway lovelies, included Betty Sundmark, a former Ziegfeld Folly dancer, who took the fancy of her future husband, Alberto Dodero, the Argentine multi-millionaire. Charlie MacArthur seldom missed a visit with his wife, Helen Hayes. His legendary thirst rivalled that of the Grand Duke Dmitri, who sometimes downed two dozen dry martinis before a meal, but Broadway's favourite son had nothing else in common with the haughty exile, now even more arrogant on his American wife's fortune.

They clashed one night at the Harrimans. Both had fortified themselves in advance, but with very different effects. MacArthur sat next to a Russian princess whom he entertained with salty recollections of New York journalism. Dmitri, stiffer than usual and anxious to be off to the Sporting Club, became more peevish by the minute. He suddenly drew Charlie's attention to several blobs of hollandaise sauce on his shirt front. Charlie retaliated by playfully rattling the ducal row of jangling medals. 'Well, I, too, am wearing my decorations' he pointed out serenely.

'Possibly, from the night before last' sniffed the Romanov with distaste. Unabashed, Charlie called out to a servant, '*Garçon*, bring the Grand Duke's hat and kiddy car'. Dmitri bowed to Mrs Harriman and departed huffily, while Charlie remained to the last drop, keeping everyone rocking with laughter. He did not become a client when the Grand Duke applied himself to selling champagne in Palm Beach, Florida, after his divorce.[2]

The Wall Street crash made little immediate impact on Riviera spending. Charles M. Schwab, a Monte Carlo regular, continued to draw his salary of $250,000 a year from Bethlehem Steel, and many of his countrymen, benefiting from the slumping franc, blithely absorbed champagne cocktails at 25 cents a throw.

In the hotels and gaming rooms lounge lizards and bright-feathered parrots pecked at an endless harvest. There was no

[2] Dmitri fell victim to tuberculosis and died in 1941. Zographos paid all his bills at an expensive sanatorium in Davos.

shortage of old men with young ideas or matrons eager for virile studs sporting the late Valentino's lacquered hair with a smooth tango. Laura Corrigan busily distributed gold cigarette cases while Maxine Elliott continued to devour mountains of patisserie with her hot chocolate. The redheaded shipping magnate, Lord Furness, had a basketful of plover's eggs flown in from Holland for his wife, Gloria Vanderbilt's twin sister, when the Hotel de Paris temporarily ran out. Its pineapples were ritually cradled in beds of cracked ice; the hors d'oeuvres tray was never without green grapes stuffed with cream cheese; and croûtes of foie gras remained almost as plentiful as black olives.

Diaghilev's troupe had disbanded after his death. Lifar went to the Paris Opéra as principal dancer and choreographer; Massine was in America; and a new company had been formed in London by Dolin, de Valois and Markova. After a couple of listless years Gunsbourg persuaded the Russian Colonel de Basil and René Blum to revive the Ballets Russes de Monte Carlo with the help of Grigoriev, Diaghilev's former *régisseur*, and Balanchine as ballet master.

Established attractions like the Monte Carlo Rally, the Grand Prix and the Tir aux Pigeons drew crowds of spectators. Up at the Country Club, where the King of Sweden engaged Tilden to coach him and Borotra kept winning the singles, the dainty little Queen of Siam used to test 'Bunny' Austin's patience by sticking rigidly to her own quarter of the court throughout every game. The Aga Khan tipped his pretty girl caddie a little sports car to celebrate holing in one, and his friends, the Maharajahs of Baroda, Kapurthala and Rajpipla, entertained open-handedly at Le Sporting's summer galas. In the Winter Sporting Club, replacing the old Palais des Beaux-Arts, chemmy was played for staggering sums by Dodero and Fritz Mandl, the Austrian armaments king.

This ostentatious wealth and extravagance backlashed locally. Already penalised by rising prices linked with a devalued franc, many low-paid workers had been driven out into the French hillside villages to make room for hotels or luxury villas. They became even more alarmed by rumours of job cuts as the SBM, strained by over-expenditure, showed a steady fall in profits. The National Council remained supine in the absence of a ruler who was often away shooting at Marchais or in Scotland, his mother's native land. He also made frequent trips abroad in search of Napoleonic souvenirs.

Prince Louis had started a small library of rare First Empire documents and manuscripts, soon supplemented by treasures like the wide tricolor sashes worn by Bonaparte during the Italian campaign, together with his hats and an Imperial Guard eagle standard pierced by two bullet holes. He was particularly proud of the white and gold silk flag with three golden bees which the Grenadiers had borne during the Hundred Days. With the hope of eventually forming a small palace museum for his collection, he instructed antiquaries all over Europe to buy up Napoleonic swords, spurs and decorations. It was not an expensive hobby for one in his position, but his subjects were naturally more concerned with the price of bread and meat than Houdon's bust of Napoleon in Sèvres biscuit.

Returning from a visit in 1930 to Sidi-bel-Abbes for the Foreign Legion's centenary celebrations, the prince was shocked by a hostile demonstration at the railway station. He reacted by dissolving the National Council. Up at the new Palace of Justice, recently built near the Cathedral in the Italian Gothic style, the bench dealt harshly with 'trouble-makers'. The agitation subsided but few cheered when President Gaston Doumergue arrived soon afterwards on a State Visit. It revived the traditional Monegasque suspicion of foreign influence, quickly reinforced when Prince Louis agreed to accept a Minister of State nominated by the Elysée. To make this more palatable, Monaco's compensation for customs duties was augmented to 3,750,000 francs a year which took into account currency devaluation and the heavy French taxes on imported goods, mainly in the luxury class.

It assisted the exchequer but gave no comfort to the SBM whose profits had slipped to barely a quarter of the 1928 figure. Deauville now had two golf courses, a race track and polo ground, while Le Touquet and Biarritz were increasingly favoured by wealthy summer tourists. Francois André's wife was also spending millions of francs to develop La Baule which advertised a casino, an excellent golf course and even pigeon-shooting among its attractions.

The Wall Street slump had bitten sharply into Monte Carlo's turnover from both gambling and tourism, although Latin American magnates still played heavily and nothing could diminish the Aga Khan's tithes from his faithful Ismailis. Americans like Drexel Biddle, movie stars and the irrepressible Peggy Hopkins Joyce seemed shockproof, but most of their compatriots were staying away. English visitors, who had stoutly resisted such horrors as the servant shortage, the break-up of large estates, the Labour Party, higher taxation and the new death duties, could no longer ignore a worsening crisis. *The Times* now condemned foreign travel and the spending of much-needed currency as unpatriotic. Britain, who had borrowed on short term and cheerfully lent out on extended credit, suddenly found herself bankrupt of gold when Germany defaulted. The monetary crisis cruelly jarred an army of retired colonels and their memsahibs whose tax-free pensions had long been cushioned by a benign rate of exchange. They packed their bags sadly, except for a few stalwarts like Mrs Wilhelmina Gloster, widow of a general who had defended Ladysmith. She had first arrived in the principality in 1892 and would not be dislodged for half a century.

In the year 1931/2 the SBM paid no dividends for the first time in its entire history, but the French resorts were in worse shape with heavier taxation on their luxury hotels and casinos. Even the foreign-run Greek Syndicate, long exempt from the usual 25% tax on its winnings, now had to fall in line. Zographos hit back by suspending play at Deauville and Cannes. He soon decided to open 'a branch office' in tax-free Monte Carlo, once the SBM agreed to allow no-limit baccarat in the Salons Privés and Sporting Club. This contravention of the 1907 agreement prompted André to lobby his friends in the Senate. He and his fellow-operators threatened to close down altogether unless steps were also taken to end Monaco's unfair monopoly of roulette and trente-et-quarante.

The Greek Syndicate had opened with a flourish at the Winter Sporting Club, the SBM taking a 49% share of the proceeds in return for its heavy investment. As André was now feeling the pinch through his Wall Street losses and the decline in tourism, Zographos seized the chance to buy out his share in the Syndicate. Soon afterwards, while continuing to run the baccarat bank at Monte Carlo through a deputy, he personally resumed operations at Deauville and Cannes when the French authorities came to terms with him over tax-exemption. He also decided to start summer play at Cannes which André had always ignored. Backed by relatives, he opened in 1933 the Palm Beach Casino at the eastern end of the Croisette. Its splendid swimming pool, open-air restaurant and dance floor quickly rivalled Monte Carlo's 'Le Sporting'.

The SBM suffered a far more crushing blow when the French government, yielding to non-stop pressure, at last permitted roulette and trente-et-quarante. In France gaming receipts at once picked up, soon matched by the Italian casinos at San Remo and Venice, where a new Film Festival would capture the headlines every year.

The Goulds welcomed more American friends to the elegant Provencal in Juan-les-Pins, and film idols like Gloria Swanson, Chevalier and Chaplin began to patronise Eden Roc rather more often than Monte Carlo's Country Club which only came briefly to life for international tennis tournaments. At Cannes the Prince of Wales would frequently visit the Palm Beach Casino, while André, eager to win back patrons, invested heavily in the Hotel Majestic and engaged leading cabaret stars for his Winter Casino galas.

Although the world trade recession had eased and tourism again began to boom, Monte Carlo now had to share the cake with too many hungry competitors. The SBM took rather panicky short-term measures like halving the usual 5% *cagnotte* at chemin-de-fer, and René Léon gained brief publicity in February 1934 by re-introducing gold, not seen on the tables since prewar days, for play in the Sporting Club. As the French Mint could not supply 18-

carat gold pieces in time, he collected American gold dollar coins in fives, tens and twenties, but the novelty wore off when winners began hoarding the coins for souvenirs.

Once the French government had come to the rescue of hoteliers and casino proprietors by cutting taxes, the SBM, already injured by its loss of exclusive roulette, found itself in deep financial trouble. The prince's subsidy accounted for 8% of its profits; the subsidising of public utilities absorbed another £45,000 a year and staff pensions alone cost a cool £40,000. The casino payroll also carried 90 full-time gardeners, as well as a 100-strong corps of upholsterers, cleaners and firemen.

The 620 croupiers earned up to £600 a year. Although carefully vetted, they were watched from peepholes and slits in the walls manned by inspectors with binoculars. In the early thirties plaques worth £1,500 were found in a croupier's lodgings. Another was suspected of dealing cards marked with tiny dots invisible to the naked eye after two Italians, both wearing tinted glasses, seemed to be winning on unusually low aggregates at chemin-de-fer. They put up an angry protest but significantly stopped playing when the inspectors reminded them that dark glasses were not *comme il faut* at the tables.

A more serious fraud was unmasked soon afterwards with the help of the Austrian police, who alerted Monte Carlo that a gang was on its way with a substantial stock of counterfeit banknotes, plaques and chips. Closely watched, they took alarm and did not pass a single note or even dare to enter the casino, giving the authorities no grounds for arrest. As their train crossed the Italian frontier, they tossed a bag out of the window. It was picked up and sent to the SBM examiners who decided that the coup would certainly have misfired. The counterfeit 5,000-franc plaques were not only too new-looking but the casino also covered its 1,000-franc counters with a paper of different design each day.

The SBM now began to chafe at luxuries like the Golf Club which needed a minimum subsidy of some £5,000 a year to stay solvent. It had 100 permanent members, but the revenue from subscriptions and a lavish bar could not possibly cover the cost of a top resident professional and a staff who pampered the greens with expensive imported super-phosphates.

The theatre also had to be kept afloat with a subsidy of over three million francs a year. After Balanchine's departure for the United States, René Blum broke with Colonel de Basil and founded his own company with Fokine as ballet master and Nemchinova heading the *corps de ballet*, but other attractions were needed. The permanent orchestra of 94 was often directed by guest conductors, including Richard Strauss, and Gunsbourg continued to engage virtuosi like Chaliapin, Rachmaninov and Kreisler whose fees put a heavy strain on the budget.

The SBM's £5 shares had contracted from their record £120 quotation in pre-Depression days to only £17 by 1935. That year the company's books disclosed a deficit of several million francs, and a debenture was swiftly issued at a heavy rate of interest. To avoid total collapse, Delpierre 'requested' all personnel to take a cut in salaries, while simultaneously cutting down staff and drastically trimming sinecures. It placed an intolerable burden on René Léon, who had kept the gaming rooms running at a profit even in the thinnest years and was not responsible for the SBM's ruinous subsidies to the principality. Each of his 20 roulette tables had an estimated turnover of over £350,000 per annum and the Greek Syndicate contributed a steady share of its revenues, year after year, but competition from the French casinos and his own enormous overheads forced him to resign. He departed to manage Hollywood's luxurious Garden of Allah, but Polovtsoff remained in charge of the Sporting Club.

In 1936 the SBM took a long-overdue step in assuming private company status. It would henceforth pay the treasury 5% of its gross receipts up to 35 million francs a year and a rising scale thereafter, subject to the government's taking over responsibility for all public utilities. Although many squealed in protest, the principality's situation was not seriously damaged. Almost 30% of its budget now derived from the customs arrangement with France and a similar proportion was contributed by residential and corporation taxes (foreign holding companies being lightly treated by comparison with France, Switzerland, Lichtenstein and even Luxembourg).

The SBM's percentage, still contributing roughly one-third of the principality's revenue, adequately guaranteed Prince Louis's income. He was frugal, disliked entertaining and spent long hours in the palace library, studying his family history and adding to his collection of Napoliana. He often visited foreign spas for medical treatment, but he was usually in Monaco when his grandson, Rainier, returned for school holidays.

Half-English himself on his mother's side, Prince Louis had insisted on his grandchildren being bi-lingual. Antoinette, then a plump and studious girl, spoke four languages from childhood. Rainier was first sent to Summerfields, a preparatory school at St Leonards-on-Sea in Sussex, where he had his first taste of caning. He took it with good humour after the initial shock, but was more affected by homesickness. 'I had never been away from home before and had no friends with whom I could even spend a week-end', he has recalled. He went on to a modern public school, Stowe, to find himself 'the only foreigner among 560 English boys'. On his very first day he ran away and was caught by the police in nearby Buckingham. Instead of a beating, he received a good tea and a sympathetic talk from his very understanding housemaster.

There were times when he longed to join his father in Paris, but his grandfather had taken the precaution of asking an English court to restrain Prince Pierre from removing the boy from the United Kingdom without his official consent and approval. Although lonely, Rainier was reasonably happy at school and could hold his own. His stocky muscular build made him a useful enough boxer to become school champion at its weight. He was also a strong swimmer and developed a taste for amateur theatricals but, already an individualist, showed no enthusiasm for team sports like cricket. He was not altogether sorry to go on to Le Rosey, near Geneva, a fashionable school and, more important at his age, both cosmopolitan and less monastic than Stowe.

He and his sister, as shy as himself, were naturally drawn

together by loneliness and their parents' broken marriage. Both gravitated instinctively to their exiled father, who was not only easy-going by nature but had a sophisticated taste for music and the theatre. They enjoyed their holidays with him in preference to their mother, who had become more withdrawn and introspective.

Rainier had soon discovered odd paradoxes in Prince Louis' character. He gave the impression of being a gruff-spoken old soldier, interested only in military history or shooting at Marchais, but he shared his daughter's humanitarian outlook. The new mental hospital of Saint-Pierre owed much to his sympathetic patronage. Although a professional soldier, he had steadily followed his father's pacifism and started a campaign to make European capitals like London and Paris 'open cities' in the event of aerial bombardment.

In Monte Carlo and the other Riviera playgrounds few took Hitler's tirades too seriously, least of all the Anglo-American visitors and residents. The League of Nations had foundered, giving place to bland optimism and self-deception over foreign affairs except among a few realists. Many Jews, aware of Monaco's corporation advantages and her neutral status, arrived from Germany and Austria to set up quickly-thriving factories for manufacturing plastics and synthetic fibres. Most others, however, were more inclined to seek a little fun in 'dear old Monte' or at Eden Roc where screen idols like Dietrich, Robert Taylor and Swanson could be glimpsed in the flesh. At 'Le Sporting' Noel Coward and Gertie Lawrence (in a pearl-studded bathing suit) were always surrounded by dazzled moths.

The Monte Carlo streets were jammed with English visitors. Stockbrokers, liberated from City serge, strutted about in livid shirts, garish slacks and sandals, their ladies sporting diamonds and varicose veins. The luxury hotels had their usual intake of royals, including handsome Prince Andrew of Greece, father of the future Duke of Edinburgh. Banished for life in 1922, after having clashed with the Greek High Command over the campaign in Turkey, he had settled into his estate at St Cloud but always spent several months a year in Monte Carlo. The prewar guest lists of the Hotel de Paris rattled with titles and tiaras. Elsa Maxwell followed in the wake of Willingdons and Queensberrys while she inhaled incense from Indian potentates like Kutch, Berar, Kapurthala and the moon-faced young Maharajah of Rajpipla, who rewarded chefs and head waiters with gold cigarette cases adorned by his crest in rubies.

Faces paled briefly as the Nazis goose-stepped into Vienna. The British colony packed its bags when the Royal Navy mobilised, and unpacked even more briskly when Chamberlain bounced back from Munich. But sad-eyed sceptical Jewish refugees continued to swarm into the hotels and *pensions*. Spy mania quickly swept the Côte with rumours of sinister activity by the Italian secret police (OVRA) in the consulates of Nice and Savoy, but the principality, certain of neutrality despite its Great War experience, seemed immune to such alarmist talk.

Monte Carlo wallowed in euphoric escapism. Smiling French reservists lolled in the cafés with flowers behind their ears. Ancient flesh was sedulously honed, needle-sprayed and vapoured in the thermal baths. Gamblers, with rolls of *mille* notes in their pockets and a roll of flesh at the back of their necks, could take their pick of the nymphs who disported outside the cabanas of 'Le Sporting' or arrived at the casino in gowns bought by lovers or on loan from the Paris fashion houses. On the decks of spanking white yachts mahogany-brown men and women sunned themselves by day and danced their nights away under fairy lights. The oil-smooth bay was striped with blue, russet and green like a Neapolitan ice. Liveried chauffeurs idled beside huge parked limousines, with the ex-King of Spain's Hispano-Suiza easily distinguishable by its coat of arms. The Hotel de Paris barman had flatteringly concocted a new 'Alfonso' cocktail of gin, Dubonnet and a dash of angostura, although a weak Bourbon might have been rather more fitting. Even with the prospect of war becoming more certain by the hour, Monte Carlo seemed so uncapsizable as a *pedalo* on the tideless Mediterranean.

In March 1939 all the locals cheered madly when their very

popular Princess Antoinette, who had by now lost her puppy fat, partnered Brugnon to win the open handicap mixed doubles. Over in Cannes the final touches were being put to the first Film Festival, but by September even Monaco could no longer whisk the facts away with a gold swizzle stick. An American destroyer called to carry off the International Hydrographic Bureau's files for safe keeping; and the athletes, who had assembled hopefully for the Eighth University Games, left the vast new £150,000 Louis II Stadium still unconsecrated. One after another the yachts had slipped out of harbour, including that of Zographos. (He established himself for the duration in Switzerland, relieving the monotonous round of ski-ing and golf with private baccarat parties for the Aga Khan and other bored refugees.)[3]

'Le Sporting' had closed down almost at once, quickly followed by the theatre. Some of the casino staff had been recalled to their units in France, but several hundred past military age or enjoying Monegasque citizenship remained on duty. Delpierre, the SBM president, appealed to them to accept a cut in salary, hinting that the company would otherwise collapse within a few months. They accepted the inevitable. In the 'Kitchen' an army of ancient addicts continued to claw at their 5-franc chips, but the Salons Privés still attracted rich polyglots who played maximums at roulette with green 20,000-franc plaques, encouraged by the management's abolition of zero for half an hour twice a day. But this trickle of business could not oil the wheels. The casino closed for three months until the 'phoney war' lull brought back a number of visitors.

Lord Furness was one of Monte Carlo's first casualties. The once-gay playboy, now frail and pathetically shrunken, lingered for a while at the Hotel de Paris. He never recovered from the loss of his son and heir, Christopher, who fell at Arras in May and was awarded a posthumous V.C. Furness died within a few months.

[3] Prince Andrew of Greece was one of the few to put into Monte Carlo during an interrupted Mediterranean cruise. He remained until his death four years later. A dignified figure to the end, he was saddened by family disruption. His wife had remained in Greece to work for the Red Cross; three of their sons-in-law were German; and Prince Philip was serving England in the Royal Navy.

Maxine Elliott departed with all flags flying. She had quickly adopted several French military units and sent lavish parcels of comforts to all the surrounding posts.

She celebrated the first Christmas of the war with a party for 200 local youngsters, providing their mothers with blankets, bonnets and shoes. She had her entire wardrobe cut down to make children's clothes and layettes for newborn babies. She collapsed on 5 March 1940 on the marble floor of her bathroom. A Chasseur Alpin stood guard outside the chateau with his head bowed over a musket.

Prince Louis had sent a handsome wreath, but he was ill and too preoccupied with official duties to attend the funeral in Cannes. His seventieth birthday almost coincided with the collapse of French resistance. For the next four years he would struggle to retain a precarious neutrality against pressure from the Italians, Vichy French and the far more formidable Nazis, who soon offered the peach of collaboration at bayonet point.

Chapter Nine

FRANCE HAD hastily put up various blockhouses and defence installations which gave the Italians a pretext to brush aside Monaco's plea of neutrality. After overrunning Menton, Mussolini's troops received a hysterical welcome from their compatriots in June 1940. Prince Louis attempted to ban demonstrations and the display of foreign flags, but had to stand by impotently while the local gaol was emptied of Italians and pro-Axis sympathisers. He was even threatened with protective custody unless he toed the line.

Somerset Maugham was among the 1,500 Riviera residents evacuated from Cannes in two old British colliers. Those who remained in Monaco were rounded up and cross-examined by the Italian secret police, who briefly interned all British nationals under the age of 70 in a camp at Sospel, near the Italian border. The OVRA was heavy-handed with anti-Axis suspects but showed little animosity towards the wealthier Jews who had come southward from Nazi-occupied Paris. Many of them joined officers on leave, French profiteers and Italian businessmen in the casino. A loss of five million francs in the first year of the war jumped to a profit of six by the end of 1941, and even that satisfactory figure quadrupled in the next twelve months, by which time over 100 new companies had been registered, mainly as cover for Nazi, Italian and Vichy holdings.

Although Italian military and secret police had occupied two of the best hotels, they continued to behave correctly and even climbed down when the casino management, supported by Prince Louis, reminded them of its strict rules prohibiting the wearing of uniforms in the gaming rooms. But they became distinctly twitchier after a daring escape by British airmen from Fort de la Revère, brilliantly master-minded by the British S.O.E. under a Belgian army doctor, A. M. Guérisse, alias 'Lt. Cdr. Patrick O'Leary, R.N.' His own escape from St Hippolyte, a fortress near Nîmes, had encouraged him to crack La Revère a classic exploit rightly acclaimed by Airey Neave and other authorities.

Dating back to Napoleonic times, the fortress was hewn out of solid rock and protected by a deep moat trussed with barbed wire and lit at night by powerful arc lamps. It had huge iron gates with each corridor heavily bolted at both ends for extra security. But O'Leary had valuable inside information of its few weaknesses, thanks to a brave Polish priest, Father Myrda, who took communion in both St Hippolyte and Fort de la Revère, and an equally resourceful White Russian, Vladimir Bouryschkine ('Val Williams'), a former basketball star in the States. After working with the American Red Cross in Paris he was recruited by O'Leary and given the excellent 'cover' of coaching the Monegasque basketball team. He always cycled up to La Revère whose commandant he disarmed with his cherubic smile and American accent. He was soon allowed to give the prisoners half a day's exercise each week in accordance with the Geneva Convention.

They made contact with the prisoners' senior officer, Squadron Leader F. W. Higginson, whom the Royal Air Force urgently wanted back in harness. Shot down in June 1941, he had already collected over a dozen Luftwaffe scalps and prudently concealed his true identity under the name of 'Captain Bennett'. Once the escape route was finalised and an invaluable hacksaw smuggled in by Father Myrda, Higginson chose his party; two officers, Barnet and Hawkins, with two N.C.O.s, an Englishman, Nabarro, and Hickey, a rather wild New Zealander. Both sergeants had previously escaped from Hippolyte but were betrayed by an Italian prostitute in Monte Carlo and sent to La Revère. Apart from Myrda and Val Williams, the prisoners could rely on three key outside contacts; Jean Nitelet, O'Leary's vital radio link with London; Tony Friend, a tall blue-eyed Australian employed in the Monaco police department, which made him an ideal source for forged papers; and finally Eva Trenchard, an elderly Jersey-born spinster, who had resided for 20 years on the Riviera and now ran the Scotch Tea House on the Boulevard des Moulins.

Higginson and the others had timed their break-out for the night of 6 August 1942 under cover of a camp sing-song. They opened the cookhouse door with a skeleton key and slid down a coal chute into the kitchen. Negotiating the moat, they made their way into a vile-smelling sewer, their tunnel to freedom, while fellow-prisoners sang lusty sea shanties. Their hacksaw broke on an iron grille but they managed to get out. By this time, however, the alarm had been raised and guards were frenziedly combing the area. The five, exhausted and reeking of excrement, hid out under some bushes, but their contacts, Friend and Nitelet, had meantime been pounced on and handcuffed by some prison guards. However, Friend flourished his police pass and convinced them they were on official business. In Monte Carlo they contacted O'Leary, who decided to make for the Scotch Tea House, their emergency rendezvous.

The party had discovered in daylight that they were not, as expected, near Monte Carlo but practically at Cap d'Ail. With only one set of forged papers between them, made out for Higginson, their situation seemed almost hopeless. Brian Hawkins had managed to stay a little cleaner than his comrades and was therefore sent off to the teashop. Within a few hours O'Leary had supplied fresh clothes and directed them to an isolated villa rented by Tony Friend. Here for the next two weeks they stayed under cover behind drawn curtains, playing cards and smoking furiously. Their only visitors, but most welcome, were Miss Trenchard and a Monegasque couple, the Guitons, who arrived with food hampers after dark. Finally, two by two, they set off at intervals for Marseilles by train, with Higginson disguised in one of Father

Myrda's soutanes and suitably tonsured by M. Guiton (now Princess Grace's coiffeur). They hid out at various points on O'Leary's smoothly-geared escape machine before reaching Perpignan, the last stop for Gibraltar.

Their break-out had immediate repercussions at Fort de la Revère. All officers were bundled off to an Italian prison camp, but the remaining aircrew and army sergeants became impatient to try their luck in a mass escape. Sixty desperate men crashed into the moat, some with sheets or ropes, others jumping. Two broke their legs and another, too corpulent to squeeze through the outlet, was wedged in the sewer. More than half of them safely reached O'Leary's hideouts.[1]

Soon afterwards, following the Allied landings in North Africa, the Nazis occupied the whole of the Riviera and took over from the Italians in Monaco. They first appointed a Consul-General, who quickly made out a case for the 'protection' of German vital interests. A panzer division arrived under the command of General von Kohlermann whose staff appropriated the Métropole. They mined the port and then set up gun emplacements and tank traps on Mont Agel, with a radar station in the golf club house.

Although there was no *maquis* activity in the principality, the breakout at La Revère and the certainty that Monaco formed a vital link in the O'Leary escape organisation stung Himmler into action. Senior Gestapo officers took over part of the Hotel de Paris, whose management had swiftly bricked up their best wines and spirits, but one of the barmen carefully removed a bottle of Winston Churchill's favourite whisky for a future victory toast.

The Gestapo HQ was established almost directly opposite the

1 Nitelet was arrested shortly after the first breakout. Higginson returned to fighter pilot duty and now farms successfully in Wales. Val Williams was caught by the Germans in 1943 but escaped, half-crippled, from Rennes while under sentence of death. He was spirited back to England. O'Leary, also captured in the same year, was released in 1945. He fought in Korea, winning the highest awards for gallantry to add to his George Cross.

In June 1946 Eva Trenchard received the King's Special Commendation for her wartime services. She was later handed the key to a Chelsea flat by Wing Cdr Paddy Byrne on behalf of many grateful p.o.w.s. In March 1965 the Royal Air Force Escaping Society honoured her 80th birthday with a celebration dinner.

Scotch Tea House which gave Miss Trenchard many awkward moments. She once had several British airmen hiding out in the backroom while some Gestapo men unhurriedly sipped their ersatz coffee. In her flat she later cooked a 21st birthday dinner for an airman, named Walsh, whose health was drunk by other RAF escapers in transit for Marseilles. They remained unaware that several German and Italian officers also happened to be celebrating in a neighbouring apartment.

As the French Resistance movement grew in size and daring, Monaco's Gestapo became correspondingly more brutal, chiefly towards the Jewish refugees, who now had to wear the yellow star at all times. Round-ups of suspects, Jew or Gentile, were enforced by humiliating orders to drop trousers for scrutiny. Many victims were beaten up and sent to concentration camps, but a great number owed their lives to the Chief of Police, Conan, whose men formally accompanied the Gestapo and often warned victims in advance of house-to-house searches. This policy had the sympathetic approval of Prince Louis, who always behaved with proper military decorum towards the German Commandant but never concealed his distaste for the Gestapo bullies.

Black market food, liquor, petrol and cigarettes were only available to the occupation forces, war-rich German and Italian profiteers or collaborators, who swarmed into the principality from France with bulky wallets of banknotes and Vichy bonds. They gambled so recklessly that the SBM showed an average profit of over £500,000 a year for the rest of the war, but the directors still refused to relax their prohibition on the wearing of uniforms. A German admiral in full naval regalia was denied admission and had to climb down when von Kohlermann, urgently summoned by Prince Louis, supported the management. Claiming that the casino was 'a cultural and historical monument', the Commandant even resisted a directive from Berlin to remove its domes for copper then much needed by the Germans.

The SBM also withstood a threatened takeover by Michel (*né*, Mendel) Skolnikoff, the Nazis's quartermaster for almost anything in short supply on the Riviera. This renegade Jew of

Roumanian origin had operated for years in shady international finance before his arrival in occupied Paris. One deal earned him a prison sentence but an astute Gestapo official drew Himmler's attention to his promising talents. He was soon buying uniforms for the Wehrmacht and developed an enormous black market organisation which supplied Himmler, Goering and French quislings with art treasures and jewellery.[2]

Bald and lantern-jawed, he would have been ideally cast as a sinister butler in some blood-and-thunder horror film, but his millions and a vast Mercedes attracted a beautiful Alsatian mistress, Hélène Sanson, complete with dachshund. 'Neutral' Monaco made an ideal springboard for his wholesale acquisition of hotels, abandoned villas and apartment houses. In Monte Carlo he bought himself the Hotel Mirabeau where he and Hélène occupied the bridal suite and gave enormous parties for high-placed visitors from Paris and Berlin, but conspicuously without von Kohlermann, who despised him even more than his Gestapo masters. From this palatial base Skolnikoff embarked on land raids like some medieval robber baron, snapping up some of the best hotels in Nice, Cannes, Biarritz and Aix-les-Bains.

A black market flourished in Monte Carlo for the privileged minority but many of the population, lacking jewels or Vichy banknotes, found themselves desperately short of meat, fish and other foodstuffs. Cigarettes almost vanished and eggs fetched up to a dollar each. Relief kitchens were opened at the Hotel de Paris and the Métropole, with the soup ration strictly limited to one litre a day. Prince Louis, who had refused all invitations to attend Nazi dinners or receptions, took his place in the soup queues until the Gestapo decided that this gesture was deliberately provocative and insisted on a palace servant being sent on his behalf.

Arriving from Paris, Rainier was nauseated by the casino's cynical policy of 'business as usual'. After his schooling at Le Rosey

[2] Laura Corrigan, like Gould, had refused to leave the Riviera. She dined in her villa in gloomy isolation, attended by her aged butler, but later went to Paris and sold many of her jewels to Goering. She passed all the proceeds to Resistance funds and richly deserved her decoration from de Gaulle after the Liberation. She died in 1948.

had been interrupted by the war, he was tutored for a while by a French naval officer before resuming his studies for the *baccalauréat* at the University of Montpellier. Debarred from war service by his country's neutrality, he spent a frustrating year at the School of Political Science in Paris where he developed a deep loathing for the Nazi conquerors.

He had returned to Monaco in May 1944 to celebrate his 21st birthday. An edict was issued a few days later by which Princess Charlotte formally renounced all succession rights in his favour. As heir to the throne he would normally have served an apprentice-ship in administration, but his grandfather locked himself away for months on end in his library at Marchais or among his Napoleonic relics. He rarely gave a second glance to the few papers sent for his signature. All important decisions seemed to be made by a secre-tariat or officials conditioned to obey the Nazis.

Within a few weeks Rainier had become unbearably irritated with the roaring Mercedes and delicatessen accents. He also objected to the Minister of State, who seemed too easygoing towards the Germans. In a huff he walked out of the palace one day and settled into a small villa on his own. Among his few visitors was his sister, Antoinette, who snatched moments from her duties with the Red Cross and running homes for war orphans and the children of men serving with the French Army.

The Americans landed in Provence on 15 August and occupied Cannes, Nice and Antibes within a fortnight. They decided to side-track Monaco but bombed seven German minesweepers in the harbour. A stray bomb hit von Kohlermann's hotel, another wiped out the thermal baths, and a third landed among the flowerbeds in the Boulingrins. Most locals took shelter in the tunnels under the Rock, but the casino remained open throughout the raids. Cheer-ing crowds rushed into the streets when a torpedo from a British submarine scored a direct hit on the German minesweeper, *La Prudente*. Winston Churchill sent the commander a signal of con-gratulation with the warning postscript: 'I hope you won't go into the casino and lose your money'.

The liberation on 3 September was something of a hilarious

anti-climax. As Monaco was still technically neutral, the Americans had decided to remain just over the French border, but two tipsy G.I.s zig-zagged across in a jeep and were hysterically mobbed. Soon afterwards, a bemused Free French officer drove about in search of a Monegasque sweetheart from prewar days. He found her in the British-owned Hotel Métropole which had already hoisted the Union Jack.

The Germans hurtled off by jeep or taxi, leaving only a token force in the fortress on Mont Agel which surrendered after an American warship had lobbed in a few warning shells. Skolnikoff had not tarried for any last-ditch stand. As soon as the first Allied troops set foot on the beach near St Tropez, he loaded his Mercedes with jewels and other portables, including a rumoured hoard of bullion. He headed for Madrid with Hélène and her dachshund, pursued by four members of French counter-espionage with orders to bring him back for trial. Another account alleges that they were, in fact, a murder squad recruited by the Resistance from the Marseilles waterfront. It appears that official representations were tentatively made to the authorities in Madrid who agreed to exchange the fugitive for two Spanish refugees held in France.

A corpse, stabbed in several places, was found soon afterwards inside a burned-out car on the Spanish side of the frontier. According to the Resistance men, who were cross-examined by the local police but vanished mysteriously, Skolnikoff had been killed while attempting to escape. The prosecution at Nuremberg branded him as a Gestapo agent who had made over £11 million in black market deals for the Nazis.

In 1951 the American novelist, David Dodge, came across an immense Mercedes on the taxi rank at Burgos. It bore traces of six bullet-holes in one of the rear doors, but nobody could unravel its past history or discover any previous owners. An obstinate theory persists that Skolnikoff went underground and the charred corpse was in fact that of a Spaniard murdered and planted in the car to deceive the Resistance agents. A few of the missing jewels were sold, but neither the bullion nor La Belle Hélène ever reappeared.

*   *   *

In Monaco a number of local collaborators were rounded up. General Robert Tryon Frederick, whose men had been fêted while they removed barbed wire and de-mined the harbour, quickly discovered a less amiable side to the smiling principality which, greedy for food and long-missed luxuries, set up a black market in PX goods and rations allocated by the American Food Commission. As a result, many were denied their fair share. The general, already outraged by the number of rich American expatriates who had sat the war out in Monaco, grew even testier after suggesting that Monte Carlo might make an ideal leave centre for his men. Prince Louis hedged, weakly pleading Monaco's 'neutrality', while his Council and the SBM produced more practical objections to accommodating 12,000 high-spirited Servicemen. As all the hotels were rundown and in need of extensive renovation, they offered to take a mere thousand or so but hinted broadly that the intake should be limited to officers.

They mistook their man. General Frederick was slight of build and inconspicuous but his peppery manner was familiar to the Pentagon which he had left, at Mountbatten's request, to command the First Special Field Force of American and Canadian troops. In Sicily he had won high praise for a daring assault, enabling General Mark Clark's army to advance after being shelled for two months. At 37 the youngest major-general in the U.S. army, and with nine war wounds, he declined to accept this insult to his enlisted men. Monaco was briskly placed off limits to all military personnel, who found more welcome billets in Nice, Cannes, Juan-les-Pins and Antibes.

Rainier was not only spared the embarrassment of having to condone this local snobbishness, but he and his sister drove over to Nice and reminded General Frederick about their grandfather's Minister of State. Once a state of war had been officially declared in the principality, Rainier volunteered for service in the French Army. He was commissioned as Second Lieutenant Grimaldi on the intelligence staff at First Army HQ and served for almost 18 months, taking part in the campaign in Alsace. He was decorated in the field with the Croix de Guerre and Bronze Star.

Rainier arrived back in a principality of peeling stucco and blistered woodwork. Hotels and villas still showed the effects of long neglect or enemy billeting. Somerset Maugham made an early return visit, took one disparaging look at the collection of furniture which could be reclaimed by its rightful owners, and declared, 'They were d-d-dammed lucky to have this stuff looted.' The wartime profiteers and collaborators had vanished from the casino, and a single trente-et-quarante table operated in the Salon Privé without enough patrons for roulette. Baccarat attracted only a few players and Zographos had significantly decided to ignore Monte Carlo in favour of Cannes and Deauville.

Despite wartime profits which had shot its capital up to a handsome 500 million francs, the SBM seemed curiously lacking in initiative. Cannes showed far more enterprise. The Film Festival was revived and brought back Hollywood's leading producers and stars. In marked contrast to the paltry £30,000 which the SBM had grudgingly allocated to redecorating its casinos and hotels, Francois André was lavishly restoring Cannes, Deauville, Le Touquet and Juan-les-Pins. He could easily afford the $1\frac{10}{4}\%$ government tax on baccarat, thanks to committed players like the Aga Khan, Jack L. Warner and Alberto Dodero, whose millions had sponsored an ungrateful Peron's rise to power. The Aga Khan had divorced his wife on the grounds of 'mutual dislike and diversity of character' and taken unto himself a fourth Begum, a former 'Miss France', with whom he settled into his huge pink villa perched high over Cannes. His son, Aly, had returned from war service with a renewed appetite for high-speed fun. He had quickly bought Maxine Elliott's Chateau de L'Horizon for £35,000 and proposed spending even more on extensive improvements.

Winston Churchill was rapturously mobbed when he came over from Lord Beaverbrook's villa at Cap d'Ail for his first post-war visit to Monte Carlo. He dined at the Hotel de Paris and asked the orchestra to play *Lili Marlene* – but never again. 'I had Rommel on the brain all night' he later told his friends. After the hotel management had formally presented him with the long-hidden bottle of Vat 69, he walked into the gaming rooms with his daughter, Sarah. All players stopped as patrons stood up to sing *Malbrook s'en va-t-en-guerre* (Marlborough went to the wars) in honour of his celebrated ancestor. Even the usually stone-faced croupiers twirled their rakes when the old warrior, pink-cheeked with delight, gave the 'V' sign in acknowledgement. It was a welcome tonic for Monte Carlo, now suffering from an acute shortage of its faithful English clientèle.

After his military service Rainier found the atmosphere forlorn and almost moribund. He had never established a close rapport with his grandfather and spent even less time in the palace when the 76 year-old ruler married a buxom actress, Marie-Francoise Dommanget, his long-time friend and companion, whose future he was anxious to safeguard.

Bored with protocol, Rainier recklessly drove high-powered cars over the mountain roads and also took up skin-diving. He soon acquired a playboy reputation and formed a close liaison with Gisèle Pascal, the glamorous film actress, with whom he began sharing a love-nest at St Jean-Cap Ferrat. When this became more than a passing infatuation, snobbish Monegasques shuddered at the prospect of a princess whose parents ran a vegetable and flower stall in the market at Nice. Still hopeful, however, that the heir might select a suitable partner like the daughter of the Comte de Paris, the French Pretender, or possibly ex-King Umberto's daughter, Maria-Pia, they grew even more alarmed when Monte Carlo's leading soothsayer confidently predicted that he would one day marry a movie star.

Chapter Ten

IN FEBRUARY 1947 a roving magazine assignment enabled me to revisit the Riviera after eight years. The Blue Train, now tawdry, rundown and chilly, was the first of several disappointments, and even the luxurious Carlton at Cannes typified the depression which blanketed the whole Côte d'Azur. Few of its 400 rooms were occupied, although Dodero had reserved several suites. The only reminder of former free-spenders was a rajah whose appetites evidently exceeded his digestion since the local cocottes referred to him behind his back as 'His Exhausted Highness'. The management mourned the scarcity of English guests no longer able to spare 1,150 francs a day without food from the £75 a year permitted by the British Government. The exchange rate was a tempting 480 francs to the pound with almost any barman prepared to offer 750 on the black market, but the once-jammed Carlton bar was still short of patrons with Scotch at ten shillings a tot.

Marooned in a sea of empty tables, one quartette used to meet regularly on the terrace at noon; Grace Moore and her husband, Val Parera; Harry Pilcer, still looking chipper and wearing clothes rather too tight and youthful for his years; and Elsa Maxwell, over-hatted and prattling endlessly about La Belle Époque and her plans to bring America's Four Hundred back to Cannes. 'I saved Monte

Carlo' she assured me, 'but it's quite *dead* now.' Pilcer echoed that coroner's verdict in his pumice stone voice, and I had to agree after driving over to the principality with Parera, who enjoyed chemin-de-fer.

The SBM would shortly open a new terrace restaurant for patrons of the Salons Privés with a panoramic view of the harbour and palace, and arrangements were also in hand for staging the European swimming championships in the magnificent pool, but these gestures only testified to a lack of co-ordinated planning. The Place du Casino looked rather like a derelict papier-mâché film set abandoned after some weeks of shooting. Half a dozen fiacres stood outside the Café de Paris with their drivers dozing in the back seats or dispiritedly playing cards. Only two tables operated in the 'Kitchen' and Parera found little action in the Salon Privé whose flunkeys pounced to empty ashtrays almost before one had lit a cigarette. The few croupiers on duty, discontented with low pay and a very depressed *tronc*, looked even surlier than usual.

But the Winter Casino at Cannes seemed to be booming. André favoured English clients with generous credit facilities and almost nominal rates at his Hotel Majestic. When I dined with him at Les Ambassadeurs, the casino's crowded night club, it was liberally 'papered' with attractive hostesses. Latin Americans, upper crust English and several French industrialists formed a procession to greet the white-haired old charmer. We were joined by Aly Khan and a plastic model with lively hips but dead eyes. He talked animatedly about the Chateau de l'Horizon and sketched plans for his new terrace on the linen tablecloth.

In the Salon Privé, perched on a high stool overlooking the no-limit table run by a member of the Greek Syndicate, André watched the baccarat. One of the heaviest punters was a young Argentinian who, earlier that evening, had paid for his drinks with a £1,000 plaque and carelessly left the change as a tip for the barman. Next morning I called on André at the Majestic where he characteristically occupied one of the cheapest-priced rooms and drank *vin ordinaire* with his bowl of bouillabaisse. He cheerfully admitted the truth of a story then circulating on the Côte. He had engaged Piaf at £1,500 a performance but deducted 80 francs for a glass tumbler which she accidentally broke during her act.

He wore his usual panama and carried an umbrella. 'I take no chances, even on the Riviera' he explained. After breakfasting on a little fresh fruit, he had run through the figures of his previous day's takings from the casinos at Cannes, Deauville, Le Touquet, La Baule, Juan-les-Pins and Aix-les-Bains, apart from the earnings of his hotels, cinemas, racecourses, golf clubs and polo grounds. As we walked round Cannes, he stroked his luxuriant white moustache and pointed out the tall newly-painted hotels, tennis courts and pampered gardens which would doubtless soon attract back former patrons and many others. He did not under-rate Monte Carlo but hinted that its huge overheads – the prince's percentage, a top-heavy staff and costly showpieces like the Oceanographic Museum – might ruin the SBM which had already been drained of most of its wartime profits.

The Chilean Marquis de Cuevas and his wife, a Rockefeller, had just formed the Grand Ballet de Monte Carlo by merging a company of French dancers with a talented American troupe, but André discounted any Diaghilev-like success. However, he had shrewdly covered himself by engaging the de Cuevas ballet, supported by leading guest stars from other international companies, to dance at Deauville and Cannes between their seasons in Monaco.

I next saw him in the early summer of 1949 at the Aly Khan-Rita Hayworth wedding reception which he stage-managed like a born impresario. A squad of white-suited violinists from the casino orchestra accompanied Yves Montand, who crooned the bride's favourite *La Vie en Rose* while the 80 guests, an odd amalgam of movie notables and robed Ismailis, attacked caviare, lobster and magnums of vintage champagne. The elaborate buffet had been prepared by a squad of chefs from Paris and Cannes. Louella Parsons, queen bee of Hollywood's columnists, was responsible for a studio handout and had edged out Elsa Maxwell, who first introduced Aly to the screen goddess at one of her dinner parties. Among the absentees was the new Prince of Monaco, whom I had recently interviewed. He remarked, with a faintly derisory eyebrow, that court mourning had *unfortunately* prevented his attendance. Neither of us could foresee that his own nuptials, seven years hence, would make the shenanigans at the Château de l'Horizon seem like a low-budget second feature.

My request to meet Rainier III shortly after the funeral of Prince Louis, the first Grimaldi to die in Monaco for almost two centuries, had met with unexpected approval. It chimed with the ending of a disastrous financial year for the SBM whose accounts showed a loss of £150,000 and a 75% decline in visitors. But the company had made a gallant attempt to keep up appearances. One caught a whiff of fresh white paint at the Hotel de Paris whose menus were up to pre-war lavishness. I was greeted, like all new arrivals, with a dozen roses and a basket of choice fruit on the dressing-table. The hotel chefs stood ready, night and day, to pander to guests like an eccentric Austrian, who always ordered a giant omelette of precisely 100 eggs for himself and his friends when he returned from the gaming tables. The sugar-loaf casino again looked fairylike by floodlight, and the Boulingrins sparkled with a new flowerbed design. In the pond a giant lily from the Amazon, 'Victoria Cruziana', was flourishing in the open air and unfurling its leaves at night. Rare species were also being imported for the Jardin Exotique whose visitors would soon be encouraged to proceed from the tropical splendour of the gardens into the cool Grotte de l'Observatoire. Its entrance cave, dating back to neolithic times, led into pillared halls and caverns ornamented with majestic stalagmites and stalactites.

A more surprising innovation was located in the casino where an array of fruit machines now lined the ante-rooms. One of the baroque salons, decorated a vivid scarlet, had been given over to dice tables, obviously with American tourists in view. Local gossip credited Edward G. Robinson with this minor revolution. While taking a break from the Cannes Film Festival he had lost a few hundred francs at roulette in an almost deserted room and was apparently overheard to growl, 'What this joint needs is a real crap game.' Others having expressed similar views, the SBM's chief croupier visited Reno where he bought several tables and engaged operators to initiate local personnel into the rites of seven and eleven. It was even simpler to install a battery of one-armed bandits which so quickly paid for themselves that an American syndicate offered the SBM $1 million as a down payment for the entire gaming concession. The National Council, hopeful that the financial slump would be arrested by reparations for war damage, rejected the proposal which Prince Rainier, who had inherited his grandfather's 22,000 shares, would certainly have vetoed. Although he had his family's distaste for being associated with the casino, it was still the major tourist attraction, quite apart from contributing a healthy sum to his privy purse. Control by a foreign gambling group was therefore quite unacceptable.

Before motoring up to the palace over which the Grimaldi standard fluttered at half-mast, I was gently urged by an official to avoid two rather delicate subjects; the casino and, particularly, Mlle Gisèle Pascal, whose continuing romance with the ruler had become even less popular since his accession. As it was freely rumoured that she could never bear children, their marriage presaged the end of the dynasty and also Monaco's special privileges if France chose to invoke her treaty rights.

Rainier seemed cheerfully unaware of these tensions. He received me in his book-lined snuggery, with signed portraits of pin-up actresses and racing drivers on the walls. He was 26, deep-chested and with the chunky build of a useful-looking middleweight. His unaccented English was as impeccable as the dark blue suit of Savile Row cut. He wore suede shoes, then considered a shade 'caddish', complemented by a Ronald Colman triggerline moustache. He chain-smoked but his manner was bland and relaxed.

He talked seriously of his country's post-war tourist problems and his hopes of restoring both the Oceanographic Museum and the theatre to their former splendour. He shrugged off accusations of personal extravagance for changing his cars every 3,000 miles and enthused instead over the recent revival of the Rally, won by a

(top) (left) Princess Antoinette with her brother. Rainier was a good horseman but soon switched to a motor bike. His passion for speed led him to racing cars. He narrowly escaped death in the Tour de France which he entered under an assumed name.

Rainier attends a Monte Carlo Dog Show with his grandfather, Prince Louis, whom he succeeded in 1949. His apprenticeship was sketchy and interrupted by the war.

Monaco's neutrality was ignored by the Italians and Germans, who mined the harbour and ringed the principality with barbed wire. But it was 'business as usual' at the Casino. A black market also flourished for the benefit of wealthy refugees and Vichy quislings.

Soon after his accession, Prince Rainier III reviews the Palace Guard. Himself a wartime officer in the French Army, he smartened up their drill and uniform.

Rainier first met his future wife on 6 May 1955. Grace Kelly came over from the Cannes Film Festival and made a conducted palace tour with the Prince acting as guide.

Prince Rainier and his bride leaving the Cathedral in Monaco after their marriage on 19 April 1956. It was covered by an army of 1800 reporters and photographers.

Back at the Palace after the ceremony, bride and bridegroom relax briefly before the reception. MGM's Helen Rose designed the wedding gown of pale caramel lace. The honeymoon was a short cruise on Rainier's yacht, *Deo Juvante*.

The Throne Room, with portraits of Monaco's princes and superb frescoes, is furnished in scarlet and gold brocade. Sumptuous velvet hangings adorn the Throne.

An aerial view of the Palace, originally built in the 13th century on the remains of a Saracen citadel. It has 180 rooms, many Holbeins and other art treasures, a stamp and coin collection, historic archives, apart from Prince Rainier's garage for vintage cars.

Hotchkiss from a record number of competitors (230). He recalled in technical detail the previous year's Grand Prix in which Farina's Maserati had swept to a thrilling victory in just over three hours, and also expressed lyrical admiration for the Argentine ace, Fangio, who had entered his powerful Mercedes-Benz for the coming event. After tea we walked through the palace gardens and he pointed down to the Stade where two teams were playing football. 'This is my free grandstand seat', he remarked with a grin.

I came away with the impression of an agreeably extrovert young man, who would eventually marry some safely eligible foreign princess and rule his pocket State in the easy-going style of his forbears. In fact he was desperately unsure of himself and had enjoyed little or no preparation to handle the delicate relationship with France or the SBM's complicated semi-official status. He was still temperamentally handicapped by an unhappy childhood, the estrangement of his parents and his grandfather's unhelpful tutorship during and after the difficult war years.

He maintained the good-time bachelor profile and showed no intention of giving up either his mistress or the racing cars, but some had noted his peppery impatience with the old secretariat, semi-fossilised by years of service with an ailing and often absentee ruler. They were ousted by younger and more forward-looking men, who had orders to draft plans for driving the railway tunnel through the Rock and reclaiming more land from the sea. Rainier also started modernising the palace and had the guards drilled by a former Foreign Legion major, who soon placed them on a strict diet.

His accession was formally celebrated at Easter, 1950, when the casino and all public buildings were decorated with bunting and floodlit. The veteran Gunsbourg had at last retired and made way for Maurice Besnard, who staged a new Lichine ballet. Massine also arrived to supervise his *Good Humoured Ladies* and arrangements were put in hand for the French version of Prokofiev's *L'Amour des Trois Oranges*. Cortot bewitched Chopin devotees while 'Gorgeous' Gussy Moran's underwear offered lighter entertainment at the Country Club whose tournaments attracted champions like Trabert and Drobny.

One of Rainier's first moves was to bring his father back from exile. Prince Pierre helped to sponsor golf and tennis tournaments but his main interests were cultural, notably the theatre. Rainier warmly endorsed his plan to establish a Literary Council which first met at the Monaco Legation in Paris under Colette's honorary presidency, supported by Maurois, Duhamel, Pagnol and other Academicians. It was decided to inaugurate an annual literary award, the Prix Prince Rainier III.[1]

The young ruler took more than a perfunctory interest in this prize. When in Paris he often slipped away to exhibitions of 'modernistic primitive art'. He also wrote poetry which Cocteau amiably pronounced, 'beautiful and sincerely felt'. After months in the claustrophobic midget principality, he would have welcomed the peace of Marchais but dreaded his mother's match-making parties. Worse, Princess Charlotte had studied for a diploma in social welfare and gave up much of the ancestral chateau to convicts on parole, some of them very ugly-looking customers indeed.

Rainier had other family troubles. His sister dutifully opened bazaars and remained an active President of the Monegasque Red Cross but she also enjoyed parties with her rather frivolous stage or ballet friends and had begun to chafe at palace protocol. The breach had widened when she went off to Genoa and married Aleco Noghues, Monaco's leading tennis star, of whom her brother openly disapproved.

Rainier's own romance with Gisèle Pascal caused many to undervalue his serious approach to official duties. He paid a State Visit to France and his meeting with President Auriol was soon followed by a treaty reaffirming Monaco's independence and the continuance of 'friendly neighbourliness and mutual administrative aid, concerning Customs, taxes, postal services, tele-communications and monopolies.' France also demonstrated her goodwill with an assurance of financial assistance which supplemented a useful sum for war reparations under Marshall Aid.

[1] Julien Green became the first lauréat, in 1951, succeeded by Henri Troyat, Jean Giono, Jules Roy and Louise de Vilmorin. Simenon was an early member of the Council which met in Paris for its final deliberations chaired by Prince Pierre.

Only 350,000 foreigners arrived in 1950, the majority of them package tourists, who stayed only a night or two en route to Italy or France after rounding off the obligatory visit to the tables with a lightning round of the Palace and the Oceanographic Museum. Most luxury hotels still shut off many of their rooms except in peak season, and few of the wealthy clientèle now reserved suites for two or three months each year.

Monte Carlo had gained revenue but lost something of the old *ton* by installing the dice tables and fruit machines in its casino. Colette continued to rhapsodise on the delights of Monaco ('a charming Principality whose flowers are its only frontiers'), but had to admit that the raucous cries of 'Baby wants new shoes' from crap players lacked charm even in gallic translation. She seldom entered the casino. Crippled by arthritis, she much preferred to sit in her wheelchair on the Hotel de Paris terrace and sign autographs. One day she was invited to watch a scene being shot on the casino steps for a movie, *Nous Irons à Monte Carlo*, for which the publicity-hungry SBM had gladly given facilities. It was a very minor epic and Colette began yawning until she spotted a gazelle-like girl in one of the small parts. She at once cabled Gilbert Miller, then preparing a Broadway production of *Gigi*, that she had discovered the ideal actress to play her heroine. Anita Loos flew in from New York and quickly endorsed her view. It led to a Broadway stage triumph, followed by a Hollywood contract for Audrey Hepburn, until then an unknown chorus girl in mediocre London revues.

The locals were far more taken with Errol Flynn, who would come ashore from his schooner, *Zaca*, for a riotous night in Monte Carlo with the Roumanian Princess Irene Ghika and his inseparable American playboy friend, Freddie McEvoy. Flynn, who once cheerfully confessed, 'my gross habits cannot be reconciled with my net income', seemed unperturbed by his recent divorce from Nora Eddington and insistent claims for back pay by his first wife, Lili Damita. In July 1950 he left his princess for Patrice Wymore, a tall red-headed starlet from Salena, Kansas whom he married at the Town Hall on the Rock on 23 October, with McEvoy as his now seasoned best man. The mayor, who wore a red and white sash with tassels, presented the couple with gold medals on behalf of the municipality. Following the civil ceremony, they were spiritually linked at the Lutheran Church in Nice as the pastors of Menton and Monaco had both declined to accommodate the twice-divorced actor.

A cold buffet and champagne reception was held in the Hotel de Paris. Since most of the shops had closed at the request of employees, all fans of their adored 'Robin des Bois', almost 10,000 sightseers thronged the gaily decorated streets. A dramatic but unrehearsed incident enlivened the proceedings when two sturdy policemen presented the bridegroom with a court summons from the parents of a 16 year-old shop assistant whom he was accused of enticing aboard his yacht and raping. They claimed £1,000 damages.

Flynn did not blink. Although his visa applications always had 'Sex' marked against 'Occupation', he appeared to be guiltless in this particular case. The writ was thrown out of court after several postponements, but Flynn henceforth avoided the principality unless he happened to be filming on location nearby. He had also lost his friend, McEvoy, who drowned when his yacht went down off the Moroccan coast during a suspected smuggling operation. Neither was much missed in the casinos of Cannes and Monte Carlo. The management could overlook Flynn's taste for wearing flaming red socks with evening dress, but not his drunken brawling at the tables when he would swear in fruity *argot* at anyone, male or female, who displeased him.

Nicky Hilton was another contemporary hell-raiser and even worse-tempered. Heir to the hotel chain, he had married Elizabeth Taylor in May 1950 and embarked on a European honeymoon tour with two major objectives; to drain the Riviera of hard liquor and break the bank at Monte Carlo. As his 18 year-old bride was not allowed in the gaming rooms, he set forth alone while the mooned about in their hotel suite. She once called at the casino and sent in a message urging him to call it a night. He emerged in a drunken fury and threw a handful of plaques in her face. Their marriage lasted all of seven months.

The Hotel de Paris preferred more stylish clients like the Baron de Rothschild, who used to engage a whole floor for himself and his nine-strong staff, including a secretary who sat up throughout the night to take any telephone calls. One of his two chauffeurs would drive over to Nice every morning to pick up fresh milk, eggs and vegetables specially flown in from the Rothschild farm near Paris.

Although the grand ducal flavour had vanished for all time, Riviera villa-owners made their ritual sorties for a night's dining and gambling in Monte Carlo. The Fiat tycoon, Gianni Agnelli, and André Dubonnet joined the Aga Khan in the Salons Privés, and guests scrambled for tickets at £15 a head for Sporting Club charity galas whenever Piaf headed the cabaret. Mme. Benitez-Rexach, formerly a flower-seller on the streets of Paris and now wife of the Dominican shipping magnate, would parade with rubies and sapphires worth half a million dollars distributed about her plump person. The Windsors were often joined by the Churchills, who usually stayed at Lord Beaverbrook's La Capponcina or Coco Chanel's former villa, owned by Emery Reeves, Sir Winston's continental publisher. Aristotle Onassis, the multi-millionaire owner of a vast oil tanker and whaling fleet, and his elegant golden-haired wife, Tina, were recent arrivals on the Riviera scene and hardly noticed in the glittering turnout of better-known celebrities.

In May 1951 they had rented Lady Burton's Chateau de la Croe, formerly tenanted by the Windsors, Leopold of the Belgians and ex-King Umberto. Its appointments included swan-shaped baths and marble basins, but Onassis entertained unobtrusively enough to assure even Garbo of anonymity. House guests had the run of a well-staffed house and swimming pool, but his yacht, *Olympic Winner*, a 1,250 ton ex-corvette chaser, was modest by Riviera standards and drew as little attention as its squat owner, who strolled around in thickly-tinted glasses with his wife and two small children. He avoided the casino and reminded an inquisitive reporter, 'My whaling fleet is out and might earn or lose me $5 million within three or four months. That's what I call gambling!'

But he had shrewdly sized up certain business possibilities. He first toyed with buying the local brewery which he dismissed after passing a shuttered and derelict building in the Avenue d'Ostende. It seemed an ideal headquarters for his shipping firm, Olympic Maritime, then based in Paris and subject to French taxation. To his annoyance, the SBM seemed disinclined to lease the property. They were perhaps influenced by the preliminary hearing of a Senate Committee investigating his purchase of war-surplus ships, together with hints of scandalous lobbying to secure contracts on his behalf. More probably, the xenophobic Board, Monegasque or French to a man, preferred to seek another tenant.

Whatever their reasoning, Onassis was not easily snubbed. He had accurately decided that the SBM was losing money at the casino but still owned some 25% of Monte Carlo's best real estate, including the largest hotels and the two Sporting Clubs, Winter and Summer, apart from the exclusive Country Club and the golf course up at Mont Agel. But overheads were high and three of its directors had been trying to raise a million-dollar loan in Paris.

Onassis saw the prospect of enlarging the harbour to accommodate not only the biggest yachts but ocean-going liners on luxury cruises. Monte Carlo also had obvious tax advantages as a business base and might form a useful conference centre for his many and varied interests. He and his wife, a willowy sun-bronzed young woman who adored water-skiing, had by now developed a taste for Riviera social life, which could obviously be indulged by ownership of the Hotel de Paris, the Hermitage and other glossy establishments.

Working through his network of foreign companies, he had no difficulty in buying up blocks of SBM stock, then modestly priced. He bought circumspectly through nominees to avoid boosting share values but could not conceal his interest indefinitely. By now the company's directors had also begun to long for a new injection of capital which would relieve them of a heavy payroll and pension list, but they had to take their cue from Prince Rainier, who could veto any decision.

His first meetings with Onassis were both amicable and constructive. The Greek seemed most sympathetic to his plans for modernisation and agreed without hesitation that the railway was an eyesore which should go underground. He seemed genuinely to favour the scheme for reclaiming land from the sea which could be utilised for laying an artificial beach and replacing 'Le Sporting' by a new club with vastly improved facilities for gaming and floor shows. He also impressed Rainier by his promise to spend millions on doubling the accommodation of the Hotel de Paris by adding a rotunda of several floors. Above all, he did not object to Pierre Rey, the prince's nominee for the presidency of the SBM, with the reasonable proviso that one of his own lieutenants, Charles Simon, should become managing director.

In this cordial atmosphere of co-operation the way was officially cleared for Onassis to acquire a majority holding of the SBM's one million shares for an initial investment of little more than £300,000. The house in the Avenue d'Ostende was leased to him at a peppercorn rent and his staff of 20 quickly settled in. He declined Lady Burton's offer to sell him the Chateau de la Croe (soon bought by his brother-in-law, Stavros Niarchos), and moved instead into the Hotel de Paris while awaiting delivery of his mammoth air-conditioned *Christina*, which was being converted in Kiel from a 1,600-ton Canadian frigate.

Rainier was among the first to enjoy a conducted tour of the world's most luxuriously appointed private yacht, manned by a crew of 50. The owner's private three-roomed suite boasted an El Greco in the spacious panelled study and his vast kidney-shaped bath was sunk into a floor of Siena marble with mosaic tiling modelled on the Minos palace at Knossos. Each of the nine double guest suites, designed and exquisitely furnished by a different artist, took its name from a Greek island. The separate marble bathrooms were equipped with gold fish-mouth taps copied from those at the Chateau de la Croe. Instant room service was of course available by bedroom telephone, plus numerous extensions for outside calls. Passengers in a hurry also had the use of several speedboats and a five-seater amphibian aircraft. To compensate for the loss of Lady Burton's grounds where they had kept many pets, including two gazelles from the King of Saudi Arabia, the Onassis children had their own dining-room, nursery and a playroom with a small electric organ and a music box shaped like a fruit machine.

Rainier's palace did not yet boast a swimming pool, and he marvelled at the Onassis extravaganza with a Minoan mosaic bottom which became a 16 square-yard dance floor when raised electrically to deck level. The dining-room, tastefully furnished in the Louis XV style, made a perfect setting for banquets prepared by two chefs, a Frenchman and a Greek. Guests could then adjourn to the poop deck smoking-room, with its grand piano and an open fireplace of lapis lazuli, or drift into the handsome bar, lined with parchment maps and models of famous sailing vessels. Its stools were covered with white whaleskin which provided a cue for the owner's routine joke whenever some beautiful guest took her perch for the first time. 'Darling', he would chuckle, 'you are sitting on the world's biggest penis'.

Rainier had long been a sailing enthusiast but only took it up in earnest when an accident cured him, if only temporarily, of his passion for racing cars. In 1953 the Grimaldi dynasty almost ended when he drove into a tree during the Tour de France which he had entered under an assumed name. He was badly concussed and alarmed his subjects then celebrating the end of his liaison with Gisèle Pascal. She afterwards told journalists, 'People resented the fact that I was not of royal blood . . . We broke up for reasons of State. The Prince had to choose between me and his people'.

In making that choice Rainier was undoubtedly influenced by his chaplain. As a devout Catholic he had often visited Rome since his accession. During one audience with Pope Pius XII he mentioned that the rather neglected parish of St Charles in Monaco might benefit from a priest, who could serve English–Catholic residents as well as the considerable Italian colony in adjacent Beausoleil. Father Francis J. Tucker was appointed Superior of the parish and principal of the American School. An Irish–American who spoke fluent French and Italian, he became a welcome visitor to the palace. Rainier enjoyed his company and later recalled him with affection as 'a very, very nice man . . . and great fun'.

Bespectacled, with white hair and a ruddy complexion, his Pick-wickian looks matched a jolly manner. He warmly welcomed visiting Americans, particularly from his home town, Philadelphia, where his old friends and former parishioners included John and Margaret Kelly, whose movie star daughter, Grace, he had known since childhood.

Following the break with Pascal, Rainier had perceptibly sobered down. He began to spend more time on practical matters like the projected railway tunnel and reclamation schemes. But he still continued to enjoy social life and became a very active member of the new Yacht Club de Monaco, sailing his own *Deo Juvante* in regattas and big-game fishing trips. White with a red funnel (the Monaco national colours), she was a converted English boat with a cruising speed of 11 knots. Alongside the *Christina* she looked rather like a tug sniffing round some Atlantic liner. Many whispered that she was a gift from the uncrowned 'King of Monte Carlo', but Rainier had in fact paid Onassis 50 million francs (then $125,000).

He soon fitted special tanks for any rare fish which might be picked up and passed on to the Oceanographic Museum, but his first long Mediterranean trip also gave him the chance to fulfil another of Prince Albert's ambitions. While cruising off the Canaries and North Africa, he put in at various places and brought back 32 animals to form the nucleus of the Centre d'Acclimatation Zoologique. It opened on Christmas Day, 1954 in an ideally sheltered corner of the principality near the Louis II Stadium. Here the animals could live in a natural environment, the mild temperature allowing them to be kept in the open air for most of the year. Rainier visited the centre almost daily and maintained an expert eye on conditions.

The *Christina*, blazing with lights and dwarfing every other yacht in the harbour, seemed to symbolise a plushy new régime.

Although Onassis was constantly jetting back and forth between Claridge's in London and his Paris apartment in the Avenue Foch, with frequent trips to Kuwait or New York to organise his new whaling fleet or launch yet another oil tanker, he had begun to stay longer in Monte Carlo. He and his wife entertained the Windsors, Margot Fonteyn and her husband, Roberto Arias, and visiting Hollywood celebrities like Clark Gable, the Bogarts, Merle Oberon and others.

Claudette Colbert preferred to play hostess. She rented Lady Kenmare's Villa Fiorentina for the summer months and gave original parties, including a memorable *luau* for 80 guests with sarongs for the ladies and a Hawaiian guitar orchestra. Maugham wore a crimson boutonnière in his white dinner jacket and sat on the ground barefooted like a true South Seas veteran. But he remembered to bring his soft cushion and also took the precaution of drinking dry Martinis instead of the lethal rum punch served by Garson Kanin.

Almost overnight Monte Carlo seemed revitalised. The SBM had streamlined its staff and swiftly moved out of the red with the return of many high-playing patrons. The hotels had received a much-needed facelift and the Place du Casino became a no-parking area with every yard of space down to the harbour massed, bumper to bumper, by sleek limousines. The local jewellers and florists registered almost pre-war profits and Madame Wanda, a former film actress who had survived Buchenwald, was kept busy in her Pets' Beauty Shop adjacent to the casino. She shampooed Mistinguett's poodle, the Begum Aga Khan's Aberdeen and a chow belonging to the ex-Emperor of Assam, Bao-Dai, who lived up to his name, 'Keeper of the Grandeur', during his years of exile. He bought himself a 30-roomed villa overlooking the sea, formed his own dance band and cruised around the principality in his fleet of six cars with a troupe of beautiful girls. But his losses at roulette finally dissipated his fortune. In his last years he played for amusement only, investing a few francs at the cheapest table in the 'Kitchen' or trying his luck on the fruit machines.

Another ex-monarch, King Farouk, arrived on the Côte d'Azur

after abdicating in July 1952. His dark glasses, immense Havana, and double-breasted suits, topped either by a stetson or a yachting cap, soon made him an unmistakable, if scarcely a popular, figure at the Carlton in Cannes whose staff lived in terror of his whims. When the maître d'hôtel, Josef, once enquired deferentially if he would like some special dish, Farouk replied, 'Yes. Your ears, poached'. His entourage laughed dutifully. It included a coffee-maker, a food-taster and a squad of bodyguards alert for any signs of the Egyptian gang reportedly hired to assassinate him.

He played baccarat with considerable success against the Greek Syndicate, both at Deauville and Cannes, but preferred to deal the cards himself at chemin-de-fer, which gave winning an added flavour. Appraised of his first visit to the Salon Privé in Monte Carlo, the management had requested all patrons to wear evening dress. Farouk, whose few virtues included a sense of humour, must have been told of this directive. He chose to make his entrance in a T-shirt and baggy shorts. He invariably kept playing until he was either on the winning side or had cut his losses to the minimum. He would sit, hour after hour, drinking bottles of Perrier or fresh raspberry juice, never alcohol. It helped to make him a redoubtable opponent for players less ruthless or self-controlled and lacking his almost endless reserves of capital.

He was at first welcomed by the Hotel de Paris to which he had transferred himself and his retinue from the Carlton. He tipped on an enormous scale but demanded round-the-clock service, however unreasonable. Whenever he returned from the casino he would call for his usual 'breakfast' of a 12-egg omelette, roast doves with a mountain of spaghetti, followed by assorted pastries. At lunch he doused his caviare with cream and disposed of a dozen lamb cutlets at high speed before seriously tackling the main menu.

Sulking one night in the Salon Privé after a bad run of the cards, he was handed a message from his first wife, Farida, who wished to discuss an important matter with him. Scowling, he scribbled on the back of the note, 'There is nothing to discuss'. Farida, who was waiting in an ante-room, turned to her companion and said quietly, 'Now there is only pity in my heart; pity, but no hate'.

His coarseness even overwhelmed Elsa Maxwell. She once refused a 'command' to dine with him and wired back, 'I don't dine with clowns, monkeys, profligates and evildoers'. He later sued her successfully for libel but had no redress for a snub from a beautiful young Englishwoman, who had steadily lost money to him at chemmy. He pushed one of his red million-franc plaques at her with an unmistakable leer. She picked up her little rake and steered the plaque towards the croupier, murmuring graciously, '*Pour le personnel*'.

The Hotel de Paris lost his patronage to the Métropole whose elderly waiters can still recall serving him with early-morning 'snacks' of six chickens. His huge tips helped to mollify the less fastidious for vulgar antics like fitting his Cadillac with a horn which, when honked, sounded exactly like a dog being run over. It was no great asset to the principality when he took Monegasque nationality in 1956 for tax purposes. This debarred him automatically from the Monte Carlo casino but he continued playing on the same scale at Deauville and Cannes, often against the Greek Syndicate or in opposition to Zanuck and Jack L. Warner.

The movie moguls, bitter studio rivals in Hollywood, seemed to enjoy their gambling sessions together. Warner, dapper, tanned and almost a ringer for the late Douglas Fairbanks Snr., was the more dashing of the two and had a disconcerting habit, dreaded by all casinos, of restlessly moving on to a rival resort after a winning run. Francois André never forgot the shock of a single night's play at the Palm Beach Casino when Warner, Zanuck and a Brazilian coffee magnate relieved the bank of £100,000 at baccarat and then drove off exuberantly to lose it all in Monte Carlo. Warner once dropped £25,000 at 'Le Sporting' in four hours' play and made for Cannes at 2 a.m. where he recouped most of his losses before dawn. Heading back to 'Aujourd'hui', the villa he had bought from Lily Pons, he drove his high-powered Alfa-Romeo into a 10-ton coal lorry. Within a few months he was back at the tables, on crutches but with all the old zest. In his high-rolling years on the Côte d'Azur he was only seriously put out once, when he locked away his winnings and took off for a business trip to Rome. One of his house guests then emptied the safe of $74,000.

Darryl Zanuck, short, dynamic and wiry, with a cigar clenched between his teeth and a man-sized Scotch at his elbow, had all Warner's card skill but laboured under a handicap named Bella Darvi, who cost him his marriage, a fortune in cash and also helped to wreck his position at 20th Century-Fox. When Zanuck first met her in Paris in 1951, she was an attractive Polish girl recently divorced from a wealthy husband. Zanuck paid her gambling debts, then a modest $2,000, and invited her to his home in Santa Monica. He also arranged a film test and starred her in one or two best-forgotten pictures. By 1954, when he followed her to France, he was completely infatuated and quite powerless to control her gambling mania. She once stripped off her rings and tossed them on the table to call a bet. Long after splitting with her in favour of Juliette Greco (another celluloid risk but, luckily for him, without much taste for baccarat), he salvaged her wardrobe which the Hotel de Paris had impounded for a long-unpaid bill.

Zanuck was not the easiest or most endearing of men, although he could be a staunch friend in adversity. One night in Antibes he was unceremoniously awakened by Orson Welles, who needed a mere $420 to pay off his cab. He had driven all the way from Italy where he had been shooting *Othello* and desperately needed $75,000 to meet his studio payroll. Although stripped through gambling losses and his already precarious position at Fox, Zanuck somehow managed to raise the cash. Welles blithely left the Hotel du Cap but turned back at the Italian frontier. Zanuck soon learned with horror that he had spent the past three nights at the Monte Carlo tables. However, he not only kept his $75,000 intact but even showed a modest profit before departing to finish his picture in Venice.

Players could enjoy reasonable privacy in the Salons Privés, where onlookers craned their necks from behind an iron rail, and the Sporting Club's gala nights, with dinner, dancing and gambling, were even more exclusive. Although it was harder to keep undesirables out of the popular rooms, a tight security system helped to discourage crooked operators. The only weak spot, as the management discovered in the mid-fifties, was the overcrowded and noisy dice tables which made supervision more difficult.

In February 1956 three Americans arrived from Los Angeles and checked in at the Hotel Ambassador. They were Jason Lee, an elderly man of Korean origin, who was ostensibly interested in buying marine salts for export to Japan; Phil Aggie, his so-called business associate; and a burly Lebanese–American, one Arif Shaker. The casino's security chief quickly recalled broken-nosed Lee and Aggie, who had a mouthful of gold teeth, as players who had lost heavily at craps during a recent visit. He very naturally assumed that they were back to try and recoup. Shaker, who had entered alone, was unknown to him.

They threw dice for the maximum of 40,000 francs (then £40) and ended a long session considerably in the red. Next night, however, their luck changed quite spectacularly. They threw so many winning sevens that the croupier suddenly raked in the dice and replaced them with another pair from his box. Lee, by far the biggest winner until then, lost a few throws before moving off to cash his considerable stack of chips. The others played a little longer, though prudently not for maximums. They also departed, but separately, and at discreet intervals.

In his office the white-haired Chief Inspector, Louis Cérisol, and his assistants were carefully examining the dice which the vigilant croupier had withdrawn from play. It soon became clear that the 'lucky' cubes must have come from the same Reno firm which manufactured the casino's own dice, but the Monte Carlo engraving, while skilfully copied, was still slightly darker than the genuine article. Calipers and scales also established the dice as a millimetre smaller, two milligrams heavier and weighted to produce a most gratifying sequence of sevens and elevens.

The syndicate was naturally disappointed by having its run interrupted but thought it prudent to leave with winnings of £5,000. Lee and Shaker checked out of the Hotel de Paris, to which they had transferred for the night, and took a taxi to Nice Airport where they booked three one-way tickets to Tangier. To avoid suspicion Aggie remained behind at the Ambassador but was already packed and about to leave when the Monegasque police courteously requested an interview. He disclaimed all knowledge of the missing couple and indignantly repudiated the slur on his honour. The police seemed satisfied but took the precaution of tapping his telephone. They were quickly rewarded by an impatient call from Nice demanding his presence at the Air France terminal where, soon afterwards, the trio were arrested. Shaker's baggage disclosed a wad of traveller's cheques, bought with the Monte Carlo winnings, and 164 pairs of loaded dice, some rather clumsily doctored to exclude inconvenient twos, threes and fives.

The accused were sentenced in Monaco but soon pardoned and sent on their way. They owed their good fortune to Prince Rainier, who had benevolently amnestied all offenders in celebration of his marriage. For Francois André and others, who had long provided such stiff competition to the principality, Rainier's wedding had a particularly bitter flavour. The romance had first taken root in Cannes' very own Film Festival.

Chapter Eleven

PRINCE RAINIER has said, 'May must be my lucky month. I was born on the 23rd, came to the throne on the 9th, and met Grace for the first time on the 6th (1955)'. She had previously visited Monaco only once, while on location for Hitchcock's *To Catch a Thief*, when Tina Onassis invited her and her co-star, Cary Grant, to lunch. Onassis miscued on that occasion by asking her, 'Are you also connected with the motion picture industry?' A surprising gaffe, since by that time Grace Patricia Kelly had practically qualified as Hollywood's First Lady after a short but spectacular career.

Her mother, Margaret, was a former fashion model and physical education instructor at the University of Pennsylvania. Her father, John Brendan Kelly, the son of an immigrant from County Mayo, had prospered from a lowly start as a bricklayer by borrowing $7,000 to found a construction business with his brother. A fine oarsman, he entered for Henley in 1920 but was rejected as a 'non-gentleman', having worked with his hands. Soon afterwards he had the satisfaction of trouncing the English champion at the Brussels Olympics. His son, John, won the Diamond Sculls at Henley 27 years later and repeated the feat in the following year. By then Grace, 17, was heading for New York and her first term at the American Academy of Dramatic Art. Her only connection with the theatre was through an uncle who had played in vaudeville, and another, George Kelly, a Pulitzer-winning playwright, but her most treasured childhood memory was being kissed, as a seven year-old, by Douglas Fairbanks Jr. when he visited the home of John Kelly, then Mayor of Philadelphia.

She was brought up in a comfortable 15-roomed house in Philadelphia and attended the Raven Hill Academy run by nuns before spending some years at Stevens School, where she acted in plays. She had briefly contemplated becoming a children's teacher but decided on a two-year dramatic course. 'We hoped she would give it up', Mrs Kelly used to reminisce, 'as these stage people live such shallow lives'. While studying in New York she did part-time photographic modelling. Contemporaries recall her as already very cool and self-possessed, insisting on being paid the full Madison Avenue rate of $25 an hour. She took her Academy diploma and made a few TV appearances prior to some experience in summer stock. She then made an inconspicuous Broadway début as Raymond Massey's daughter in Strindberg's *The Father* in which she caught the eye of a Hollywood producer. Her film test caused very little excitement. The cameraman firmly declared, 'She generates absolutely nothing,' but it led to a part in a low-budget suspense thriller.

High Noon, opposite Gary Cooper, first registered her in the affections of movie fans, and MGM were quick to offer a seven-year contract, soon justified by *Mogambo* in which she was excitingly partnered by Clark Gable. Even her warmest admirers could not rank her as an actress in the Garbo or Bergman class, but a shrewd connoisseur like Gable came nearest perhaps in assessing her unique appeal; 'her cool looks seem to hide a promise of smouldering sex, and every man thinks he could be the one to ignite the flame'. There were rumours of a secret romance but, already in his fifties, Gable was drinking heavily and had the unattractive habit of removing his dentures with shaky hands to demonstrate his 'irresistible smile'. When he broke with MGM and went to 20th Century-Fox, she sidestepped his plea to co-star in *Soldier of Fortune* and, as a strict Catholic, any thought of becoming his fifth wife.

Framed by corn-gold hair, her face had an Ingrès-like delicacy. She was rather squarer of jaw and shoulder than her celluloid image and also looked less tall off-screen, but audiences were captivated by her serenity and an aura of reticence which not only complemented to perfection such varied personalities as Gable, Cooper, Stewart, Milland and Crosby but thawed delightfully in light comedy. Hitchcock, one of the earliest to sense her 'sexual elegance', directed her in several successes, followed by *The Country Girl* which won her an Oscar for the Best Actress of 1954.

Rivals, jealous of her success with an income averaging £70,000 a year, considered her over-rated and hinted darkly at the advantages of family wealth and connections. She was undoubtedly spared the traditional casting couch preliminaries or having to pose for cheesecake publicity stills, but her independence proved far more valuable in the long term by giving her some freedom to choose her own rôles. Her large pale blue eyes were myopic, but she could still see and understand the fine print on any contract. Equally important, she remained level-headed despite her very rapid sequence of box-office hits. Although fun-loving and squired by a succession of glamorous leading men, she avoided wild parties and remained immune from the usual Hollywood gossip, commuting placidly between California and New York where she spent most of her time sketching or taking pictures developed in the privacy of her apartment. Voted among the World's Best Dressed Women and pursued by photographers, it was impossible to avoid malicious tittle-tattle. The absurd rumour that Ray Milland was so infatuated that he had left his wife sent an alarmed Margaret Kelly hotfoot to Hollywood. Oleg Cassini, the fashion designer, may have come closest to any firm romance, but, as a divorced man, he was judged ineligible by the strictly Catholic Kellys.

Arrangements had been finalised for *High Society*, with Sinatra and Crosby, when Grace arrived in Cannes for the 1955 Film Festival. As the guest of Elsa Maxwell, she dined one night with Van Johnson, Charles Boyer, Olivia de Havilland and her husband,

Pierre Gallante, then a director of Paris *Match*, who suggested that his magazine might welcome a picture story on Grace. He considered Monaco an ideal background and Rainier readily agreed to act as palace guide.

Grace arrived, coolly elegant in a flowered dress with her hair in a chignon, without hint of having survived a windswept journey from Cannes in which she narrowly avoided a head-on collision. Rainier showed her round the palace and they went out to view the harbour from the ramparts while the cameras clicked away. The visit ended in less than an hour after Grace had nervously admired two Sumatra tigers newly arrived for Rainier's Zoo. She was startled when he put his arm through the cage to embrace one of the animals. 'I think she was more used to poodles', he drily commented. The film party were in too much of a hurry to stop even for a cup of tea although arrangements had been made to entertain them. It had been a rather formal meeting, with the magazine publicity an obvious priority, but Rainier had taken a liking to his visitor, who seemed refreshingly different from all he had heard or read about pampered screen goddesses. Grace later confided to her mother that his courtesy and shyness, unexpected for a prince, flatly contradicted reports of the playboy reputation. She wrote a cordial thank-you letter to which he replied amiably, but with nothing on either side to promise a more intimate relationship.

He was preoccupied throughout that summer by a serious financial crisis. The semi-official Monaco Banking and Precious Metals Society had over-invested in a group set up to exploit Monte Carlo's commercially sponsored radio and TV stations. It collapsed into bankruptcy, leaving the government responsible for almost half the £3 million deficiency. Many depositors lost money in the bank which remained closed for three months, while accusations of incompetence, and possibly worse, flew around. Rainier had hurriedly reshuffled his government and also appointed more reliable members to the bank's management committee, but the only hope of salvage came from a French consortium who, among other assets, acquired from the liquidators half the 74,000 shares in

'Images et Sons', the holding company which owned the transmission station up at Mont Agel.

During this unsettled period Rainier could not press his economy-minded Council for action on either the tunnel or further land reclamation. He was also thwarted by the long absence of Onassis, who had gone to Washington to face accusations of having fraudulently acquired a contract to carry Saudi-Arabian oil in his tankers (an obvious threat to powerful American interests, like Standard Oil) and demands to refund the earnings from American surplus ships which he was alleged to have obtained illegally. The criminal charges were dropped and a settlement laboriously reached by which the Onassis interests paid $7 million in compensation. He then formed a $20 million Trust in favour of his children, Alexander and Christina, both American-born, and guaranteed the building of new tankers in the United States.

His savage handling by the Maritime Commission and others rankled long afterwards. He once commented wryly, no doubt with Zaharoff in mind, 'In England I would have been knighted; in America I was indicted'. The undertow of scandal tugged him even more strongly towards Monte Carlo where a new social secretary, supplementing his high-powered public relations expert, issued details of the *Christina*'s glamorous celebrity guests. In that winter of 1955, with Onassis still licking his wounds, the prince made his first trip to America, but in very different circumstances.

When Gisèle Pascal married the French actor, Raymond Pellegrin, in October, Monaco again began speculating whether Rainier, seemingly rooted in his bachelor ways, would ever marry. He mentioned in a TV interview that his 'dream girl' would have 'blonde hair, be very feminine and have clever blue eyes'. Nobody took this remark as anything but lighthearted, except perhaps Father Tucker, who had noted Rainier's sudden enthusiasm for Grace Kelly's films, and Russell Austin, an oilman from New Jersey, who met the prince that autumn during a pleasure tour of Europe and declared afterwards that 'he talked of nothing but

Grace'. She had urged 'Uncle Russ', a family friend, to telephone Prince Rainier for any special facilities he might require while in Monaco. He took the hint on discovering that all tickets had been snapped up for a gala at the Sporting Club. A telephone call to the palace was switched to Father Tucker, who was instructed to present two tickets with the prince's compliments. Austin called next day to thank Rainier and cordially invited him to visit if ever he found himself in the United States.

The opportunity came very quickly, thanks to Father Tucker, who had arranged to return home to renew his religious vows. He had no difficulty in persuading Rainier, who had long promised himself an American trip, to cross the Atlantic with him. They sailed from Le Havre on 8 December, Rainier having vaguely explained his absence from Monaco at Christmas by his need of a check-up at the Mayo Clinic and the chance of some barracuda fishing.

There seemed no time either for fishing or the medical examination. Rainier travelled incognito as 'Mr Grimaldi' but was accompanied by an Italo-American bodyguard whom the State Department had insisted on providing. He rented a car and headed for Florida where he visited the winter quarters of the Sarasota Circus. They stayed at a modest hotel in Tampa run by one of the Big Top's proprietors, who only discovered their identity when Rainier's picture was splashed over every newspaper. 'Grimaldi and Cresci?' he exploded later, flourishing his hotel register. 'Heck, I thought they were a spaghetti-bender tumbling act I had hired!'

Rainier returned north to spend Christmas Eve in Margate, New Jersey, with the Russell Austins, who also passed on an invitation for him to dine next day at the Kelly home in Philadelphia. He and Grace danced after dinner to gramophone records. He stayed the night and next day went on to Wilmington for Father Tucker's religious ceremony. The upshot was a visit by the priest to Grace's father who learned, not without some surprise, that the couple had come to 'an understanding'. He gave his provisional consent on being assured that the prince was 'not only noble by birth but in deed and character'. But Monaco still had no inkling of the romance when the prince recorded a Christmas message in which he cheerfully assured his subjects that 'the Principality is known and loved here'.

He followed Grace to New York where they met several times during the next few days. He formally proposed and was accepted at a private New Year's Eve party. Reporters soon scented the truth and, on the 4th, bluntly asked Grace at the Stork Club 'to confirm or deny'. She smiled non-committally. Following a family celebration lunch next day in Philadelphia, Rainier telephoned the palace and authorised his Minister of State to announce the engagement. He returned home in February after spending a month in Hollywood where his fiancée was working on *High Society*.

The world's press bubbled with stories of a lightning romance, but Rainier later declared firmly, 'It was not love at first sight. Ours was a gradual falling in love. We were both ready for marriage'. He was then 32, six years older than Grace. He still smiles indulgently when recalling Father Tucker's slightly noveletish account of his alleged lovesickness: 'The prince telephoned me one day and said, "Father, I have met *the* girl"', admitting that it was Grace Kelly. "My Lord Prince, that's the kind of girl I want you to marry." And he said, "Father, you'll have to help me out", and I carried on from there'.

As soon as the wedding date was announced for 18 April 1956, Monaco was almost submerged under an avalanche of gossip. It embarrassed Rainier whose publicity office was more geared for casino chit-chat than a real-life de Mille extravaganza. Gossip crackled back and forth across the Atlantic. MGM announced that the bride would start a new picture six weeks after the wedding, but Rainier doubted that his wife would ever act again. Father Tucker told reporters that Gisèle Pascal was 'a very nice girl', adding a mite ungallantly, 'For six years I have been trying to prevent the Prince marrying the wrong woman'.

Every scrap of news, true or false, was being chewed over round the world. Even the gifts made front page stories. The casino's croupiers presented an ivory hand-carved chess set but nobody would have been surprised if they had formed a wedding arch of crossed rakes to counteract the welter of publicity from the bride's native land. MGM's chief designer, Helen Rose, was responsible for the wedding gown and the studio presented the bridesmaids' dresses created by Neiman Marcus of Dallas, Texas. All the clothes worn in Grace's last picture, *High Society*, formed part of her £15,000 trousseau. Eight sponsors, including Lanvin, Coty, Slenderella and Purex Cleaning Tissues, backed the TV and radio coverage. When Mrs Kelly heard that the Peter Pan Girdle and Brassière Company would also participate, she snorted, 'Brassières! That's the last thing Grace needs.'

Prince Rainier had his own pre-nuptial troubles. He graciously accepted a Rolls-Royce Silver Cloud from his subjects and complimented Onassis on his choice of an exquisite ruby-studded bracelet, but the National Council fared less well with their £35,000 necklace which turned out so tasteless in design and setting that they hurriedly decided to buy something more acceptable. A distasteful lawsuit ensued when the jeweller refused to return the deposit and demanded full payment.

The Kellys arrived a week before the wedding in the American liner *Constitution* which put in first at Cannes to unload two truckfulls of baggage. It had been an uncomfortable eight-day crossing for the bride, not a good sailor at the best of times. Rainier sailed out to meet her in his yacht, but a heavy swell made it difficult to come alongside and a carpet of red carnations slid down the gangway into the angry sea. Grace finally boarded the *Deo Juvante*, clutching her terrified poodle, Oliver, who looked unprepared for hundreds of ship's sirens, a 21-gun salute from anti-aircraft cannons lent by the French and a mammoth firework welcome from the *Christina*.

Of the 1,800 reporters, cameramen and publicists who had converged on Monaco for 'the Wedding of the Century', a considerable quota was assigned to cover the bride's arrival. Some photographers, who had paid up to £100 for a place in the launch to meet the *Constitution*, became exasperated when Miss Kelly appeared at last in a huge mushroom hat which almost hid her features. They were even more put out by the scramble aboard the

Deo Juvante where the 76-strong Kelly party crammed into a tiny saloon with Monegasque notables and tried to sip champagne served by a corps of waiters in tailcoats and white gloves.

Rooms at the palace were reserved for the bride and her parents, now on the warmest terms of informality with 'Ray', who dutifully reciprocated by addressing Mr Kelly as 'Pop'. Other guests stayed in hotels, already bursting at the seams, and hundreds of visitors had to take to the hills. Many of the bride's American friends fretted over their accommodation or demanded seats in the Cathedral which could hold only 600 maximum. Grace kept an appearance of calm during the frantic round of last-minute fusses and salaams from local functionaries, who protested that the Hollywood contingent was leaving them only crumbs from the publicity wedding cake. The photographers, demented by unseasonable rain, made it almost impossible for Rainier or his bride to venture beyond the palace walls. When they managed to escape for a picnic, a French magazine photographer pursued them into the mountains and practically threw himself under the wheels of Rainier's car.

Only Father Tucker, plainly relishing his rôle of Cupid in a cassock, seemed to be enjoying himself. He gave almost non-stop interviews – on paper, radio and TV – and reminded Art Buchwald with a chuckle, 'Sure, marriages are made in heaven, but safety matches are made by man'. Still glowing with sentimentality, he offended the devout by preaching a wedding-eve sermon in which he reminded the congregation, 'The Prince is keeping an oath that cost him a young man's love. He is keeping an oath for you, his people'. Although politically well-intentioned, this whisper from Rainier's past romance was unlikely to cheer the couple, but Grace's first broadcast pleased her future subjects. She assured them, 'The Prince, my fiancé, has taught me to love you'. Others were more grandiloquent. Two actors on TV read Cocteau's florid 'Tribute to the Prince of Monaco', and Robert W. Service, since 1946 a local resident in Monte Carlo where he still took two sea dips every day at the age of 80, rashly decided to turn Poet Laureate. He wrote some commemorative verses which only a sadist would reproduce in full. Readers will be mercifully spared more than a teaspoon of his treacle:

> *To G.K.*
> Princess, what magic pen was dipped
> In radiant colours of romance
> To write the wonder of your script,
> Your fairy tale of chance . . .
> A people we, proud of our Past,
> From modern urgency afar,
> Long have we hoped with faith steadfast
> To hail with ecstasy a Star.
> Sweet Princess, may our dreams come true –
> Our Star be you.

Monaco's hard-pressed police were understandably less lyrical after several Old Masters had been ripped from the walls of a local villa. A bridesmaid lost jewels worth £3,750 while attending the wedding rehearsals, and thieves snatched a batch of stamps issued for the occasion. An even worse shock was the appearance of a notorious gentleman cracksman, René ('Swagger Stick') Gigier, formerly France's Public Enemy Number One. Elegant in a tight-fitting white uniform, he flourished his official pass as chauffeur to Princess Charlotte, the bridegroom's mother, whom he had driven down from Marchais. 'I thought the air and sun would do him good' she told reporters. 'His health is delicate after his years in prison'·

'René La Canne', who had been paroled to her custody while serving a 20-year stretch for armed robbery, had previously crashed two of her cars. He fared no better after she had optimisti-cally set him up as a bookseller in Rheims when he tired of garden-ing at Marchais. Knowing he was being watched in Monaco, he trod warily and avoided his old chums from the Marseilles underworld. Nevertheless, the local gendarmerie shared Rainier's intense relief when René at last headed north with his employer.

On the morning of 18 April a civil ceremony was held in the Throne Room, preceding the solemnisation next day in the Cathedral. After weeks of hammering rain, the sun at last shone from a clear blue sky. The tiny-waisted First Lady of Monaco, wearing a gown of 'pale caramel lace', walked up the nave on her father's arm, soon joined by His Serene Highness in full dress uniform with a red and white sash and a breastful of medals. The couple took their vows under a merciless battery of flashlights with TV and movie cameras poised to record the tiniest twitch of an eyelid as the rings, presented on white satin cushions by two pages, were nervously exchanged. One or two unauthorised reporters, masquerading as cassocked priests, had to be winkled out, and a photographer, smuggled into the orchestra, almost succeeded in focussing his Long Tom camera from a bassoon while the Archbishop, flanked by a beaming Father Tucker, pronounced the Benediction.

At five that evening the couple sailed out in the *Deo Juvante* to the screeching of sirens and with rockets linking the flags of Monaco and the United States by parachute. As the sea was rough, the yacht anchored for the night at Villefranche before proceeding on the six-week honeymoon cruise to Majorca and round the Spanish coast. From Valencia the newly-weds motored to Madrid where Franco entertained them to lunch.

The inevitable stampede to run 'festivals' of Grace Kelly films supported MGM's exuberant prediction that she would soon be resuming her Hollywood career. Only the London *Times* hinted at longer-term benefits for a principality still reeling from its recent banking disaster: 'After this famous romance Monte Carlo will be found graven on every romanticist's heart. More to the point, perhaps, it will be printed bold on the luggage labels of Americans bound for a holiday in Europe'. It was a shrewd forecast. Henceforth even the casino would have to share star billing with Princess Grace as Monte Carlo's main tourist attraction.

Some time afterwards I drove with Francois André along the Croisette past the luxury hotels, new apartment blocks and thronged beaches towards the site of the huge marina near Palm Beach Casino. He pointed his umbrella in the direction of Monaco and declared wistfully, 'Here at Cannes we hold all the cards – except the Queen of Hearts.'

Part Three

THE YEARS OF GRACE

Chapter Twelve

ON HER 12th wedding anniversary Princess Grace told an interviewer, 'When I married Prince Rainier, I married the man, not what he was or who he was. I fell in love with him, no matter how it might all turn out. What followed was a good deal more difficult than I had thought. I am basically a shy person and do not like being with people I don't know. I had to get over that . . . My husband is a very shy person too. I think that in a way we helped each other along.'

She had to adapt to the slower and more formal European tempo, quite apart from familiarising herself with local complexities like the political and economic upheavals which continued to disturb the principality long after the collapse of the Monaco Bank. Her first task was to supplement her schoolgirl French with colloquial lessons. Fortunately, her acting experience had made her 'a quick study' and she made rapid progress with Rainier's help. It was less easy to conform to the stiff palace protocol on curtseying, precedence and other alien incidentals. She found it tiresome to have 15 footmen ritually in attendance at dinner and offended some dignitaries by inviting them to buffets and even replacing the formal banquets with intimate parties at which guests sat less primly at a number of small tables.

For her first official appearance at a Cathedral Mass to celebrate

America's Independence Day, she broke an unwritten law by wearing a rather low neckline and, perhaps worse, a large picture hat which made photography unrewarding. At a Sporting Club gala she unwisely went to the other extreme in a simple white gown unadorned by jewels. It did not endear her to the more ornate fashion plates on parade.

Homesick at first without her family and old friends, she shipped over most of the furniture from her New York apartment, together with three of her nursery dolls which would later be passed to her own daughters. She visited her parents in October and confirmed reports of her pregnancy. She and her husband were received by the Eisenhowers at the White House but returned with some relief to Monaco after reporters had quizzed Grace incessantly about her 'interrupted' film career. She was professionally skilled in fielding troublesome questions but Rainier, long accustomed to privacy, showed less patience with journalists and studio opportunists. He stubbornly refused to allow her old films to be shown in the principality and won an injunction in Paris against a gramophone company, who wished to issue a record of Grace's *High Society* songs in a folder bearing the arms of Monaco with their portraits.

While awaiting the birth of her first child, the princess set about modernising the palace by installing lifts and central heating. She also supervised the layout of a beautiful tropical garden to fringe their new pool where swimming was possible for at least five months a year. 'She has brought a much-needed feminine touch to the social look of the Principality, and certainly the palace is now more of a home' Rainier declared gratefully. 'It was a bit mothballish before she arrived.'

She liked sailing – in smooth waters – but fretted during their first summer together when Rainier skin-dived alarmingly off Corsica to test some new underwater equipment. She had never felt comfortable in the *Deo Juvante* which Rainier soon replaced with a 40 year-old Spanish cargo boat. The *Costa del Sol* was refitted at Toulon with four bathrooms and a small oceanographic laboratory, but Rainier had to admit, 'without bananas in the bottom, it still rolls'. The *Christina's* stabilisers became even more attractive to the seasick-prone princess, who enjoyed short cruises with the Onassises, despite ill-founded gossip that Tina resented being deposed as 'Queen of Monte Carlo'. She gave a lavish party at the Hotel de Paris to honour Rainier's birthday and he sat down at the drums to accompany Ari's exuberant guitar solo.

But he now tended to avoid parties and surprised advisers by his serious application to official work. Domesticity suited him. After the daily round of visits or audiences, with at least three hours before dinner allocated to talks with his ministers, he and the princess preferred a light meal followed by a session of gramophone records. He would put on his collection of Negro spirituals or Al Jolson songs, and they danced cheek to cheek to Stan Kenton standards and new slow foxtrot discs sent over by Mrs Kelly. Most evenings they settled down in their small private cinema. Grace usually had her way after giving him his fair ration of Westerns and detective thrillers which were less to her taste. They would often be joined by Prince Pierre with whom Grace had established a warm and lasting rapport. With Rainier's approval, they helped to inaugurate open-air summer concerts in the Cour d'Honneur, with the Heracles Gallery forming a romantic background between two white marble staircases.

Relations with her mother-in-law were less happy after various embarrassments like Princess Charlotte's appeal to the police to have 'René la Canne' moved from Marchais as she could no longer guarantee his parole. Malicious gossip also started when Princess Antoinette, a very popular figure, relinquished her long-time presidency of the Monaco Red Cross to her sister-in-law, who would perform the rôle with much energy and devotion. Antoinette, who divorced Noghues in 1954 and now lived at Eze with her three children and a small menagerie of pinschers, black poodles, cats and birds, had dutifully acted as First Lady until her brother's marriage. She remained a dedicated patron of child welfare but inevitably took a backseat when Grace initiated a municipal crèche and took a very active part in the reconstruction of Monaco's hospital.

Good sense and dignity on both sides avoided fuelling stories of a vendetta, invented by irresponsible French magazine hacks, but Antoinette's visits became less frequent and practically ceased altogether after her second marriage, in the Monegasque Consulate at The Hague, to Maître Jean-Charles Rey, one of Rainier's strongest critics on the Council. Some noted that Antoinette was no longer invited to receptions in honour of foreign dignitaries, and she limited her palace appearances to formal family gatherings like the christening of her niece, Princess Caroline.

The baby was born on 23 January 1957 in the four-poster which Rainier and his wife had shared since their return from honeymoon. The event was accorded a 21-gun salute. Few shared the gloom of an English resident, who noted that the cannon were trained on the casino and growled, 'I only wish they were loaded.' His sentiment was fully endorsed by another disappointed gambler, Robert E. Sherwood, the six-foot-four playwright and former speech writer to Roosevelt. He took the pledge one night on discovering painfully that the green baize was indeed an idiot's delight. After a last drink at the casino he declared emphatically, 'None but the brave chemin-de-fer.'

Ava Gardner had been among the first to call at the palace with flowers. She was one of Princess Grace's many Hollywood friends to become regular visitors to the principality. Danny Kaye arrived to give a concert and moved Grace with reports of his UNICEF travels on behalf of deprived children. He has never forgotten his first visit to the casino. Looking up at the ornate ceiling where a cigar-smoking nymph had only draped her feet, he commented, 'She looks scared that the water's going to bite her.' His guide smiled and pointed out a distinguished old lady tremulously risking her 5-franc chips in the Kitchen. She had posed for that very painting back in 1903.

Grace shared her husband's distaste for gambling and once cheerfully admitted that, while she liked watching horse racing, she was 'far too stingy' to enjoy a bet, however small. A devout Catholic, she had been impressed during her first Easter in the principality by the Good Friday torchlight procession when the

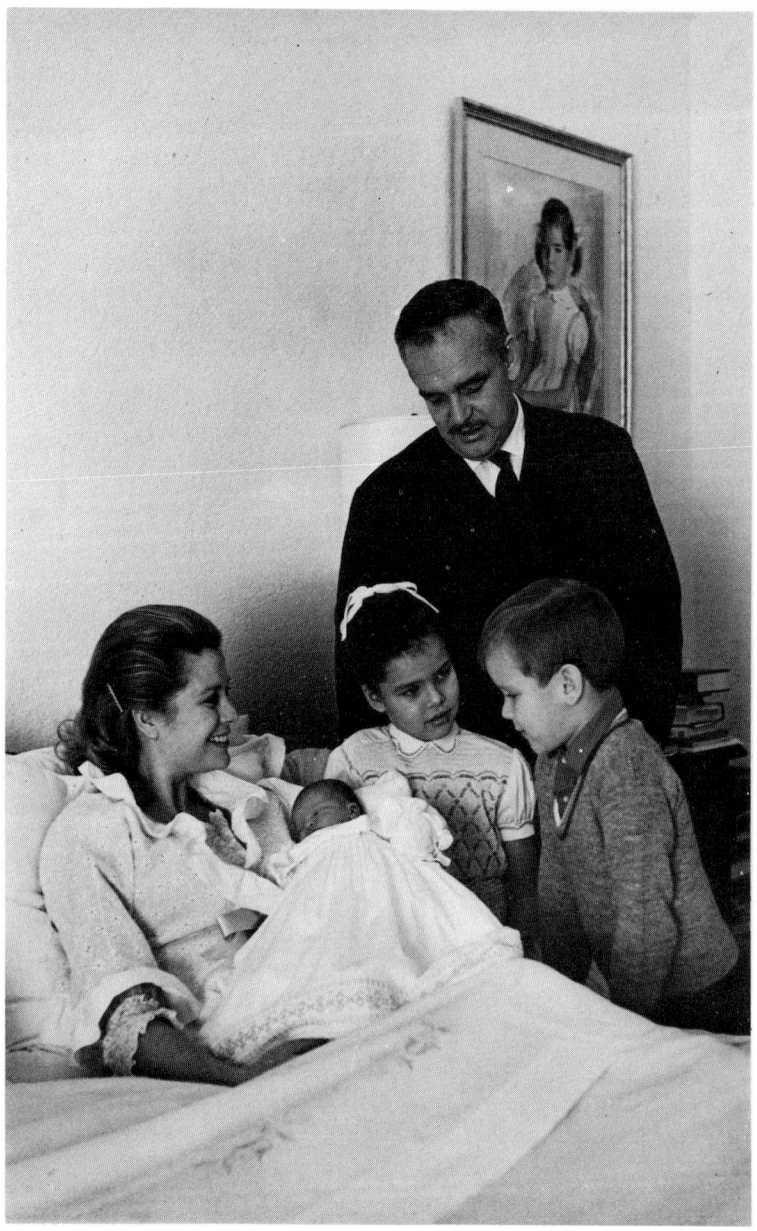

The Palace of Monaco, February, 1965. Princess Grace introduces her baby daughter, Stephanie, to her husband, Caroline and Albert.

Grace in galley of the 3 double-bunked *Carostephal*. That day she cooked a meal of spinach tart, salad and spaghetti.

President de Gaulle stops for a word with Caroline during a State Visit, October 1960. Two years later, friendly relations broke off over alleged tax evasion by French residents.

Onassis with (left) the novelist, Françoise Sagan, and his first wife, Christina, who later married Lord Blandford and then Stavros Niarchos (her sister's former husband).

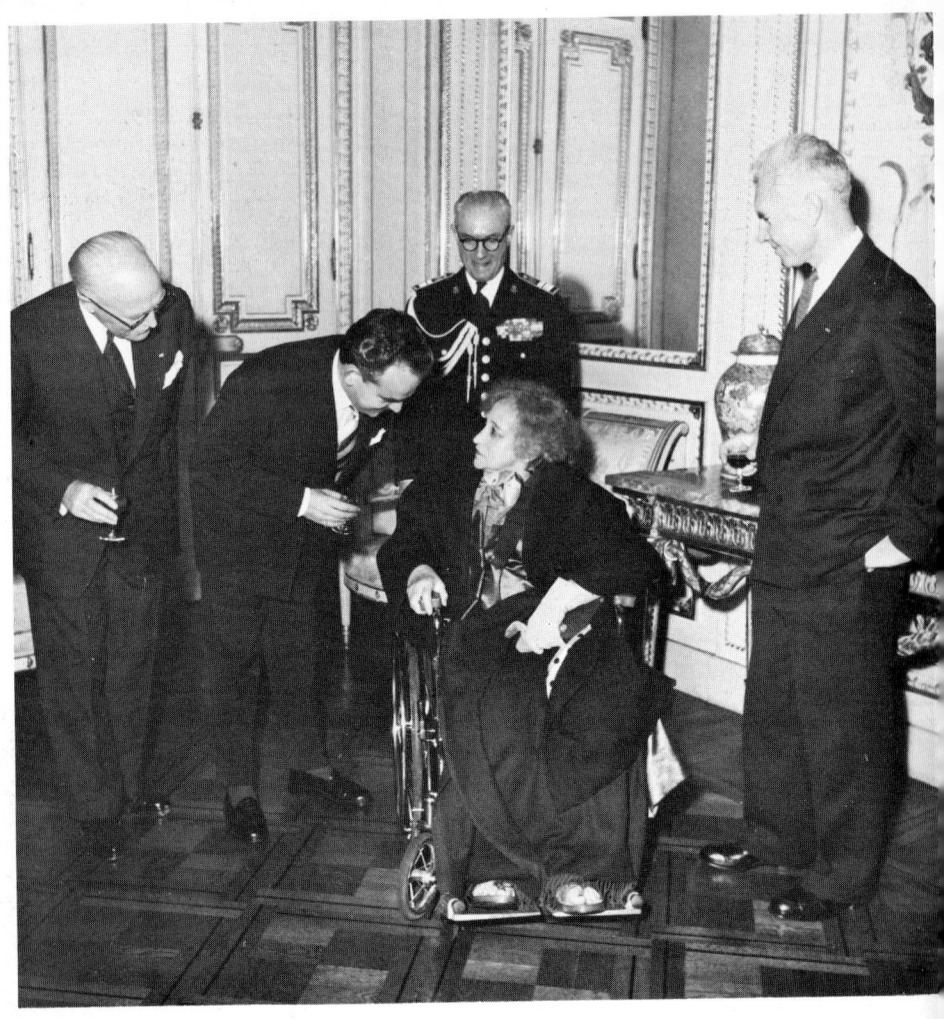

Prince Rainier greets Colette at a Hotel de Paris reception. She once described Monaco as 'a principality whose only frontiers are flowers'.

Prince Rainier, Princess Grace and their children in the Palace drawing room.

Rainier gives Albert a steering lesson
aboard the family yacht, *Stalcia,* a
69-tonner manned by a crew of two

Rainier welding in his workshop at
Roc Agel, the ranch house over the
French border where the family ofte
retreats at weekends or in the summ
months.

David Niven, a close friend of the Rainiers, dancing with Maria Callas.

The Begum Aga Khan, a former French beauty queen, came over from her villa near Cannes.

The new Summer Sporting Club

Gala opening June 1974

Prince Rainier partners his vivacious 18-year-old daughter, Caroline, always a target for the cameramen.

Aerial view of the crowded harbour. (Left) the Stade Nautique Rainier III, ringed by the now familiar skyscraper apartment towers and office blocks. Only Monaco-Ville (the old town, with the palace and administrative buildings) still retains its mediaeval charm.

figures of the dead Christ and those present at His Passion are solemnly carried through the narrow streets of Monaco-Ville. But she was horrified to learn that the casino remained open for play in the afternoon of the holiest day in the Christian Calendar.[1] The authorities remained intractable on this point but she won a minor campaign for the abolition of pigeon-shooting. Rainier conveyed her views to Onassis, who good-humouredly agreed to ban this attraction although reminded by others that rival resorts like Deauville and San Remo were less squeamish.

The loss was more than compensated by Grace's photogenic appeal. The palace revenues benefited at once from the sale of thousands of picture postcards and souvenir stamps, but the princess firmly discouraged autograph hounds, who attempted to accost her whenever she went shopping in Monte Carlo. Brash French photographers and over-familiar fans, with her adoring countrywomen in the majority, soon discovered that she had no intention of posing eternally on a Christmas tree like some glazed sugar plum fairy. But no other playground could guarantee such sure-fire coverage when the glamorous ex-Hollywood star opened fêtes or took the floor with her husband at the Sporting Club's galas.

In the palace she played charming hostess to Stirling Moss and Fangio, whose Maseratis won the Grand Prix in successive years, followed by Jack Brabham, who lifted the trophy in a $2\frac{1}{2}$-litre Cooper-Climax. Rainier, a racing car buff himself, and still taking mountain roads rather too fast for his wife's comfort, sympathised with Brabham's ordeal. On a day of blazing heat, with his feet almost roasting in the cockpit, he crossed the winning line after averaging 107 kms/h. in under three hours.[2] That 1959 Grand Prix drew a bumper crowd of spectators, who had not only come to see the race, with Princess Grace afterwards presenting the winning trophies, but were stimulated by a recently-shown colour documentary, *Invitation to Monaco*. Rainier had done some

[1] Apart from Good Friday night, the gaming rooms close only on the 1st of May.
[2] Brabham went on that year to capture his first world championship but never again won the coveted Monaco Grand Prix.

skin-diving and baby Caroline upstaged both her parents, as well as Sinatra, who made a guest appearance.

The success of this picture, worth untold millions of francs in potential tourist revenue, may have encouraged Grace to advocate an International TV Festival to counteract the Cannes film junket. The first, held in January 1961, showed entries from a dozen nations including the U.S.S.R. It soon became such an established attraction that Rainier began pressing for more co-operation from Onassis on the entertainment front. Despite the casino's huge profits which had soared almost from the royal wedding day, the SBM seemed to be dragging its feet, particularly over plans for a new Summer Sporting Club.

The projected tunnel to remove the railway had at last started on 12 April 1958, but it was making slow progress and costs mounted, month after month. Meanwhile, Rainier kept reminding Onassis that middle-income visitors, many on package tours, needed less costly hotels and *pensions*, a good stretch of beach, and more imaginative entertainment generally than the casino's fruit machines or a tour of the Oceanographic Museum.

Onassis argued blandly that he had sunk over a million sterling in adding four floors of suites, each the last word in luxury, to the Hotel de Paris. This rotunda was dominated by 'Le Grill', a roof-top restaurant with wrought-iron lanterns, antique roasting spits and an electrically operated sliding roof for warm summer nights. Rainier, then pre-occupied with plans for building factories and workers' apartment blocks in the reclaimed Larvotto quarter, disappointed Onassis with his muted approval of this new haven for well-heeled sophisticates.

They had begun to draw apart, although Rainier still enjoyed the Greek's company and spoke of him as 'a very pleasant man and great fun on his boat'. His meetings with the prince were rarely formal and usually ended in good-humoured banter. Onassis once observed that the Jews excelled at business, but not shipping. 'What about Noah?' Rainier asked teasingly. 'You've got something there' Onassis agreed with a wink. 'However, don't forget the damn fellow had a monopoly!'

But a touch of acidity had entered their relationship. Both were too disposed to make off-the-cuff remarks which looked rather less flippant in cold print. Rainier took offence when the shipowner lightly confessed to having 'only two toys; the *Christina* and the SBM', while Onassis, sensitive to his origins, did not appreciate the prince's aside that 'Monte Carlo is getting more like Monte Greco every day'. Another possible cause of friction was Princess Grace's sympathy with Tina Onassis over the Maria Callas liaison, vulgarised by so much unpalatable newspaper gossip. She and Rainier took the Vatican's disapproving line and supported the prima donna's husband, who stubbornly opposed an annulment.

The SBM emerged as the only beneficiaries from this unhappy affair when a mysterious wave of buying, mainly through hard-to-trace nominees, sent its stock spiralling. It was freely rumoured that Tina's father, Stavros Livanos, nettled by the break-up of her marriage, aimed to destroy his son-in-law's hegemony in Monte Carlo. Onassis had to increase his majority holding by buying more shares at an inflated price.

Rainier still considers that Tina's divorce action, soon followed by her marriage to Lord Blandford, the Duke of Marlborough's heir, soured her ex-husband's disposition and made him even more intractable. 'He may have taken an unconscious dislike to Monte Carlo' Rainier told his biographer, Peter Hawkins. 'All at once I discovered that there was no longer any dialogue possible with him'. But this view of an embittered Onassis does not easily square with the socialising years that followed when Churchill and other celebrity guests were regally entertained at the Hotel de Paris or aboard the *Christina*. It can also be argued, with at least equal validity, that since his own marriage and notably after the birth of his son and heir, Rainier had himself grown more self-willed and intolerant of all opposition to what he considered Monaco's best interests.

Individualists both, they saw the principality's future from widely divergent positions. Rainier would constantly maintain that the Greek's primary interest was 'press coverage and social standing – it gave him a visiting card to get his business going, and it was a good place to get started socially, too'. True, no doubt, but Onassis also rescued the SBM from near-bankruptcy and certainly helped to restore Monte Carlo to almost its pre-1914 splendour. As an autocrat, whose tanker and whaling fleet operations involved billions of dollars, he naturally disliked subjecting himself to a prince, who had power through a docile bureaucracy to veto building permits even on the SBM's own sites.

Another source of friction was lack of contact. Onassis paid only short visits to Monaco, which necessarily ranked as merely one of his manifold global interests, while Rainier, unlike his absentee predecessors, was spending at least nine months of the year in his principality. His short annual trips to the United States had also made him enthusiastic for transatlantic business drive and enterprise. At the palace he welcomed American industrialists, vacationing on the Riviera, and always asked searching questions about the latest mechanical gadgets and developments in electronics. Within a year or two of his marriage he had already begun to resent rubber-stamping legislation under 'advice' from his Elysée-appointed Minister of State, and he chafed even more at the time-honoured Grimaldi dependence on a stipend from the SBM.

The whole situation was rich in paradox. Onassis, self-made and with a reputation for ruthless thrust, seemed obsessed with preserving Monte Carlo's Edwardian image of gilt and crystal chandeliers at the Hotel de Paris and the Hermitage. By contrast, the heir to eight centuries of tradition veered more towards corporations like 'Holiday Inns' which had put out tentative feelers to erect a new hotel complex for package tourists and business conferences.

The Greek had underrated Rainier's growing toughness, soon exemplified by his rough handling of the Dockers. In retrospect that episode has all the elements of *opéra bouffe*, but in blasting the *Shemara* clean out of the Côte d'Azur's territorial waters, Rainier also served clear notice that he was no longer an easy-going and malleable princeling.

Norah, the attractive blonde wife of industrialist Sir Bernard Docker, her third millionaire husband, favoured a life-style which included gold-plated Daimlers and a taste for pink champagne. Hospitable and generous, she was popular in London's 'café society' but inclined to become over-exuberant and too outspoken. The Dockers entertained lavishly both in Mayfair and aboard their 863-ton *Shemara*, whose yellow funnel was often seen at Monte Carlo. Bought for £100,000, it was the largest private yacht under a British flag with eight cabins and a main deck measuring 214 feet, although hardly justifying Lady Docker's dismissal of the *Christina* as 'a converted banana boat, you know'. She liked roulette and used a little silver bell from Capri as a lucky charm. One night, excitedly tinkling it after her number had won, a squad of croupiers trooped in, assuming that a new session was starting. But she always tipped handsomely and was forgiven.

The SBM president, Prince Jean-Louis de Faucigny-Lucinge, showed less tolerance at a Red Cross gala dinner in the Sporting Club when she rightly observed, 'The cabaret was awful. Couldn't you have put on something better than a fashion parade?' He ordered her to leave his table. Onassis smoothed things over, but another incident just before the wedding, to which she and her husband were invited, again threatened the peace. Lady Docker, having asked several guests to dine at the casino's night club, objected fruitily when told that His Serene Highness had booked it solid (in fact, Grace Kelly's father had reserved it to entertain his family and other wedding guests). Lady Docker protested so sharply to the palace that the British Consul was asked to convey Rainier's displeasure. But this, too, ended in a friendly spirit, although Lady Docker did not improve matters by criticising the commercialisation of the wedding which she covered for a London newspaper and the New York *Herald-Tribune*.

A 101-gun salute signalled the birth of Monaco's hereditary prince on 14 March 1958. Church bells pealed joyfully and all the yachts in the harbour, including the *Shemara*, sounded their sirens. A month later the Dockers were asked to a palace reception following the christening of Prince Albert whom they had presented with a coin of his namesake's reign tastefully mounted on a gold watch from Cartier's. They requested an invitation for Lance Callingham, Lady Docker's son by her first marriage, who happened to be celebrating his 19th birthday on the day of the christening. This was refused – over 400 others had to be similarly excluded – but Norah Docker took it as a personal affront and angrily stayed away from the reception. That night she became very excited in the casino's club and, according to gossip-mongers, made some caustic observations about the Rainiers. Next day, lunching at the Hotel de Paris and still seething, she knocked over a tiny crêpe paper flag of Monaco resting in a bowl of flowers on her table. She picked up the flag and allegedly ripped it to shreds, remarking to her husband, 'We shan't be needing this any more, Bernard. We'll go where we're more welcome'.

They left for Cannes and received back Prince Albert's watch, coldly returned by his parents, together with the news that Lady Docker had been banned for life from Monaco 'for indulging publicly in demonstrations offensive to the Principality'. As this prohibition extended automatically to all the French provinces adjoining Monaco, in accordance with the 1918 convention, many thought that Rainier had over-reacted. 'I was surprised – and amused – at the tetchiness of the bristling little Prince and his bride from Walt Disneyland' snorted the columnist of a London tabloid. The Dockers sailed off to the Caribbean and other less troubled waters. 'It made me mad to have imagined that we could ever miss Monte Carlo' the irrepressible exile wrote in her memoirs. 'We've heard they've missed us more!' She and her husband later settled in Jersey, a pleasant enough island and twice the size of Monaco, though no serious rival in Docker terms of glamour.

Rainier's action was naturally applauded by his subjects, but within a few months, he lost popularity by peremptorily dismissing his National Council. 'I cannot tolerate any pressure whatsoever which might undermine my complete rights' he declared over the radio. In attacking 'administrative paralysis' he also denounced 'those who wish to impose old ideals or satisfy their personal ambitions', an obvious side-swipe at Onassis.

The constitutional crisis had been precipitated by the Council's objections to Rainier's demand for an increased allocation to the Oceanographic Museum where Commandant Jacques-Yves Cousteau, co-inventor of the aqualung, had recently become director at a handsome salary. He planned to build new laboratories and well-lit aquaria, a 'marinarium' for dolphins and porpoises, and an underwater 'floating laboratory', anchored off the coast, where nuclear and other advanced techniques could be applied to marine research. It proved to be one of Rainier's most inspired appointments when Cousteau's books and his voyages in the research ship, *Calypso*, followed by Oscar-winning films, brought swarms of tourists to the Museum, but the long-term contract had displeased a reactionary Council now in its terminal stage of galloping inertia.

With the railway tunnel making only snail's progress and other schemes still mouldering on the drawing board, Rainier saw no alternative but to seek fresh investment capital from abroad. He soon gave his blessing to the Monaco Economic Development Corporation, jointly masterminded by Martin Dale, the young ex-American Vice-Consul at Nice, and Yves Laye, a shrewd lawyer from French Algeria. Leading firms in America and Europe began receiving glossy brochures proclaiming the tax advantages of moving into the principality, with reminders of its ideal location for sales conferences. The response was swift and almost overwhelmingly cordial. Hundreds of business men, American, British and German, together with returning French exiles from Algeria, Morocco and Indo-China, eagerly transferred their companies or subsidiaries to Monaco. A miniature real estate bonanza started almost overnight with office blocks and apartment towers a top priority.

A huge Italian labour force crossed the border daily to man the cranes, scaffolds and pneumatic drills. Pay dirt encouraged them to cut even the sacred siesta to unheard-of brevity, and some achieved the feat of simultaneously handling a hunk of salami with a cement mixer. Many villa-owners migrated to neighbouring French villages after disposing of their deeds at fancy prices.

Sam Cummings, a Philadelphian like the princess, was among

the first of the new arrivals. A former U.S. Army Sergeant, he had served with the CIA in Korea where he first sensed the long-term potential in captured weapons. One of his early coups was the purchase of 600,000 Lee Enfield rifles from the British government. A fresh-faced and bear-like young man with a bushy crop of hair, his Ivy League clothes and charm concealed a razor-sharp brain. By his early thirties he was already a multi-millionaire and had founded the International Armament Corporation (Interamco) with agents in 70 countries and clients like Batista, Chiang Kai-Shek, Sukarno of Indonesia, the Dominican Republic's Trujillo and smaller fry like Sudan's mounted cavalry, whom he equipped with lances. Within a few years he was indisputably the world's biggest independent arms dealer and could offer an attractive range of tanks, heavy or light artillery and the latest line in jet fighters. He had been living in Nice with luxurious *pieds à terre* in London, Washington and Switzerland, when Dale's brochures decided him to establish his permanent headquarters in Monaco.

Other newcomers were more transient. The principality attracted many shady operators, who used Monegasques as guinea-pig 'presidents', and dozens of 'letter-box' companies eagerly paid £20,000 and upwards for office suites with a shiny name plate and little more than bare walls behind. Rainier would later deny that Monaco gave unrestricted asylum to tax-evaders, claiming that as many as 40% of the applications, obviously bogus, were turned down in a single year.

Although property values had gone sky-high, with penthouses commanding prices equal to prime sites in the Champs Elysées, 150 new companies were registered in 1959 alone, many with American and Canadian capital which de Gaulle would have welcomed in his stagnant eastern regions.

But there was still no outward sign of disharmony when the Rainiers paid a State Visit to Paris, which de Gaulle cordially returned within a few months. The prince took care to affirm that his country had 'no other interest or ambition but to prosper and expand while maintaining the friendship that binds it to France', but he was not helped overmuch by Emile Pelletier, the Minister of State, recently appointed at a tax-free salary of £12,500 a year. This former French cabinet minister, almost as tall and stiff-mannered as the President, was not the most sympathetic of administrators for a progressive-minded ruler but, in the absence of a Council, they pulled together in reasonable comfort.

Even Rainier's opponents had to admit that he was showing remarkable stamina and resilience under pressure. He seemed to thrive on paper work demanding long office hours, but was consoled by seeing cash cascading into the treasury from corporation and sales taxes, stamp duties and many other lucrative incidentals. He could at last accelerate progress on the railway tunnel and help finance the costly operation for reclaiming land from the sea, an obvious priority with such an unquenchable thirst for building space.

Cousteau could now afford to push ahead with his underwater laboratory buoy and work in collaboration with the Scientific Centre, founded in May 1960, on a wide range of research on marine radioactivity, microbiology, maritime pollution, apart from developing his latest Observatory for the study of seismology and meteorology. Funds were also being deployed for many other long-dormant projects, including the inauguration of a museum of prehistoric anthropology, the handsome Princess Caroline Library, clinics and primary schools.

The prince approved the building of the Stade Nautique Rainier III, a vast swimming pool adjoining the port and up to Olympic Games standards. Well-equipped and also suitable for water-polo, it was envisaged, above all, as a welcome amenity for residents or middle-income tourists, who preferred not to scramble on the pocket-handkerchief strip of public plage and found the Sea Club pools or exclusive Monte-Carlo Beach far too costly. One of Rainier's deepest satisfactions was the emergence of the Monegasque soccer team several of whose crack players won places in the French eleven. When Monaco, the little outsider, shocked gallic pride by winning the national Cup Final, he presided with Princess Grace at a victory dinner in a Paris hotel. Two years later the team went on to win the coveted double – the Cup and the French League – and qualified for the European Championships.

During Monaco's boom period he would gratefully escape for a little sailing in his launch, *Albercaro*, (a hybrid of his children's names), which had replaced the unwieldy *Costa del Sol*. Most weekends and in the two hot summer months, he and the family retreated to their 'ranch' house up at Roc Agel, which he had built on Provencal *mas* lines, with massive beams and sturdy stone walls. Here he had his own hut for carpentry and metal work, drove a tractor and took an almost professional interest in his orchard and a miniature dairy farm started with two cows. Grace ran an excellent garden and cooked expertly, specialising in curries, Chinese dishes and her husband's favourite, an American version of Polynesian food.

Since the birth of their children the Rainiers always flew in separate aircraft and limited themselves to short but enjoyable foreign trips, particularly to the United States or London where they remained incognito at the quiet Connaught, shopped, saw the new plays and usually had a palace tea with the Queen and the Duke of Edinburgh. One of their happiest breaks (in June 1961) was a holiday in Eire. They were received by President de Valera and drove on to County Mayo to see the three-roomed thatched and white-washed cottage where Grace's grandfather was born.

Rainier seldom relished either making or receiving State Visits which he thought tedious, costly and time-wasting, but 'royals' were made welcome when they passed through or happened to be staying nearby. They both adored the former Queen Ena of Spain, one of Prince Albert's godmothers, and often received Michael of Rumania and his wife. Rainier liked to talk car 'shop' with Prince Bernhard of the Netherlands, who rarely missed the Grand Prix and would afterwards spend happy hours in the palace garage where the prince kept his vintage models. He had started this collection modestly with a gem dating back to 1898, followed by a 1902 De Dion-Bouton 6 CV, a sturdy 1910 Renault and other treasures, like an early American Maxwell. He bought with discrimination and refused to pay exorbitant prices, favouring cheap wrecks which he and his chauffeurs could overhaul and resurrect.

An inspection of this 'museum' was ritual for Rainier's circle of friends, including neighbours like David Niven and Gregory Peck whose wife, Véronique, had formerly worked on *France Soir*. The Paul Gallicos, permanent residents of Antibes, came over frequently and, like the others, delighted in Cousteau, an unfailing joy whether discoursing on penguins, philosophy or rare wines. The decorative Maharanee of Baroda, another engaging raconteur, wore beautiful saris and smoked cigars in a ruby-studded holder. Two years after her 1956 divorce she had become a citizen of Monaco which, apart from its social and fiscal attractions, was ideally located for jetting between Paris couturiers, racecourses and casinos. One of the world's richest women, with jewels conservatively estimated at some £4 million, she was a valued resident of the Hotel de Paris but, as a Monegasque, now played her baccarat in French casinos where she handled 5,000-franc plaques like tiddlywinks.

Ex-King Peter of Jugoslavia and his wife had also settled into a suite at the Hotel de Paris but lived very quietly, rarely attending official receptions or even the theatre. While Alexandra busily wrote books and articles under a pseudonym, her husband drove about in a big English car or took solitary walks, but always with a police bodyguard as he had a chronic dread of being ambushed by Titoists. Both were keen tennis players and often came up to the palace for parties until one unfortunate incident, which Rainier deeply regretted. When Van Cleef et Arpels, adjoining the casino, were robbed of £750,000 in diamonds during a daylight raid, Peter took alarm and demanded round-the-clock police protection. Some economy-minded official then suggested that the ex-monarch might move down instead to a suite overlooking the jewellers and share the same guard. Peter objected and angrily installed himself and his wife in the Métropole until their departure for the United States.

With hotel bookings at an all-time peak, and the casino grossing huge sums, the SBM had every reason to be satisfied. Only the more fastidious deplored the transformation of the once-elegant and exclusive Café de Paris into an American-style drug store with magazine racks, souvenirs and a snack counter, plus the universal rows of clanking fruit machines. Simenon was among those assaulted by the principality's new Miami architecture and noisy vulgarity. He had arrived to seek casino local colour for a novel and paid £15,000 for a disastrous spell of roulette in the Salon Privé. He settled the hotel bill early next morning and took off in some haste for his Swiss retreat.

Ian Fleming had little good to say for the casino's new clientèle, infinitely preferring Le Touquet's sporty elegance or the quieter little gaming salon at Beaulieu. 'What used to be a pastime has become a rather deadly business of amassing tax-free capital gains' he reported to the *Sunday Times*. 'Monte Carlo and its casino were designed for flamboyants – for Russian Grand Dukes, English milords, French actresses and an occasional maharajah, but now the beautiful stage is occupied by the scene-shifters who have inherited it from a race of actors that is bankrupt or dispossessed'. Distracted by the fruit machines, the crap games and a number of jowly, graceless Italian business men, who made it impossible for him to concentrate on chemin-de-fer, he moved on thankfully for a chat with Cousteau about his new aquarium.

One might have expected an even more waspish attack from a notorious snob like Evelyn Waugh but his sensibilities had apparently been anaesthetised by the cuisine and wine list of the Hotel de Paris. 'I go often to Monte Carlo for simple love of the place' he told the *Daily Mail*. 'For one thing it has one of the best hotels in the world . . . It was part of Francois Blanc's civilising mission to introduce classic French cooking to the frugal Italian Monegasques and to supplement the drab little wines of the district with importations from his homeland, from Burgundy, and from Champagne. And the tradition survives . . .'

Sir Winston Churchill, his palate still miraculously unimpaired at 85, fully endorsed this tribute. To celebrate the new four-storeyed rotunda, the management had replenished its cellars, chiselled from underlying rock and honeycombed with a maze of tiny passageways. They could now offer 130,000 bottles of vintage wines, champagne and liqueurs, together with the rarest of cognacs in oak casks. As the honoured guest of Onassis, Sir Winston could not only command the pick of this bottled treasury but the most assiduous service at all times from an adoring staff.

When his publisher, Emery Reeves, began to fail in health, he decided to move from the Roquebrune villa where he had spent many pleasant vacations. Onassis at once placed the *Christina* more or less at his disposal together with the exclusive use of a luxuriously furnished three-roomed suite on the top floor of the Hotel de Paris with a panoramic view of the harbour, distant Corsica and the mountainous Tête de Chien. Unhappily, the view was too much for Sir Winston's beloved budgerigar, Toby, who preferred his garden at Chartwell or, failing that, a bracing yacht cruise. One morning while his master was still in bed reading the newspapers, Toby flew out to explore the Boulingrins flower beds. He hopped joyfully between the cacti before perching on a palm tree.

The alarm was quickly sounded. Waiters and *commis*, with aprons flapping, rushed into the Place du Casino like manic penguins, soon joined by a cream clot of white-uniformed gendarmerie waving clubs while the fire-brigade tore into action with ladders. Jean Broc, the hotel manager, tried to direct operations, with Churchill simultaneously coaxing his pet and barking orders at the mixed force of helpers. Unnerved by all this excitement or possibly savouring the delights of liberty, Toby issued a final ungrateful cheep before taking off into the blue yonder in the general direction of the *Christina*. Churchill took this blow almost as hard as his rejection by Britain's post-war electorate. He remained inconsolable for days and Onassis, who mourned with him, would doubtless have sacrificed one of his tankers for Toby's safe return.

He could not do too much for his hero and generously entertained all his friends, even the newspaper proprietor, Lord Beaverbrook, whom he disliked, an antipathy heartily reciprocated. But Onassis could be ludicrously over-protective in his anxiety to shield Churchill from the smallest irritation. One summer in 1959, during the early stage of their association, he gave a cocktail party on the *Christina* in Churchill's honour and invited John F. Kennedy and his wife, who were staying with the Senator's father at Cap d'Antibes. 'I'm afraid your visit will have to be a very short one' he warned them. 'I must ask you to leave not later than 7.30 as Sir Winston always has his dinner at 8.15 sharp'. Nothing could disturb the ritual punctuality of that meal, followed by a film showing for the star guest.

The Kennedys did not leave until well after nine, Churchill having engaged the Senator in a long conversation about his presidential chances. 'It will not be easy' said J.F.K. 'I'm a Catholic, you know'. The old man sipped his whisky and chuckled, 'If that's the only difficulty, you can always change your religion and still remain a good Christian.' Onassis meantime conducted Jacqueline Kennedy over the yacht, obviously gratified by her ecstatic approval of his exquisite 18th-century furniture, paintings and mosaics.[3]

With the threadbare treasury now practically mink-lined, Rainier had somewhat mellowed towards the SBM who backed his bowling alleys and the opening of a Sunday Go-Kart Club. Onassis still resisted any large-scale investment but had made a token gesture with the Piscine des Terrasses, a new salt-water indoor pool sited below the Hotel de Paris and connected with it by an underground tunnel. Maintained at a constant temperature of 28°C, it also offered patrons Finnish saunas and massage, private cabins, a solarium, with cocktails and expensive snacks served on the terrace overlooking the yacht-filled harbour.

The grand opening of the Piscine was celebrated by a fancy dress ball at which Rainier appeared in a bald wig and a masher's curling moustache, while Grace sported a padded rubber mask, a fraulein's false braids and underwater flippers. Soon afterwards they joined Onassis, Callas and the Maharanee of Baroda on the

[3] Soon after the Kennedys' departure, Monte Carlo buzzed with talk of a mysterious young American, who had asked probing questions concerning the Senator's previous visits, with pointed reference to women friends and his sessions at the gaming tables. He claimed to have up to $10,000 available for 'information', but as this seemed hard to come by, he had moved on to Eden Roc and Cannes which proved equally unrewarding.

His identity remains puzzling. He was almost certainly a hired private investigator, yet the mind's eye can almost discern some diligent trainee starting his long apprenticeship to Watergate!

Christina to attend the launching of the new £3 million Hotel Son Dida, near Palma, in which Rainier had invested. In the ballroom Onassis attempted a Neapolitan love song with Elsa Maxwell at the piano, Callas shaking the maraccas and Rainier on drums. Next day the prince suddenly jumped the rails at a bullfight and made some mock matador passes while the crowd cheered and Grace looked on nervously. On their way back to Monaco, she went ashore at a French port to join a two-day pilgrimage to Lourdes. She attended Mass in the Grotto with a crippled Monegasque girl, Anna Spaiani, whose fare and expenses she had secretly paid.

In Monte Carlo everyone was whizzing about on a merry-go-round with little patience for the disbanded National Council or others who grumbled at the non-appearance of the promised new Constitution. The cash registers set up a continuous tinkling all along the Boulevard des Moulins whose florists, jewellers and perfumers grossed pre-Depression turnovers. The good Monegasques, debarred by law from their own crowded casino, could still stand hopefully at the fruit machines in the Café de Paris with little tin cups at the ready or drive off to the gaming tables of Nice in their shiny new Simcas. The theatre attracted glittering audiences and supper tables were at a premium in all the leading hotels and restaurants.

For a Sporting Club gala, with Ava Gardner as the Rainiers' principal guest, 12,000 roses adorned the ballroom where several dozen violinists played Strauss waltzes until dawn. When fire broke out at another ball organised by Princess Grace on behalf of the Monegasque Red Cross, it was doused with magnums of champagne from Karim Aga Khan's table. Onassis continued dancing with Callas but Jack L. Warner, impatient for action, went off to the tables. He dropped £10,000 in precisely ten minutes and returned while the audience was still applauding Nat King Cole's cabaret version of Grace Kelly's 'True Love'.

Hugh O'Brien, currently escorting ex-Queen Soraya, had his slice of beginner's luck. One night he made a quiet exit from the crowded hotel lounge and wandered down the tunnel into the casino. He asked for the rules of baccarat to be explained to him and swiftly pocketed £8,000 with all Wyatt Earp's nonchalance. These were small pickings compared with the run later that summer in Le Sporting by a baccarat syndicate from Italy, South America and the United States. Headed by Joseph Saphi, a stocky textile magnate from Kentucky, who had arrived in Monte Carlo with a wife and two Cadillacs, they dry-cleaned the bank for upwards of £300,000 in ten nights. Zanuck and Warner punted against them for a while but dropped out to watch with Gregory Peck, Charles Clore and others.

Sam Spiegel punted heavily and often showed a profit but, win or lose, he gave the liveliest parties on his yacht. His Hollywood soulmates included the ebullient scriptwriter, Harry Kurnitz, who was typing on deck one afternoon when a gust of wind blew all his notes overboard. He dived in, fully-dressed, bespectacled and with the eternal cigarette on his lip. Someone pulled him out and even salvaged most of the manuscript. 'Thanks,' drawled Kurnitz. 'It was in mid-air that I remembered I couldn't swim.' None the worse, he went out on the town that night. Asked afterwards about the statuesque local charmer who had partnered him, he gave the matter some thought. 'Well, I've been in Volkswagens smaller than she was,' he decided solemnly.

Although the real estate bubble showed no sign of bursting, Rainier was perhaps over-euphoric in ordering himself a new 125-foot luxury yacht for £250,000 from an Amsterdam shipbuilder. He disregarded criticism of his so-called extravagance and once remarked off-handedly, 'Monaco's a small place. People live on top of each other and watch what each one does. It's like an aquarium.' But it became less easy to ignore glum reminders that the railway tunnel, originally estimated to cost £2 million, was already heading for treble that figure and with no firm date for completion. Moreover, almost three years had passed since he had disbanded the National Council without as yet much prospect of a new and more liberal Constitution.

Parallel to these political grievances, aired behind closed doors in the absence of a Council and any local newspaper, the cafés hummed with sneers at favouritism or even graft in the allocation of building permits. Disgruntled property owners reported harassment by speculators, while others complained of being evicted or asked prohibitive prices when their leases ran out.

In March 1962 Princess Grace became the target for a creeping barrage of innuendo. It was all the more painful and unexpected as, since their marriage, she had commanded universal respect and affection in the principality. This changed overnight when the palace announced that she would star in a new Hitchcock film based on Winston Graham's novel, *Marnie*. Fans rejoiced all over the world except in Monaco where she was criticised for shelving her responsibilities for a reported million dollars in salary and percentages. She had in fact earmarked her potential film earnings to endow a local children's charity foundation and was naturally all the more distressed at being accused of cynically disregarding her duty.

The project had been spearheaded by a persuasive Hitchcock, backed by Rainier, who knew that his wife occasionally missed acting and thought she might enjoy a brief 'sabbatical' from her almost year-long round of official functions and palace housekeeping. Shooting schedules had been carefully tailored to fit in with a two-month holiday visit to the United States with Rainier and their children. While these facts were belatedly made public, Grace had already tired of the sniggering gossip. She withdrew from the film, firmly resolved never to be tempted again.

The hubbub had barely subsided when Rainier received six months' notice of de Gaulle's intention to abrogate the 1951 convention guaranteeing friendly relations and administrative aid between the two countries. It was argued, not without some justification, that Prince Rainier's concessions to French tax-evaders had breached the treaty of 1918 with its built-in pledge to respect France's economic interests.

De Gaulle's spring offensive was no overnight decision. He had long resented the principality's bubbling economy and now saw his chance to humiliate the *pieds noirs*, who had followed up their defiance in North Africa by impudently settling into the tax haven of Monaco. Ironically, however, the crisis was triggered by Rainier's resistance to further infiltration of French capital investment which threatened his television monopoly.

Since the Liberation, Radio Monte-Carlo had gradually fallen into French hands until Monegasques on the board were outnumbered by six to one. The yearly royalty paid by the company was acceptable but it did not compensate for Monaco's loss of all real influence on policy. Rainier had even found himself in the humiliating situation of receiving threatening letters from O.A.S. sympathisers for supporting the network's pro-de Gaulle bias! He could not disturb its status quo but was determined at all costs to preserve the independence of his TV station, which had expanded rapidly during the boom years and now accounted for over 30% of the national revenue. Its programmes went out to the whole Midi and even North Africa in competition with France's State-operated non-commercial system.

The French Government's substantial share holding in Télé-Monte-Carlo, allocated after the collapse of Monaco's Bank, had been steadily increased in the boom years until Rainier became alarmed by the nightmarish prospect of a take-over. He had therefore decided in January 1962 to issue an ordinance prohibiting the further sale of company stock on the Paris Bourse. It was countersigned by the Minister of State, who at once received a stinging reprimand from de Gaulle. He pleaded in his defence that he had signed 'inadvertently' while awaiting an urgent operation for prostate trouble.

De Gaulle brushed this aside. Late one night Pelletier was awakened by a telephone call from the Elysée ordering him to inform Rainier *immediately* that the ordinance would have to be cancelled. He arrived at the palace shortly after midnight, wearing a formal black suit and looks to match. Rainier received him in his study where he had been reading a novel and chain-smoking after the Minister's urgent request for an audience. He wore a polo sweater with flannel slacks and seemed relaxed until Pelletier opened the discussion by stammering, 'In the name of the Government of the French Republic . . .' Angry words were exchanged. Rainier accused his so-called Minister of State of being nothing more than de Gaulle's messenger boy and wholly failing to present Monaco's case. However, he had no alternative but to climb down and rescind his ordinance.

De Gaulle, the military strategist, was now encouraged to press home his advantage and widen the field of operations. The affair also stiffened Rainier's determination to re-assert his authority. Not long afterwards two vehicles left Monaco almost simultaneously but in different directions. The Rainiers and their children sped off to Switzerland in a grey Alfa-Romeo for a short holiday while an ambulance headed for a Nice clinic with M. Pelletier, who had been told in the plainest terms that he was no longer *persona grata* to His Serene Highness.

The situation was now developing into a classic *High Noon* confrontation. The brave loner, who saw Monaco's sovereignty under threat for the first time since the French Revolution, had until October to come to heel by virtually sacrificing his country's fiscal autonomy. He had the support of a beautiful heroine, who shared his faith in a just cause, but Charles de Gaulle was simply too big and sharp-elbowed for this script. He saw himself not as the baddie but a righteous marshal protecting his folk from corruption by a wide-open saloon town across the border.

Chapter Thirteen

THROUGHOUT THE tense summer months of 1962 public opinion in France was being subtly revved up for the expected drive against Monaco. In the Paris boulevard cafés one heard barbed comments on Princess Grace's retention of her American passport, coupled with reminders of her husband's refusal to apply for membership of the United Nations where, in accordance with the 1918 Treaty, Monaco could not have avoided voting automatically with France. Monaco's adhesion to UNESCO, the World Health Organisation and other international bodies was ignored by those who considered Rainier's independent diplomatic stance as snidely pro-American, particularly when de Gaulle had built up gold reserves and adopted a deflationary policy to hit back at the dollar. The automatic reduction in France's domestic living standards also made an uncomfortable contrast to her impudent little neighbour's roaring prosperity.

Rainier took strong exception to being labelled as francophobe. He felt as deeply rooted in the culture and traditions of France as any of his ancestors, most of whom had fought under her colours throughout the centuries. His own war record was exemplary and he had valued his promotion to the rank of colonel, in December 1954, almost as highly as his Knight's Cross of the Légion d'Honneur. But he swallowed his resentment and wrote three personal letters to the President, volunteering to come to Paris and discuss outstanding problems in a frank and friendly spirit. As further evidence of goodwill, he initiated a fiscal survey to disprove exaggerated stories of undercover fortunes. He also invited tax officials to make an on-the-spot investigation of all French corporations in his territory. These suggestions, like his letters, went unanswered. The President seemed deaf to all arguments but his own, echoed by Couve de Murville and other entrenched opponents of Rainier's policies. Significantly, the French Consul-General was ordered home for attempting to act as conciliator after Pelletier's dismissal.

The end of the six-month ultimatum approached without sign of any thaw in de Gaulle's glacial isolation. If anything, his attitude had hardened. His implacable contempt for Monaco's *pieds noirs* was now almost as obsessive as his distrust of the State Department's growing influence in NATO. Every American or French company registered in Monte Carlo must have seemed an act of treachery to the lonely megalomaniac in the Elysée Palace. It helps to explain his use of an elephant gun for butterfly-hunting that October.

The tragi-comedy opened with a threat to cut off Monaco's gas and electricity supplies. It was not taken too seriously but near-panic set in as a squad of French customs officers arrived at the frontiers with portable barriers. Two companies of Nice gendarmes were reportedly standing by on a two-hour alert to place a cordon round the rebel State, while excitable palace visitors almost swore that the guards had been issued with tommy-guns.

The so-called 'Siege of Monaco' was raised without any demand for unconditional surrender, but Rainier had no doubt that, failing a reasonable compromise, his country faced possible annexation or a whittling of autonomy which could reduce it to the status of a *sous-préfecture* like Grasse. He continued to seek a settlement in almost a cold war atmosphere as delegations shuttled warily back and forth.

Rainier won local support for refusing to be rattled by de Gaulle's sabres, but he clearly saw the need for uniting public opinion during the prickly negotiations. He therefore expedited his grant of a Constitution to introduce 'a new spirit into the old framework and dedicate modern principles without relinquishing tradition'. Promulgated on 17 December, it was no millenium but some advance at least on the one-man autocracy of the past three years. The principle of hereditary monarchy was maintained but rule by divine right renounced. The Supreme Court, whose judgements would apply even to the prince, now became the custodian of fundamental rights and liberties, guaranteeing full equality before the law. The death penalty was abolished and preventive detention limited to 24 hours. The Constitution also confirmed the rights of trade union association and strike action. The principality would continue to be governed by the sovereign's authority but through a Minister of State (nominated as before by France, subject to his approval) with three Councillors appointed by the prince; Monegasques for Finance and Public Works, and a Frenchman as Minister for the Interior.

Braced by the newly-elected National Council, who swiftly gave him its full vote of confidence, Rainier pursued the negotiations which ended in a Franco–Monegasque Fiscal Convention signed in Paris on 8 May 1963. French nationals, unable to prove five years' residence in Monaco previous to 13 October 1962, would have to pay their home country's standard rate of income tax. As from 1 January 1963, all French companies deriving over 25% of their revenues from direct foreign transactions or activities outside Monaco also became subject to a local profits tax.[1]

These fiscal restraints had an immediate effect although not wholly up to de Gaulle's expectations. Two-thirds of the 16 billion francs invested by colonials found their way to Switzerland. But many French-owned businesses closed and almost all new investment from Paris dried up. Local property values nose-dived and several speculators found themselves left with hundreds of un-

---

[1] The treaty, unlike all previous pacts between the two countries, omitted any reference in its preamble to Monaco's sovereign status. But Article One of the 1962 Constitution had clearly specified that 'the principality of Monaco is a sovereign and independent State in the framework of the general principles of international law and its special treaty agreements with France.'

wanted apartments or office suites, so recently at a premium. Some Frenchmen, terrified of tax probes, disposed hastily of their apartments and moved on to Menton, but a few others sat tight on discovering that they would still pay less than the French company tax for business done outside the principality. International tycoons like Sam Cummings, whose armament business continued to roar ahead, remained comfortably insulated from the crisis. Monte Carlo had become so congenial in all respects that he bought a luxurious 12-roomed mansion on the Avenue Hector Otto for himself, his Swiss wife and their twin daughters. He was followed early in 1964 by Boris Vlasov, who moved his headquarters and a 200-strong staff from Genoa. A man of Russian origin with a mania for privacy surpassed only by Howard Hughes, his vast empire covered cargo and passenger ships, tankers and bulk carriers.

With his country's economy still depressed by the building slump, Prince Rainier austerely cancelled an order for the latest E-type Jaguar but still had to pay the agreed £250,000 for his new yacht, *Albercaro II*, which seemed singularly ill-fated. Before he could take delivery in Amsterdam, a fire broke out in the engine-room and put her out of action for a year. He and his family had enjoyed only three brief cruises to Portugal, Majorca and Greece (for King Constantine's wedding) when he decided that the upkeep of the vessel, with its crew of 12, was an unnecessary extravagance. He sold her within a few months to an oil-rich sheikh and took his time before buying an Italian-built motor cruiser for a more realistic £75,000.

The *Christina*, serenely riding all the local squalls, continued on her champagne course, although with Sir Winston less frequently aboard. He received treatment at the Princess Grace Clinic after a fall at the Hotel de Paris and had to be flown home with his leg in plaster. But Onassis did not lack for prestige cargo. In the late summer of 1963 he was dining in Athens with the Radziwills when they learned that Jacqueline Kennedy had lost her new-born baby,

Patrick. Lee Radziwill thought her sister might benefit from a sea holiday, and Onassis promptly extended an invitation. Mrs Kennedy soon joined him, his married sister, Artemis, the Radziwills and Franklin D. Roosevelt Jr. for a cruise among the Greek islands during which the President often called his wife on the radio telephone. Onassis acted as guide when they went ashore at Istanbul and Ithaca. He lavished so many costly trinkets on Mrs Kennedy that her sister jokingly complained to the President of having been fobbed off with 'three dinky little bracelets that Caroline wouldn't wear to her own birthday party!' Onassis heard of the Dallas horror while launching one of his new tankers in Hamburg. He was among the first to call on the widow and express his sympathy before flying back to rejoin Callas in Monaco. He found Rainier in a mood of exasperation and far less receptive to vague promises.

The new Minister of State, Jean Reymond, was infinitely more congenial and tactful than Pelletier, but he very reasonably saw his primary rôle as that of peacemaker between Monaco and President de Gaulle. He sympathised with the ruler's ambitious projects but could do little to sway the National Council, who baulked at voting supplementary budgets although Rainier argued impatiently that an upswing in tourism was crucial to any significant economic revival. He and Princess Grace, whose practical judgment he valued increasingly, agreed that plushy night clubs like the Hawaiian-style Maona (a tender coupling of 'Maria' and 'Onassis') or the £15 a day Boudin-striped bathing cabins and chic boutiques at Monte-Carlo Beach had no appeal for visitors in need of medium-priced accommodation and entertainment.

An alarming number of package tour operators had already turned to Spain, Italy, Greece and Yugoslavia. It was obviously no longer enough to offer a 10% reduction on hotel bills for over five-day visits or free entrance to local parks and museums. The few boosted novelties like clay pigeon shooting had also fallen flat. The Rally and Grand Prix, the regattas, the TV festival, Davis Cup tennis and such permanent attractions as the changing of the Palace guard at noon, with possibly a glimpse of Princess Grace, could not compensate for a lack of sandy beaches and cheaper hotel rooms. Even the traditional flutter at roulette had become far less of a novelty to British visitors, who now had their own flourishing casinos in London and the provinces, while international jet-setters had meantime found new playgrounds and exclusive watering holes in the Bahamas, Jamaica, Prince Hohenlohe's Marbella complex and Sardinia's Costa Smeralda, heavily promoted by the young Aga Khan.

A severe challenge had also been mounted by Cannes since the recent death of François André, who left a fortune of some £20 million. His nephew and successor, Lucien Barrière, renewed the gaming concession and cheerfully met the municipality's demands for expansion by laying out a polo ground, improving the two golf courses and agreeing to maintain a full symphony orchestra. The company, like all French casinos, had to pay 55% of its receipts in local and State taxes and could only obtain a small relief by using the cash to improve its associated hotels, but Barrière spent far more to maintain André's entertainment standards. He also continued his uncle's policy of inviting celebrities and high-staking gamblers as guests at his hotels and golf clubs. Yet Monte Carlo's SBM, despite its satisfactory and very lightly-taxed profits, still quibbled at subsidising new operas and seemed content to floodlight the casino gardens or put on peacock Friday night galas at the Summer Sporting, which was now plainly showing its age.

Rainier bluntly vented his dissatisfaction in a New Year, 1964 message to his people. He did not spare timidly obstructive government officials but reserved his harshest indictment for the SBM: 'How can we make possible our dreams of a new life if those who get the largest profit from our tourism continue to wallow in lethargic inaction?'

He had now persuaded himself that Onassis was becoming socially bored with Monte Carlo and, encouraged by Callas, might set up a rival holiday complex. He had already bought Skorpiós, the 500-acre Greek island, for £60,000 and was apparently enlarging its harbour to accommodate the *Christina*. Such reports confirmed Rainier's suspicion that he had lost all real interest in the principality's development and simply hoped to divert the casino's profits into high-rise apartment and office blocks.

Onassis minimised their growing divergence on policy. He told the Paris correspondent of London's *Daily Express*, 'We cannot really turn the place into a second Brighton, because there is just not enough beach – the place is too small.' He then declared with a beaming smile, 'It is my sincere hope that agreement will be reached soon'. But they arrived at yet another impasse when Rainier hinted that the Greek might consider selling his SBM shares to one of several interested foreign groups, including the Banque de Paris. At one meeting Ari gibed, 'I think there should be no gambling in Monte Carlo. It's a shame to have gambling. It's immoral.' Rainier retorted icily, 'Really, Mr Onassis, I don't think you are in any position to tell me what's moral or immoral.'

This skirmish, like so many others, ended in protestations of mutual goodwill, but since the prince chafed for action and Onassis continued to visit the principality only sporadically, opportunities multiplied for misunderstanding and ambivalence. The opening of the new railway station and 3,783-yard tunnel on 13 December 1964 finally cut through all these arabesques. By releasing several acres which could be land-filled from the huge blocks of excavated rock, Rainier was at last in a position to implement his scheme for creating 'Monte-Carlo Bord-de-Mer' on the Larvotto, to the east of the principality. He and his advisers envisaged an entirely artificial beach, 500-metres long, gouged from two filled-in reclaimed areas, with a system of groynes and jetties to prevent the material being washed away by the swell. Pedestrians would have access to a promenade, bordered by bathing cabins, restaurants and shops. A wide two-way road was planned with underground parking for hundreds of cars. Space was now also available for the Holiday Inn group's plan, the brainchild of William B. Walton from Memphis, Tennessee, to put up a 3 Star hotel with over 300 rooms, restaurants, shops, a conference hall and swimming pool.

All this would be ancillary to the longer-term project of the replacing the Summer Sporting by the most luxurious gaming and entertainment complex in Europe. Bathers, who could afford it, would still enjoy the Sea Club with its cluster of pools fringing the Mediterranean or drive out to Monte-Carlo Beach for their exclusive strip of artificial sand, with water-skiing, boutiques, coiffeurs, cabanas and the salt-water pool. As owners of much of the real estate where 'Bord-de-Mer' would take shape, the SBM was expected to help finance a scheme which would take years to complete and might cost many billions of francs. But Onassis remained reluctant to pledge a huge investment until agreement had been achieved on tourist policy and, more important to him, some limitation of the prince's absolute veto power over building permits.

He was a generous man and often touchingly eager to pamper status symbols like Churchill, but he had not survived in his harsh world of tankers, whaling fleets and airlines by handing out open cheques. It was therefore fully in character for him to play for time until other parts of the principality's large-scale 'urbanisation' plan had safely taken off. In the following February, shortly after the birth of Stéphanie, Princess Grace's third child, Onassis was asked by a British journalist in Paris to clarify his views on the principality's future. 'I'm rather worried,' he answered, but without looking *too* concerned. 'The Prince wants to institute a 10-year Plan for Monaco. Fine. But the SBM has not yet been given details of this plan – so how can it approve or disapprove?'

When the Rainiers accepted an invitation to visit President de Gaulle that April, it turned out to be more than a social call. The old wounds had not yet healed and the princess, in particular, had been nettled by French hostility to America's rôle in South Vietnam, but there was complete accord over Rainier's proposals to expand his economy which would obviously boost France's revenues from goods and services. De Gaulle left them in no doubt of his sympathies. Soon afterwards Rainier told *Le Monde* that, if the SBM continued to neglect Monaco's interests 'by systematically slowing down improvement plans', he might have to nationalise the Onassis holdings. 'I am assured of the French Government's support' he declared solemnly.

That summer the Rainiers enjoyed a pleasant holiday in England. It included a visit to Henley Regatta where the Princess's brother, John, was coaching a crew from his old club in Philadelphia. They crossed to Ireland with the children but found their little ranch even more welcome after being dogged by reporters and photographers, often with telephoto lenses. Up at Roc Agel the children rode ponies, Rainier had a small nimble colt from the Camargue, and Grace galloped a hunter over the rocky ground which often made her husband nervous. Wearing jeans or denims, he drove his tractor and chopped wood, while Grace looked after the baby and prepared all the meals, with their own milk, eggs, butter, fruit and fresh-grown vegetables. As special treats they sailed out in the *Carostephal*, which was radar-equipped and had two engines with a cruising speed of 27 knots. They could make Corsica in only five hours and had three double couchettes in the cabins for themselves, the children and occasional schoolfriends. As the family photographer, Grace used to involve the youngsters in games for little sequences shot with her ciné-camera.

Caroline and Albert returned in the autumn to their local schools. Their parents were in full accord on the important question of education. Recalling his own unhappy schooldays, with vacations spent either alone in Monaco or with estranged parents, Rainier had firmly resolved that his own children should enjoy a settled and normal home life during their formative years. They were bilingual from early infancy and their English nanny, Maureen King, was followed by a French Swiss girl. But Princess Grace remained very close to them. It became ritual for her and the prince to be up for breakfast, even after late night engagements, before the children left for school at 8.30 sharp, always on foot except in the worst weather. Caroline attended a convent school, the Pensionnat des Dames de Saint Maur, and her brother had settled in at the Lycée Albert Premier where he was encouraged, like his sister, to make friends of his own age without any class distinction. Both soon discovered that some of their schoolmates had more pocket-money than themselves, but Grace, thrifty-minded and anxious not to spoil them, resisted all coaxing for an increase. Rainier was particularly emphatic that the boy should come to know his fellow-pupils, some of whom might one day be his ministers or councillors.

Throughout that winter, while his relationship with Onassis steadily deteriorated, the prince busied himself with the long-term urbanisation without, however, ignoring preparations for Monte Carlo's first centenary. He saw the celebrations not only as a much-needed boost to tourism but, with the launching of his Ten-Year Plan, an affirmation of confidence in the principality's future. The year's crowded programme opened with the formal creation of the Prince Pierre of Monaco Foundation in memory of Rainier's father. It would incorporate the Literary Council (under the presidency of Maurois) with a Committee set up to award annual prizes for outstanding new musical compositions. Princess Grace also inaugurated a new annual International Ballet Festival whose first performances were staged that June in the palace courtyard. 1,200 spectators watched Fonteyn and Nureyev dance Prokofiev's *Roméo et Juliette*. The Paris Opéra Ballet was followed by an exhilarating series of programmes on the lawn of the Louis II Stadium from the National Hungarian Ballet, who had brought a thousand costumes with them. Operagoers enjoyed the première of Poulenc's saucy *Les Mamelles de Térésias* and also recitals by Birgit Nillson and Joan Sutherland.

In the flurry of galas, official receptions and parties at the palace, where the Duke of Edinburgh was a guest, Princess Grace presented cup after cup and opened exhibitions of jewels, paintings and postage stamps, but Rainier had not overlooked the principality's more serious objectives. He had timed his long-threatened takeover of the SBM for Centenary Year when Monte Carlo would be crowded with visitors, including many potential investors. The official poster, designed by Cecil Beaton, portrayed an elegant crinolined lady on a balcony gazing down on an Offenbach-like ballroom scene. Ironically, it symbolised the spirit of traditional Monte Carlo revered by Onassis, but he no longer doubted that his régime was over. He had very pointedly sailed off to avoid taking part in the festivities.

Rainier himself owned only 22,000 SBM shares and the State had a similar number, against the Onassis majority holding of 520,000 shares in the million issued. But the moment had at last arrived to call *rien ne va plus*, only this time with the prince holding the bank. On 23 June 1966, while Van Cliburn was enchanting an audience in the Salle Garnier, a Bill was quietly introduced authorising the issue of 600,000 new shares, each at 5 NF to be paid for by the government. The preamble, drafted by Rainier's advisers, sharply reminded the electorate that the monopolistic SBM had refused to make the investments necessary to develop tourism. The government was therefore forced to stop the 'progressive paralysis' of the country's economic life.

The National Council's approval by only eight votes to six encouraged Onassis to contest the Bill's validity before the Monaco Supreme Court. He also objected to the valuation of the existing shares at only 80 frs. (£6 or $15) and demanded independent arbitration. Both his pleas were rejected. Now isolated and without a majority holding, he had to sell his stock to the State. Under protest and still asserting that his holding was worth at least double, he accepted a cheque for close on 40 million francs (£3 million or $7.5 million) for shares which had been bought for a fraction of that sum 14 years earlier.

He sailed off to Sardinia and the Caribbean before finding anchorage for the *Christina* on Skorpiós. He was reported to be more exasperated by Monaco's cavalier treatment than the disputed cash settlement. If so, it was understandable. Whatever his policy differences with Rainier, his business drive and investments had rescued the SBM from near-bankruptcy, while the mere presence of his yacht in Monte Carlo's harbour, with Churchill, Callas, Garbo and other headliners aboard, had paid incalculable dividends in social prestige and publicity. However, to the relief of his corps of tax-exempt employees, now risen to 180 from the original handful, he decided against closing down his shipping insurance offices in the Avenue d'Ostende.

The SBM's last balance sheet under the Onassis régime showed a healthy profit of £420,000 (over $1 million). This sagged to a £762,000 ($1.8 million) deficit a year later, but it took into account the heavy buying-back of shares and new facilities like a yacht to entertain VIP guests rather less critical than the Duchesse de la Rochefoucauld. She took one agonised look at a coachload of tourists feeding up to 21 coins into each of the new electrically-operated fruit machines and announced, 'I can't bear to set foot in the Monte Carlo casino. I have no objection to Italian maids and such like, but I cannot see why I should lose money in their presence'.

She was in a minority. Within two years the SBM's annual takings had soared to over £4 million to which Harold Robbins made an involuntary contribution. In one night's play, after losing $160,000, he sold his car on the casino steps to pay his bill at the Hotel de Paris and buy a ticket home. After that experience – he was served with a writ for back taxes on arriving in New York! – he gave up gambling and refused to be tempted, although his 85-foot yacht *Gracar* was anchored only an olive stone's-throw from the Cannes casino.

With its gaming revenue now out of the red, the company could justify a heavy programme of expansion. The oldest salon, dating back to 1861, was scrapped in favour of a spacious foyer whose showcases displayed chips, plaques and gold louis from the past, together with famous ballet posters and Sem caricatures re-calling 'La Belle Epoque'. More contemporary tastes were serviced by the new air-conditioned Salle des Amériques, with piped music and a red and gold Second Empire décor to lure patrons of craps, black jack and double-zero roulette. The one-armed bandits clanked on in a separate temple. The architect, André Levasseur, also transformed the former Salle Schmit into the Salon d'Europe with onyx pillars and ornate panels designed by fashionable artists. The SBM now encouraged charter flights of American punters, who could celebrate their wins and console themselves for losses in the renovated Black Jack night club or jig until dawn in the St Louis Club, a bar-discothèque with a New Orleans décor.

The old SBM hierarchy had been smoothly replaced by men versed in international banking and hotel finance, all with conspicuously American backgrounds. Wilfred Groote was a graduate of North Carolina, who had worked in the tobacco industry, American Machine & Foundry, and had later planned many hotels for Pan-Am. Max Blouet, general manager of all the SBM's hotel properties, had trained in France, England and the United States, afterwards working managerially at the Georges V in Paris, the Drake in New York City and Chicago's Ambassador. He succeeded the much-respected veteran, Jean Broc, who left the Hotel de Paris after 16 vintage years. Another new top SBM executive was the French financial expert, Guy de Brignac, a product of the Harvard Business School, with extensive experience in the Paris branch of the First National Bank, the Olin Mathieson Chemical Corporation and other powerful groups.[2]

These appointments, paralleled by the huge skyscraper projects in Monte Carlo, started rumours that Princess Grace seemed bent on 'Americanising' Monaco. Her influence was magnified by gossip but Rainier acknowledged at the time, 'I have always found it worthwhile to discuss particular problems with the Princess'. He also paid tribute to her 'intuitive' gift for correctly analysing people and questioning motives which he had 'too casually' overlooked. No doubt she found the new SBM executives more congenial than their Onassis-dominated predecessors.

Both were unreservedly opposed to General de Gaulle's anti-American stance over Vietnam. Throughout that unhappy war the whole family wore bracelets, each engraved with an American

[2] Others have replaced them. The 1975 Board now includes Georges Würz, a long-time resident and founder of the Lancaster beauty products combine, and the Directeur Général, Jean-Pierre Delanney, a former Vice-President of Trans-International Air Lines.

prisoner's name, and Princess Caroline wrote regularly to their families. With two of her own cousins fighting in South-East Asia, Grace was moved to invite ten wounded servicemen to spend Christmas, 1967 at the palace. Some weeks later she told an interviewer of her disgust with the French TV and newspapers, who glorified the Vietcong as heroes against imperialism. 'I think there are a lot of French people who do not go along with General de Gaulle on that' she declared stiffly. Relations did not improve when the U.S. warship *Constitution* chanced to sail into Monte Carlo on Monaco's National Day to a tumultuous reception from holiday-makers.

Rainier's personal détente with the SBM, who had kept their pledge to invest in 'Bord-de-Mer', was cemented by the promotion in March 1970 of his third cousin, Prince Louis de Polignac, to company boss after three years as Vice-President. A jovial and rotund figure but no guinea pig executive, he came to his new post from successful working directorships with Lanvin and the Pommery champagne firm. He and his fellow-directors approved the lavish redecoration and refurnishing of the Hotel de Paris and the Hermitage, both of which benefited from several more new suites and were directly linked with each other and the casino by corridors and lifts. The Hotel de Paris recaptured something of its former gastronomic grandeur when the Maître-chef, Bonsignore, was invited by the Shah to prepare the 'Dinner of the Century' in Persepolis to celebrate the 2,500th anniversary of the Persian Empire. The menu was later reproduced in full for hotel guests, with delicacies like 'Paon à l'Impériale', 'Oeufs de Cailles aux perles Pahlevi' and a memorable wine list which had tactfully included a Pommery & Greno Brut Rosé 1961. Soon afterwards the hotel staged a Curnonsky banquet to commemorate the centenary of the 'Prince of Gastronomes', an accolade envied by every restaurateur in France.[3]

[3] Maurice-Edmond Sailland (1872–1956) took his pseudonym from the Latin, 'Cur non' (why not), with the 'sky' added for a Slavic touch. His statements and writings on *haute cuisine* became axiomatic. He was a devoted friend of Colette, who often regaled him at Monte Carlo with dishes by Escoffier and other masters.

The extensions to the Hotel de Paris and other luxury establishments merely scratched the surface of an acute problem. The residential palaces serviced affluent refugees in search of a sunny retirement or business opportunists hungry for tax benefits, yet most tourists remained shackled by a serious lack of accommodation. Monte Carlo needed to double its room capacity which left hotel owners with an apparently insoluble dilemma. They turned away business during the peak season and for highlights like the Grand Prix weekend and the TV Festival, but stayed half-empty for several months in between. The SBM therefore took the logical step of supporting a year-round programme of entertainment supplemented by off-season hotel rates. The smaller hotels and *pensions* were also encouraged to improve their premises with long-term low interest State loans in the hope of attracting charter flight tourists.

This combined strategy soon proved effective though at some cost to the skyline. Monte Carlo's cramped space, mushrooming in value, was particularly vulnerable to speculative development to which the municipality turned a blind eye or only half-heartedly opposed. Little concession was made to overall planning. The imposing new Mirabeau block, with several hundred rooms, suites and service flats, overshadowed the eastern wing and open-air pool of its neighbour, the elegant British-owned Métropole.

The general problem still remained of more evenly spreading the intake of hotel guests. Rainier took a strong personal initiative by pressing for off-season conferences. He reminded his advisers that, dating back to Prince Albert's reign, Monaco had attracted international scientists, jurists and many other groups who had found the neutral principality an ideal venue for politically-free discussions and symposia. The high-powered SBM executives, long familiar with the American conference system, began a skilful canvass of business firms. They had the assistance of Monaco's world-wide network of influential honorary consuls and its full-time legations in several capitals. The response was immediate and gratifying. Monte Carlo's geographical position and climate seemed to exert a magnetic appeal on conference men whether engaged in discussing the elimination of radioactive waste, acupuncture or the finer points of sanitary engineering. They began arriving in sufficient numbers between seasons to calm even the most nervous hoteliers.

This development, although important, was necessarily incidental to the SBM's main objective of attracting rich socialites to its casino and Le Sporting, the Country Club, hotels, night spots and all the other money-making units in its empire. It became less of a problem when visitors surged in from the prospering E.E.C. countries, reinforced by international pleasure-seekers who had discovered that Monte Carlo was again fashionable. As always, they soon tripped over each other's ermine tails for the best hotel suites and the beach's prized cabanas. Régine, the carrotty-haired night club queen, opened a glittering new disco, Jimmy'z, and brought jigging insomniacs from 'le tout Paris' as her week-end guests.

Monte Carlo quickly breezed back into the social gossip columns. The Maharanee of Baroda's son, 'Princey', posed in a maxi-length white mink coat before slipping into his new Rolls-Royce, both birthday gifts from his mother. Photographers pounced on the blonde Duchessa Serra di Cassano, heiress to the Beretta arms fortune, who, much to the chagrin of the SBM, barred herself from all casinos for five years after losing almost £1 million at Cannes. Mme Ricarda Smith, wife of a Danish fertiliser magnate, gave a party in her villa where she received Lady Bird Johnson, Josephine Baker and other guests in a toilette topped by a huge Braque-designed topaz.

The yachts were again bobbing in the harbour, with the Niarchos 3-masted black schooner *Créole* moored in the privileged southern jetty station formerly assigned to the *Christina*. (For good measure, Tina Niarchos also took over the sumptuous 8th-floor suite in the Hotel de Paris which she and her former husband, Ari Onassis, had always occupied). Other yacht-owners, like the Duke of Westminster, Lord Cowdray's heir and Elizabeth Burton, wearing diamonds only slightly bigger than the Ritz, arrived for the Grand Prix. Before Graham Hill, Rindt, Brabham and Stewart started revving their engines to scream round the circuit, the vintage cars went on parade with a noisy ovation for Rainier's 1903 De Dion Bouton.

In November 1968, after again seeing the movie *Genevieve* in the palace cinema, he could not resist entering for the London-Brighton run. Paul Gallico made all the arrangements. Rainier drove in a fur-lined coat, corduroy trousers and black boots to arrive finally at the finishing post with Grace and their two daughters as passengers. She confessed afterwards to having 'cheated' a little by following in her warm blue $3\frac{1}{2}$-litre Rover, only joining him just outside Brighton for the photographers' benefit.

The casino was regularly drawing over half a million visitors a year, with the French and Italians accounting together for almost half that number and Americans and British another 25%. Although the croupiers' black ties outnumbered the patrons', who wore anything from elegant Puccis to drip-dry sweaters and blue jeans, the play ran so high in 1973 that the former top-priced plaque of 10,000 francs was replaced by another worth 40,000. When the wife of an Italian film producer had a losing run at roulette and demanded that the 20,000-franc maximum should be raised, she was discreetly accommodated and lost a good deal more.

Every room, from the 'Kitchen' to the Salons Privés, even with a stiff admission charge and higher minimum stakes, became so jammed that closed-circuit TV was installed to monitor the tables. This caused the croupiers to down rakes during one Grand Prix weekend in protest at the implied slur on their honour. They had to be enticed back with a pay increase, but the monitors remained and will doubtless grow bigger and still less brotherly by 1984, when the company is due to renew its gaming concession.

For the year ending 31 March 1973 Prince Louis announced a profit of over £1 million ($2.4 million), with a further increase in the following year, mainly from the casino whose fruit machines alone accounted for a take of 10 million francs. The SBM shares had risen in value by over 40% and the company could easily afford a payroll for 30 full-time gardeners. They planted and re-planted the Boulingrins and casino terraces each season with thousands of cyclamen, petunias, begonias and many rarer species. Princess Grace kept an expert eye on every change in landscaping design. She had been an enthusiast from her girlhood days in Philadelphia where the family garden included several Japanese cherry trees. Julia Clements came over from England to judge the first Monaco flower design show which proved so successful that a Garden Club was started under the Princess's active patronage.

Monte Carlo needed all its gardens, floodlighting and the new busts of Churchill and Diaghilev to distract the eye from its block-wide areas of excavation. As old houses toppled, the skyline was steadily shredded into a cut-out of pinnacles and towers against the turquoise sky. New luxury skyscrapers like the Château Périgord, the Bahia and the Estoril were snapped up, often at a premium, almost before the architect's blue-prints had dried. $500,000 cheques swiftly changed hands for apartments leased mainly by affluent Germans and, even more often, Italians, nervous of political unrest at home or anxious to preserve their profits from inquisitive tax collectors. An army of sharp-nosed bankers, under-writers, lawyers and accountants marched through the revolving doors of new office blocks to occupy suites with immense teak desks, deep-pile carpeting and winking crystal chandeliers.

Squinting through the sunlight often hazy with brick dust, some of the old guard complained bitterly that Monte Carlo had be-come 'a millionaire's concrete slum', but the much-increased working population was less critical. Many gratefully left their ancient rundown districts for modern low-rent houses in the Condamine or the thriving industrial suburb of Fontvieille with its pleasant gardens and easy proximity to new air-conditioned factories. Not all the cement-mixers were churning out a quick profit. More free schools, primary, secondary and technical, had emerged, together with one of the best-equipped hospitals in Europe.

Land reclamation was steadily enlarging the principality by almost a square mile. By 1973 the huge cash outlay by the State, the SBM and foreign investors already showed positive results. The Holiday Inn had opened and reported excellent business in its first year. The whole 'Bord-de-Mer' project took shape even ahead of schedule. The free public plage on the Larvotto now offered summer bathers 15,000 square metres of artificial beach space with good cabins, on hire for a couple of francs, and every shop and café on the promenade terrace was let at stiff rents.

The S.A.D.I.M. group completed a major feat of engineering to the west of the principality by sinking a protective dyke, resting on a substructure of rock, to a world record depth of 35 metres. Prefabricated cellular coffer-dams of reinforced concrete had been floated all the way from Genoa to build the sea wall. They were filled with sand before being sunk into position. The new land area of Fontvieille was rapidly networked with roads to serve the apartment blocks, quickly occupied, and a variety of factories for light industries, including cosmetics, printing, clothing, ceramics, precision engineering, plastics, machine tools and brewing, apart from various research laboratories. The larger of the two pleasure ports was designed to take up to 300 boats.

'Les Spélugues', an equally spectacular but smaller-scale operation, was started in the autumn of 1972 with a three to four-year deadline. Located below the casino terraces on the site of the former railway station and clay pigeon shoot, this mammoth building complex has an area of over 23,000 square metres. It rests on a platform extending over the sea but with access by tunnel to the harbour and town centre for motorists or pedestrians. The project was jointly financed by the principality, Loew's International, the American hotel corporation, Federal Germany's Neue Heimat syndicate and the Manera S.A., France's post-war building giant. Loew's have now built and run a 660-room luxury hotel, with coffee shop, night club, beauty salon and other amenities, including gaming rooms for black jack, craps and American roulette operated by the SBM. In preparation for the September 1975 opening, ten croupiers were sent on a two-month course at Las Vegas. An adjoining block of 150 apartments, financed and built by Loew's and Manera, is serviced by the hotel. The State-owned Convention Centre, due to be opened in 1976, will occupy four floors with a seating capacity of 2,000, ample space for exhibitions and facilities like simultaneous translation in five languages, tape recordings and studios for radio and TV productions.

It had been hoped that most of the 'urbanisation' programme might be completed by mid-1974 when Rainier celebrated his Silver Jubilee as ruler, but this proved over-sanguine. Nevertheless, it turned out to be a vintage year in Monaco's social history, despite minor irritations like the cancellation of the Rally, due to the fuel crisis, and a lightning pay strike by the Hotel de Paris staff, who deprived guests in the £100 a day suites of their luncheons, telephone calls and room service on the eve of the Grand Prix.

The *Christina* was back in harbour and Mr and Mrs Onassis surprised many by lunching up at the palace. 'There was never a feud,' Rainier blandly informed reporters. 'We simply had a business disagreement.' The reconciliation was motivated by sympathy for Onassis, still obviously stricken by the tragic death of his son, whom the Rainiers had known since his early childhood. But others in Monaco had little affection for the socially ambitious 'Golden Greek'. For some weeks past harbour watchers had goggled and giggled at the new leviathan, owned by Stavros Niarchos, his hated business rival. The 2,586-ton *Atlantis*, 380 ft. long, completely upstaged the *Christina* with an oval pool heated to 28°C., a dining salon adorned by a Renoir, an Utrillo and two Degas, and a bar designed by Warhol who threw in his original tin of Campbell's Soup. She boasted a dozen guest suites, apart from little extras like a gymnasium, a 40-seat cinema and a fully-automated bridge whose ITT Navigator maintains contact by computer with an orbiting satellite.

Between the towering Greek palaces, both flying the generous flag of Liberia, Prince Rainier's little secondhand 69-tonner, *Stalcia*, bobbed modestly at anchor. The young princesses made their own beds and helped with the cooking, while Prince Albert was expected to lend a hand with deck-swabbing. It typified the practical firmness and sense of responsibility with which the royal youngsters have been raised since infancy.

Rainier's heir, Prince Albert, continues to attend the *lycée* until he and his parents decide on the next stage of his education, possibly at an English or American university. A keen soccer fan, he papers his bedroom walls with pin-ups of teams and international idols. He is shortsighted like his mother and often wears glasses, but he swims expertly, enjoys Judo and has the Kelly taste for sculling. A soft-spoken boy and rather more thoughtful than most teenagers, he mixes unself-consciously with friends in his own age-group but remains quietly aware of his responsibilities. Without interfering with the normal school curriculum and rules, Rainier has gradually familiarised him with protocol. From his early years, Albert has accompanied his parents to social and official functions and is now self-confident enough to go out alone and present cups or prizes. His sister, Stéphanie, followed Princess Caroline to the local convent day school. She also takes lessons in classical dancing and piano and has obvious artistic gifts. Although the youngest and already showing signs of a strong-willed disposition, she has not been spoilt by her parents.

Since leaving her school in Monaco, Princess Caroline has become the most publicised of the Rainiers' children. She has bloomed into a pretty and vivacious brunette, although not quite the social butterfly of magazine gossip, which her mother hotly resents. She spent two years as a boarder at St Mary's, a Catholic college near Ascot, where she took all her O. levels and three A.s. She quickly mastered the piano and flute and has become an all-round athlete, excelling at water-skiing, riding and skating. She has a flair for languages and plans to add a fifth to her fluent English, French, German and Spanish.

She went to an exclusive academy outside Paris, followed by studies at the School of Political Science. The pressures on an attractive and high-spirited girl, with such a glamorous background, have steadily increased. Although chaperoned and with a plain clothes detective hovering discreetly, she cannot always shake off photographers and reporters who link her name romantically with eligibles like the Prince of Wales, the Grand Duke Henri of Luxembourg and Martin Giscard d'Estaing. Princess Grace often stays at the family apartment in the Avenue Foch now that Stéphanie has started attending a convent school in Paris.

Caroline frequently returns to Monaco for sailing and informal weekends at Roc Agel. She broke off her law studies for the gala opening of the new Summer Sporting Club in June 1974. The family party was completed by Princess Antoinette, still very decorative and now taking more part in the principality's social life. The 'Sporting', a Moorish ochre-coloured fantasy, was put up at a cost of some £3 million. Built on the Larvotto peninsula overlooking the bay, its centrepiece is the Star Room which seats up to 1,200 who can dance or watch the cabaret on a two-tiered revolving stage. A huge curved roof opens to the sky in precisely three minutes. The white marble foyer is subtly sloped to lead into the green-carpeted gaming salon with a smoothly undulating décor designed, admit the architects, 'to put people into a state of euphoria'. Roulette, trente-et-quarante and chemin-de-fer are supplemented by craps and black jack in separate '*ravissantes petites salles*'. The adjacent Maona offers Tahitian delicacies, with lavish greenery and multi-coloured parrots attracting patrons to a separate Brazilian section. For late night owls Régine has provided another Jimmy'z, a discothèque riotous with jet-black lacquer, chrome, blue table candles and a purple carpet. An open-air cinema over the lagoon shows a different film every night throughout the season.

The 400 guests specially invited, at the SBM's expense, for a house-warming menu of caviare, lobster and fireworks, needed only Lady Docker to complete the gold-plated parade of Monte Carlo, past and present. The stately dome of Telly Savalas sparkled agreeably against a frieze of titles, ancient and modern. Princess

Grace inevitably took star honours in a tiara and Dior's white chiffon ahead of Maria Callas, the Begum Aga Khan, Mme Dewi Sukarno and Liza Minelli.

Sammy Davis Jr had consented to head the cabaret without any fee, apart from some $30,000 in expenses and a specially chartered yacht for his ten-day visit. Apparently, he was dissatisfied with arrangements for his official welcome at Nice Airport and took even graver offence at being overlooked for a palace tea party which the Rainiers gave for tennis players in the Country Club tournament. He and his 20-strong entourage sailed off in the direction of St Tropez some hours before the gala opening. There was no shortage of volunteers but, after frenzied consultation, party pieces were contributed by Bill Crosby and Burt Bacharach as curtain-raisers for Josephine Baker, who had come over for the evening from her villa at Cap Martin. She once again set all the mascara streaming with *J'ai Deux Amours*, tactfully adapted to 'Mon Pays et Monte-Carlo'.

The SBM's gaming profits for that year easily accommodated such hospitality. One punter, a building magnate from Rome, dropped £800,000 ($2.70 million) in a night's play. Stakes have soared with an enormous increase in the number of gamblers, a trend equally noticeable on the French Riviera.

In November a quartette of sheikhs arrived in Monte Carlo to open a gambling blitz not seen since the Nineties. They started playing roulette at midnight in a private room and unsmilingly insisted on raising the maximum stakes. They were soon attended by the prettiest of local 'mascots' who, like the flunkeys, each received tips of 2,000 francs. After a night or two, and rarely breaking off before dawn, they had won the equivalent of £1 million but lost it all back and considerably more by the end of the week. Their lavish style attracted so much more unwelcome attention than in the discreet private London clubs that they decided to move on to Divonne-les-Bains, the French resort handily adjacent to their Swiss vaults. The SBM did not present them with a bill at the Hotel de Paris and observed an almost confessional reticence about their losses, but one of the directors, watching the last of the

Cadillacs depart, commented wistfully, 'It was a pleasure to do business with them'.[4]

Many other speculators, although less flamboyant, contributed to Monte Carlo's finances in that year of booming prosperity. With inflation rampant throughout Europe and in the United States, gambling in every form had become a tempting outlet. Some threw their cash on the tables; others saw the tax advantages of investing in the principality's 700 thriving companies or buying real estate which, with local building at last slowing down for sheer lack of space, had become one of the safest rising markets in Europe. Sotheby's arranged to hold fine art sales in the Winter Sporting from which the principality has benefited by a handy 10% commission. Objets d'art offered by the Barons Guy de Rothschild and Alexis de Redé yielded £469,748 at a single day's sale in May 1975. The Maharanee of Baroda, at a privately held auction, raised some £1,500,000 in pocket money for part of her collection which included a diamond given to the Empress Eugénie by Napoleon III.

But amid the galas, sports festivals and such artistic events as an open-air recital by Rostropovitch in the Cour d'Honneur, the popular tourist trade was skilfully coaxed with a TV film made by a French company. *The Monaco of Prince Rainier*, unabashedly commercial, had a somewhat gift-wrapped appeal for viewers, who saw the mediaeval old town, the sun-dappled toy harbour and gardens like sumptuous party gateaux. One barely glimpsed the dun-coloured and still rather bleak expanse of Fontvieille as the prince, recalling the recent landfills, presented a genial prospectus of his tiny realm as 'a nice place to work in and a very nice place to relax in'.

Some nostalgics, myself included, may have regretted that too much pink stucco has been replaced by concrete, but the ingratiating cameras glided on like head waiters. Seen from the

---

[4] Press rumours that the sheikhs had 'broken the bank' were exploded by the SBM figures for 1974/75 which disclose record gaming receipts of nearly £13 million ($32 million), almost equalling the combined revenues of the French casinos at Divonne, Nice and Cannes (Palm Beach).

palace ramparts, without hint of bulldozers or cement-mixers, the distant skyscrapers sparkled invitingly like frosted tumblers, with the casino's rococo splendour adding to the flavour of Offenbach on the rocks.

Monte Carlo, photographed in gauzy soft focus, still looked as imperishably delectable and wrinkle-free as Dietrich in long shot.

Postscript

Visiting the palace to check final research details with Prince Rainier, I found it impossible not to recall our very first meeting, soon after his accession, when the principality was crumbling into a near-bankrupt anachronism. During his reign the business turnover has multiplied, with a remarkable development of light industries despite a local lack of raw materials. Monaco's buoyant economy and general well-being now stand out by comparison with the most prosperous countries in Europe, although its area, even with land reclamation, is still barely half that of Central Park.

The traditional exemption from income tax and military service remains an unique bonus. Would-be nationals, who can only qualify by a 10-year continuous residence or 'exceptional services to the State', form a lengthy queue. No beggar can be seen in the streets, unemployment is non-existent, and the per capita income provides cars for one in every two of its people, the highest ratio in the world, although at some cost in clogged roads and air pollution during the summer season. The health service is admittedly less complete than Britain's, but free hospital care is available for the needy few, with up to 80% reimbursement for prescriptions. A plan for *médécine de travail*, open to workers of any nationality, preceded that of France. The system of free education in all sectors, with generous social security benefits and pensions, ranks among the best on the Continent.

Prosperity and slum clearance have helped to keep Monaco virtually crime-free. Mugging is unknown and no adolescent drug problem exists ('maybe because we have no university', Rainier comments ironically). The little prison, cut into the Rock of Hercules near the palace, holds only 30 inmates, who doubtless appreciate their showers and TV. It is rarely more than half-filled with small-time offenders like pickpockets or passers of bad cheques. They serve up to three months, mostly spread over weekends. Longer-term prisoners go to the far less comfortable French gaols.

The numerous local police wear dark glasses and blue uniforms with revolvers on their hips. Briefed to the benefits of tourism, they act more like suave travel guides than tough cops, notably towards visitors, but their mobile night patrols are as efficiently radio-controlled as in any big-city force. Not long ago a college teacher was picked up for a minor motoring offence. At the police station he lost his temper and unwisely shook his fist at a portrait of the prince over the sergeant's desk. He drew a fine and a 12-month suspended sentence, a sharp reminder that it is wise to stay in line even in paradise.

Rainier continues to rule as an absolute monarch, subject only to the Supreme Court and the various civil liberties safeguarded by the Constitution. But it is difficult to see how such a tiny country, with a specialised economy based mainly on foreign investment and tourism, could be run more efficiently by committees or some other intricate system of government. Tongue in cheek, Rainier keeps a straight face in reminding foreign observers that his National Council currently includes an avowed Red. Since there is no communist party in Monaco, this has as much political significance as if the Marquess of Cholmondeley, Lord Great Chamberlain of England, decided whimsically to stick a diamanté hammer-and-sickle pin into his cravat for Royal Ascot.

The treasury contributes £750,000 ($1.8 million) a year towards the upkeep of the palace with its staff of over 150. They patrol and maintain the vast State Apartments which include a number of Breughels and Holbeins.

Two chefs and several aides prepare meals for the Rainiers, their guests and personal staff. The garage superintendent is in charge of eight chauffeurs and mechanics, who drive and service the royal cars as well as maintaining the prince's vintage collection. He still resents, but now philosophically accepts, sporadic criticism of his 'huge fleet' of Rolls-Royces and Cadillacs. He uses these chauffeur-manned chariots only on unavoidable official occasions, much preferring to drive his Mercedes and a G.S. Citroen station wagon. His yacht is crewed only by an English engineer, Percy Cracknell, with the help of a former French naval officer who used to serve in the palace guard.

Stalcia was chosen as a family retreat with guest accommodation limited to one or two of the children's schoolfriends. The Rainiers can easily afford a more opulent vessel. Princess Grace's considerable film earnings, shrewdly invested, were supplemented by a share in her father's estate. Rainier's civil list donation is 5,316,950 francs (about £600,000 or $1.4 million). Unlike past Grimaldis, he is no longer dependent on the SBM which now accounts for only 2.50% of the principality's total revenue. But although the company's direct contribution is small and only half that from postage stamps, its casino and other attractions help to boost Monaco's revenue from tourism to over half the national income. The balance comes from the very lucrative commercial TV and radio, purchase and corporation taxes, State monopolies of beer and tobacco, and compensation of at least £1 million a year from France in lieu of customs dues.

Rainier received me in his office late one evening after seeing a succession of officials for several hours. He moved from the large table, piled high but neatly with documents, and settled back in an armchair with the inevitable cigarette. A veteran at responding to interrogation, he poked fun at those who still see Monaco as a glossy *pays d'opérette*, untouched by international economic and currency problems.[1] 'The future of the world is rather frightening' he said. 'As a father and a Chief of State, I want to make decisions that will give protection, both moral and physical, for my children and my people'.

He switched characteristically from such solemn pronouncements to a manner somewhat recalling the Duke of Edinburgh's jaunty and forthright style. He tends to become over-magisterial when addressing his own people, and some of his younger subjects privately mimic his rather pontifical fireside talks. He is far more at ease away from the TV cameras. When I hinted at past troubles with Elysée nominees like Pelletier, he commented that Ministers of State can now technically serve up to nine years but few last more than three. 'They seem relieved to get back to Paris for other, perhaps lighter, duties' he chuckled. He also implied a strong distaste for the Monegasque tradition of sinecures and hinted that the principality could not afford to carry passengers in its drive for industrial expansion.

He has cut down heavily on ceremonial flummery and sees himself less as a prince than 'the president of a business corporation, responsible to both shareholders and workers'. He works long hours although with enviable fringe benefits like a miniature Escorial as his 'head office'; the family retreat at Roc Agel; a Paris apartment; and reasonable breaks to ski at Gstaad or spend a short holiday most years in the States. His one regret is a lack of opportunity for more extensive travel, particularly to the Far East which he has never visited.

'I have little time to read' he told me ruefully. 'Maybe, as I have to study so many administrative documents, I've lost the urge. I enjoy fiction by authors who write in a good but easy-to-read style . . . Graham Greene, Paul Gallico, Gerald Durrell, Steinbeck, Marcel Pagnol . . . I like paintings that mean something to

---

[1] Nevertheless, Monte Carlo continues to serve its traditional antidotes. Several hundred refugees from the world's problems scrambled for tickets at the Sporting Club's Bal de la Rose during Easter, 1975. The tickets, priced at 400 francs (£45 or close on $100), did not include champagne, but guests could enjoy dinner and a cabaret with a gipsy orchestra of 100 violins playing waltz music.

me personally and I have a strong feeling for El Greco, Ribera, Dufy and the French impressionists.' His passionate interest in animals and circus life has also made him a Laura Knight enthusiast. Last Christmas he sponsored the first International Circus Festival in Monte Carlo with performers and acts from all parts of the world. Afterwards he said wistfully, 'If I were not a prince, I would have enjoyed being an animal trainer'. At other times he has confessed to missing the chance of a naval career or, even more, a farmer's life. Without his privileged background one can visualise his energy and grasp of modern technical problems employed in a high-powered executive post by General Motors or with some smaller European concern like Lotus or Ferrari.

As Monaco's 'corporation president' he freely acknowledges a lasting debt to Princess Grace's support and practical understanding of their duties, both in and out of the palace. She has set uniquely high standards in the rôle of 'company wife'. Her looks alone, backed by the long-lasting Hollywood glamour, would have carried her through the formal duties of First Lady, but she has given much more. Both at home and abroad, where she has become the principality's model ambassador in every sense, she is almost typecast in reflecting and often improving the principality's image of cosmopolitan sophistication. But quite apart from the routine entertaining, prize-givings and stone-layings, she has dedicated herself to an almost schizoid variety of personal causes like the Princess Grace Foundation to encourage local artists and craftsmen. Danny Kaye and others also stimulated her to become Honorary President of the international Association of the Friends of Children.

Although an admirer of playwrights like Tennessee Williams, she deplores films and TV programmes which glamorise violence and crude sex. In the principality she campaigns vigorously against the sale of pornographic magazines. 'When I pass a news-stand selling them, I tell the vendor exactly what I think' she says, but sadly admits that copies continue to slip under the counter and local enthusiasts now make the journey to nearby Antibes or Nice.

Wide press coverage and her regular appearance among the

World's Best Dressed Women maintain the image, which she resents, of an eternal film star princess. 'My life is not all lying about eating peeled grapes by a swimming pool' she once sharply reminded a friend of mine. She takes charge of what Rainier calls 'the social calendar' which involves making arrangements for luncheons, dinners, receptions and the comfort of staying guests. Points of protocol, seating and the like are discussed with her husband, but as châtelaine Princess Grace makes the final decisions with the palace chefs.

She is a keen and discriminating collector of antiques. Her taste in décor is evidenced at Roc Agel but also throughout the 10-roomed suite of private apartments in the palace's East Wing, from the pink-washed ante-room to the Grand Salon, two storeys high with a marble floor and huge glass wall. She receives visitors in her drawing-room whose table is adorned with silver-framed portraits of relatives and royal friends, including Princess Anne, who stayed at the palace during a British Week. At her writing desk she deals with a formidable daily correspondence which frequently requires an extra hour or two after dinner. An almost round-the-clock schedule demands careful timing, but Princess Grace has sometimes been criticised for unpunctuality. She has confessed to a weakness for day-dreaming. When a forest fire threatened Roc Agel, she admitted afterwards that her first thoughts were for the safety of her children, Rainier's petit-point waistcoat, which she had been trying to finish for five years, and – above all – her address book.

At 45 she still looks almost as beautiful and slender as the golden ice-cool blonde of her screen days, but this has not been achieved without effort. Unlike Rainier, who indulges in short bursts of violent exercise and prefers driving to walking, she covers a hefty mileage on foot in the course of her duties. She becomes easily car sick and does not enjoy accompanying her husband on long journeys, particularly over twisting mountain roads which he takes at boyish speeds. She prefers driving her own Rover and, even more, shopping or visiting in a converted London taxi, a gift from Rainier. Exquisitely upholstered and appointed, it manoeuvres splendidly on Monaco's crowded roads and has the advantage of being high enough not to disturb her coiffure. To withstand the threat of rich Provencal dishes and the relays of party canapés, she pedals a bicycle machine before her open bedroom window for 15 minutes most mornings. Her mother, still very vigorous at 75, has initiated her into the benefits of wheat-germ, yeast and other health foods, but the social round demands sterner disciplines. She goes on an alcohol-free régime from mid-August until her birthday on 12 November.

Since her arrival in the principality 19 years ago, Princess Grace has acquired fluency in French and a regal though unstarchy touch. But quite apart from retaining her native passport, she still conveys the overall impression of a crisp American salad with French dressing. It complements Rainier's blending of the Midi and Manhattan, with the former predominant. 'What impresses me in the United States is the size, the proportion of things and conceptions' he wrote to me recently. 'They represent another dimension compared with Europe, even their way of thinking. I have always been impressed by American hospitality, their generosity as a people and as a nation, and their efficiency. But I do not much favour their way of living. As a Mediterranean, I find it too fast, too frantic. Time is money for them. For me, time is life and it has to be fully employed and enjoyed.'

But he continues to generate enough ideas of his own to keep any Madison Avenue promotion department ticking over. He was long enthusiastic for a new helicopter station to link up with Nice Airport, but the operating costs would have been too high. However, this summer an enterprising new company, Héli-Monaco, have started a thrice-daily service which shuttles between the airport and principality in ten minutes flat for a fare of 100 francs. He also nurses the hope of one day building a big film and TV studio.

One of his more practical ambitions is to set up an international inventors' centre in Monaco. It will not be easy for any patentee, however ingenious, to rival the sheer alchemy which, in little over a century, has transmuted a barren promontory, valued at a few centimes a square metre, into solid gold nuggets.

Appendix

Facts and Figures (current exchange: 9 F. to £).

Area of Monaco: 190 hectares (469 acres).
Population: 4,529 Monegasques. 23,285 other nationalities.
Work force: 19,956 (approx. one-third with trade union membership).
National flag: half red, half white in horizontal bands.
Religion: a See of the Roman Catholic Church.
Climate: 260 days of sunshine. Average temperature, 16°C. 62 days of rainfall (yearly average).
Budget (1975): Revenue, 406,248,600 Fs. Expenditure: 387,401,970 Fs.
Railways: 1.6 Km. main line operated by SCNF.
Monte Carlo Rally (January). *Grand Prix* (May).

Société des Bains de Mer (SBM)

Chief Shareholder. The Principality (69%).
Contribution to State Budget (1975): 2.5%.
Capital: 9 million Fs. (1,800,000 shares, 5F. nominal).
Share value on Bourse (1975): 42.60 Fs.
Employees: 1,935.

Establishments: Casino. Theatre. Sporting Club. 3 luxury hotels (Hotel de Paris, Hermitage, Old Beach). Café de Paris. 4 night clubs. Monte-Carlo Beach, Sea Club and Piscine des Terrasses. Golf Club and Country Club.

Bibliography

In addition to archive and other official material to which the author has been given access, special acknowledgement is due to such primary sources as *Monaco and Monte Carlo* by Adolphe Smith (Grant Richards, 1912); Charles Graves's *The Big Gamble* (Hutchinson, 1951) and *Royal Riviera* (Heinemann, 1957); *Prince Rainier of Monaco* by Peter Hawkins (Kimber, 1966); *Wizard of Homburg and Monte Carlo* by Egon Corti (Butterworth, 1934); *The Big Wheel* by G. W. Herald and E. D. Radin (Robert Hale, 1965 and William Morrow, 1965); *They Have Their Exits* by Airey Neave (Hodder & Stoughton, 1953); *The Way Back* by Vincent Brome (Cassell, 1957); *The Princes of Monaco* by Françoise de Bernardy (Arthur Barker, 1961); and *Onassis* by Willi Frischauer (Bodley Head, 1968).

Other sources consulted or quoted:

Adleman, R. H. and Walton, G., *The Champagne Campaign* (Frewin, 1973).
Ball, Adrian (Ed.), *My Greatest Race* (Hart-Davis, MacGibbon, 1974).
Balsan, Consuelo, *The Glitter and the Gold* (Heinemann, 1953)
Bocca, Geoffrey, *Bikini Beach* (W. H. Allen, 1963).
Carlson, Oliver, *The Man who made News* (Duell, Sloan & Pearce, 1942).
Coborn, Charles, *The Man who Broke the Bank* (Hutchinson, 1928).
Docker, Lady N., *Norah* (W. H. Allen, 1969).

Dodge, David, *A Rich Man's Guide to the Riviera* (Cassell, 1963).

Dudley, Ernest, *The Gilded Lady* (Odhams, 1958).

Fleming, Ian, *Thrilling Cities* (Cape, 1963).

Forbes-Robertson, Diana, *Maxine* (Hamish Hamilton, 1964).

Frischauer, Willi, *An Hotel is like a Woman* (Frewin, 1965).

Graves, Charles, *The Riviera Revisited* (Evans, Bros. 1948).

Graves, Charles, *None but the Rich* (Cassell, 1963).

Gunsbourg, Raoul, *Cent ans de Souvenirs* (Monaco, 1959).

Gussow, Mel, *Zanuck* (W. H. Allen, 1971).

Haedrich, Marcel, *Coco Chanel* (Robert Hale, 1972).

Haskell, Arnold, *Diaghileff* (Gollancz, 1955).

Haskell, Arnold, *Ballet russe* (Weidenfeld & Nicolson, 1968).

Hoyt, Edwin P., *The House of Morgan* (Dodd, Mead, 1966).

Jackson, Stanley, *The Great Barnato* (Heinemann, 1970).

Jackson, Stanley, *Caruso* (W. H. Allen, 1972).

Jenkins, Alan, *The Twenties* (Heinemann, 1974).

Karsavina, Tamara, *Theatre Street* (Constable, 1948).

Ketchiva, P. de, *Devil's Playground* (Sampson, Low, 1934).

Kschessinska, Mathilde, *Dancing in Petersburg* (Gollancz, 1960).

Kurtz, Harold, *The Empress Eugénie* (Hamish Hamilton, 1964).

Lewinsohn, Richard, *Sir Basil Zaharoff* (Gollancz, 1933).

Lifar, Serge, *Serge Diaghilev* (Putnam, 1940).

Lifar, Serge, *Ma Vie* (Hutchinson, 1970).

Mackintosh, Alistair, *No Alibi* (Muller, 1961).

Massie, Robert K., *Nicholas and Alexandra* (Gollancz, 1968).

Maxwell, Elsa, *The Celebrity Circus* (W. H. Allen, 1964).

Métivier, Henri, *Monaco et ses Princes* (La Flèche, 1860).

Nabarro, Derek, *Wait for the Dawn* (Cassell, 1952).

Neumann, Robert, *Zaharoff* (Allen & Unwin, 1935).

Nijinsky, Romola, *Nijinsky* (Gollancz, 1933).

Otéro, Caroline, *My Story* (A. M. Philpot, 1927).

Painter, G. D., *Marcel Proust*, Vol. II (Chatto & Windus, 1965).

Paoli, Xavier, *My Royal Clients* (Hodder & Stoughton, 1911).

Pless, Princess D. of, *From my private Diary* (John Murray, 1931).

Polovtsoff, Pierre, *Monte Carlo Casino* (Stanley Paul, 1937).

Pound, Reginald, *Selfridge* (Heinemann, 1960).

Ray, Cyril (Ed.), *The Gourmet's Companion* (Eyre & Spottiswoode, 1963).

Ritz, Marie, *César Ritz* (Harrap, 1938).

Robert, J. B., *Histoire de Monaco* (Presses Universitaires, 1973).

Skinner, Cornelia O., *Elegant Wits and Grand Horizontals* (Michael Joseph, 1963).

Standish, Robert, *The Prince of Storytellers* (Peter Davies, 1957).

Stoeckl, Agnes de, *Not All Vanity* (John Murray, 1952).

Turnbull, Andrew, *Scott Fitzgerald* (Bodley Head, 1962).

Westminster, Loelia, Duchess of, *Grace and Favour* (Weidenfeld & Nicolson, 1961).

Williams, A. H., *No Name on the Door* (W. H. Allen, 1956).

Index